Instructor's Resource Manual with Test Questions

to accompany

Adolescence

Sixth Edition

Laurence Steinberg
Temple University

Prepared by
Dale Grubb
Baldwin Wallace College

Boston   Burr Ridge, IL   Dubuque, IA   Madison, WI   New York   San Francisco   St. Louis
Bangkok   Bogotá   Caracas   Kuala Lumpur   Lisbon   London   Madrid   Mexico City
Milan   Montreal   New Delhi   Santiago   Seoul   Singapore   Sydney   Taipei   Toronto

McGraw-Hill Higher Education

A Division of The McGraw-Hill Companies

Instructor's Resource Manual with Test Questions to accompany
ADOLESCENCE, SIXTH EDITION
LAURENCE STEINBERG

Published by McGraw-Hill Higher Education, an imprint of The McGraw-Hill Companies, Inc.,
1221 Avenue of the Americas, New York, NY 10020. Copyright © The McGraw-Hill Companies,
Inc., 2002, 1999, 1996, 1993. All rights reserved.

This book is printed on acid-free paper.

1 2 3 4 5 6 7 8 9 0 QPD QPD 0 3 2 1

ISBN 0-07-241457-X

www.mhhe.com

Contents

Preface

This instructor's resource manual is designed to accompany the text *Adolescence (6th Edition)*. It is intended to assist both novice and experienced instructors in the preparation of courses on adolescent development.

This manual is divided into three sections. The first section of this manual contains general information pertaining to the design of adolescence courses, and should be consulted before the semester begins. The second section contains summaries of each chapter of the *Adolescence* text, as well as suggested classroom activities and supplemental lecture topics. The final section contains a test item file that includes 75 multiple-choice questions and 5 sample essays for each chapter. This test item file is available on CD-Rom in both IBM and Apple/Macintosh formats. Please contact your McGraw-Hill representative for details.

The first section provides general information on the following topics:

1.	Selected Resources for Instructors of Psychology	Includes materials on teaching students as well as a list of computer on-line services for networking.
2.	Examinations	Provides the instructor with examination formats as well as suggestions on how to deal with different issues related to giving exams.
3.	Term Papers	Provides suggestions for term paper format and presents alternative ideas for term papers.
5.	Film and Video Distributors	Lists the names and addresses of the distributors for the films and videos described in each chapter.

The second section is organized by chapter. Eight areas are covered in each chapter:

1.	The Total Teaching Package Outline	This outline integrates the various resources available to help instructors cover the material in each section of the chapter.
2.	Learning Objectives	The learning objectives consist of a list of concepts the student should know after reading each chapter of the text.
3.	Key Terms	This is an alphabetized list of key terms from the chapter.
4.	Chapter Overview	To enable instructors to better anticipate the text's coverage, these summaries provide an overview of the topics covered in each chapter of the text. All headings listed in the chapter appear in the overview, followed by brief summaries of the corresponding text material.

5.	Lecture Topics and Supplementary Readings	Each chapter in the manual contains two suggested lecture topics, selected either to expand on topics covered in the text chapter or to introduce new material. Each lecture topic is supplemented by a list of references, which may be assigned to students as supplementary readings or used by the instructor as resources in preparing lecture material.
6.	Classroom Activities	The suggested activities are designed to involve students in the lecture material.
7.	Outside Activities	This section provides instructors with a variety of activities that can be conducted outside the classroom. Some of these activities will be assignments for the students to complete on their own, while others involve trips the entire class can make.
8.	Film and Video List	This is an annotated list of films and videos that pertain to the contents of the chapter.

The third section of this manual contains the test item file:

At the beginning of this last section is a description of the types of questions presented, as well as some suggestions for evaluating student performance on exams. After this, you will find 75 multiple-choice questions and 5 essay questions (with detailed answers) for each of the 13 chapters (excluding the introduction) of the *Adolescence* text. The essay questions can also be used to generate class discussion or as a review of the material before the examination.

Acknowledgments

Before concluding this Preface, I would like to thank a number of people whose efforts and support were crucial to the successful completion of this manual. I am grateful to the *Instructor's Manual* authors who preceded me. Far from being generated in a vacuum, this manual is an outgrowth of earlier versions by Nina Mounts, Anne Fletcher, and Elizabeth Cauffman, and would have been infinitely more difficult to complete without the firm foundation they provided. Also, I owe a debt of gratitude to Larry Steinberg for authoring the wonderful learning tool that he has given my students and me. Rita Lombard from McGraw-Hill provided a perfect blend of gentle prodding and stress-reducing flexibility that served to maintain healthy levels of productivity and sanity. Peg Jones from my own department is deserving of special recognition for her efforts on the Test Bank portion of this manual; her work was simply heroic. Finally, I am, as always, indebted to my wife, Lisa, and my children (Emily, Megan, and Jeremy) for their support, patience and understanding throughout this project.

Please note that McGraw-Hill offers the following additional resources to help you teach your Adolescence course. Please contact your local McGraw-Hill representative for details concerning policies, prices, and availability as some restrictions may apply.

Instructor Resource CD-ROM
This tool offers instructors the opportunity to customize McGraw-Hill materials to create their lecture presentations. Resources on the CD-ROM for instructors include the *Instructor's Manual*, PowerPoint presentation slides, the Computerized Test Bank, and the Image Database for Adolescent Development.

On-Line Learning Center The official web site for the text at http://www.mhhe.com/steinberg6. contains a variety of resources for both you and your students. The password protected Instructor portion of the site includes:
- This *Instructor's Manual*
- PowerPoint Presentations
- Adolescent Development Image Gallery
- Recommended readings
- The text's new chapter concluding **Web Researcher** feature.

This web-based critical thinking question appears before the summary in each chapter and challenges your students to apply concepts learned, and do on-line research via recommended hot links on the text's on-line learning center. Additional multiple-choice questions further test your students' understanding and offer comprehensive feedback on all chosen answers so that you fully grasp the reasoning behind correct or incorrect answers.
Again, log on to http://www.mhhe.com/steinberg6

McGraw-Hill Developmental Psychology Supersite http://www.mhhe.com/developmental
This website provides valuable resources to help you and your students such as Interactive exercises and simulations and links to some of the best developmental psychology sites on the web.

PageOut!
Build your own course web site in less than an hour.
You don't have to be a **computer whiz** to create your own course web site, especially with an exclusive McGraw-Hill product called **PageOut**™. The program walks you through constructing a site for your course, but requires no prior knowledge of HTML. No long hours of coding. And no design skills on your part. Use PageOut! to add a new, interactive dimension to your course at http:// www.pageout.net.

Problematic Behaviors During Adolescence

By Jeffrey J. Haugaard, Cornell University

This is the only text to examine some of the most prevalent problematic behaviors and provides students with a consistent framework for understanding *how these complex behaviors develop*. Each chapter comprehensively defines the behavior, establishes its prevalence, examines its development, and then offers suggestions for prevention strategies. The use of high-interest chapter opening vignettes along with boxed features such as **Broadening Perspectives** and **Helping Yourself or Others** makes the text immediately accessible and comprehensible to students.

The AIDS Booklet

This brief but comprehensive text has been recently revised to provide the most up-to-date information about Acquired Immune Deficiency Syndrome (AIDS).

Annual Editions – Adolescent Psychology

Published by Dushkin/McGraw-Hill, this is a collection of articles on topics related to the latest research and thinking in adolescent development. These editions are updated annually and contain helpful features including a topic guide, an annotated table of contents, unit overviews, and a topical index. An Instructor's Guide containing testing materials is also available.

Please note that the following resources are available to your students:

PowerWeb
This dynamic Web site, accessible to students by using their password card, shrink-wrapped for free with each new copy of *Adolescence*, Sixth Edition, offers a suite of original web-based materials for the adolescent development course. PowerWeb is the first Internet tool to help you learn how to research online. The site offers daily and weekly course updates, access to key articles on important course topics, and self-assessment built into the site.

Study Guide to accompany Adolescence. Sixth Edition
By Nancy Dodge Reyome, State University of New York at Potsdam, and Christopher A. Bjornsen, Longwood College
This offers a wealth of resources to your students including chapter outlines, learning objectives, extensive chapter-by-chapter quizzing, critical thinking exercises, and section tests.

For your students with "Print Disabilities" including blindness, visual impairment, learning disabilities or other physical disabilities, please check out the **Recording for the Blind and Dyslexic website** at **www.rfbd.org/** or call customer service at **(800) 221-4792**. This educational library has 77,000 taped titles including textbooks, and reference and professional materials for people who cannot read standard print because of a disability.

Section I:

General Information

Resources for Instructors of Psychology

A number of valuable resources are available to teachers of psychology. Below is a list of publications and organizations that can be of assistance.

Materials on Teaching

1. The *Activities Handbook for the Teaching of Psychology* describes a multitude of demonstrations and experiments that can be utilized in the classroom. This resource is published by the American Psychological Association (APA).

2. The division on the Teaching of Psychology (Division II of the American Psychological Association) publishes a monthly journal entitled *Teaching of Psychology*. Each issue contains activities and demonstrations for the classroom, as well as articles concerning broader issues in the teaching of psychology. Subscriptions are available to Division Two members. To become a member, contact the membership chair of the division. This information may be obtained for the APA's central office and is published every June in the *American Psychologist*.

3. The APA also sponsors a free newsletter for psychology instructors at two-year colleges called *Network*. It is published three times a year and can be obtained by contacting the Educational Affairs Office at APA. This newsletter may also be obtained by contacting the Educational Affairs Office at APA. This newsletter may also be of interest to psychologists at four-year colleges and universities.

4. Each year a number of prominent psychologists participate in the G. Stanley Hall Lectures at the national convention of APA. These lectures provide up-to-date information on selected topics in introductory psychology and are published by APA.

5. An electronic discussion group for instructors of psychology is available on the Internet. If you are not familiar with computer lists and need assistance, ask the computer consultants at your institution to help you. TIPS is a list for instructors who "teach in psychology." Send subscription request to:

    LISTSERV@FRE.FSU.UMD.EDU. (Internet) or
    LISTSERV@FRE.FSU.UMD.EDU@CUNYVM.CUNY.EDU (Bitnet)

Examinations

Generating Test Items

Buchanan and Rogers (1990) have found that students themselves are an excellent resource for generating test items. This technique not only aids the instructor in the generation of test items, but also alleviates the problems of cheating and stolen exams that are found on some campuses. Students are told that they can submit potential examination questions. The format for submission of questions includes: (1) students can submit up to 10 questions per exam; (2) all questions must be written or typed on a 5"by 7" index card; (3) the correct answer must be identified; (4) the source of the question (e.g. page of the text, date of lecture) given; (5)the student's name provided. Lastly, students are provided with the following motivation to generate test items: (1) the instructor will identify the author of the exam question if the student wishes; (2) the student is likely to get the exam question correct if he or she wrote it; (3) the student is given two additional points on the exam for each question chosen (equal to the value of one correct exam question). Be aware that many of even the best questions submitted may need some rewriting. Also, try to reward as many students as possible; the authors try to accept no more than two questions per student per exam.

Buchanan, R.W. (1990). Innovative assessment in large classes. *College Teaching*, 38, 69-73.

Makeup Examinations

Makeup exams are troublesome from everyone's point of view. The instructor must generate a new exam (or trust that the student doesn't speak to anyone else in the class), decide who will be allowed to take a makeup (you may have heard just one too many excuses), arrange a time and place for everyone to retake the exam, and make sure it is a "fair" makeup exam. To deal with this situation, Buchanan and Rogers (1990) have proposed the following solution. First, construct the course so that examinations of students involve three objective tests and an optional final. Students must take the optional final is they miss any of the three objective tests. Given this, no makeup exams are offered. If desired, students are allowed to take all four exams and "drop" their lowest grade, which can be either a poor performance on an exam or a missed exam. Students do not need permission to miss a test. If the student misses a second test or the final, he or she will fail the course. And lastly, no makeup exams will be given for any reason! Buchanan and Rogers found that the implementation of such a system resulted in a decrease from 15 to 25 percent of students wishing to take a makeup exam to approximately 5 percent of the class missing any one exam.

Buchanan, R.W. (1990). Innovative assessment in large classes. *College Teaching*, 38, 69-73

Taking the Heat

After examinations, some students may exhibit frustration and even hostility regarding specific items on the exam. Whitford (1992) has found the following format to work quite nicely: (1) have students write their name and offending question number on a piece of paper; (2) tell the students to look up the answer in the test or lecture notes and write a minimum of a paragraph explaining why their answer is better than your choice; and (3) require students to bring this paper to your office hours and discuss the question with you. Whitford has found that disgruntled students submit the written format 5% of the time and come to office hours to discuss the questions 2% of the time. The majority of the time (about 95%) the students are misinformed about the nature of the question, and this system provides them with immediate feedback, both from the process of looking up the answer as well as discussing it with the instructor. Some students, of course, may have valid complaint; Whitford encourages giving them credit for their efforts.

Whitford, F.W. (1992). *Teaching psychology*. New Jersey: Prentice Hall.

Term Papers

Suggestions for Term Paper Assignments

The Development of an Adolescent Psychologist

This topic is adapted from Galotti's (1989) alternative type of term paper on the development of a developmental psychologist. Students should choose a psychologist whose work has influenced the field of adolescent development (e.g., Bradford Brown, Jeanne Brooks-Gunn) but should be discouraged from choosing such prominent psychologist as Piaget. (There will be just too much information!) The paper should include the following information:

1. The specific area of development that is the focus of the psychologist's research.
2. The development of the psychologist's ideas and research program.
3. The reactions of other psychologists to this individual's work.
4. An evaluation of the psychologist's contribution to the field of adolescent development.

Galotti suggested that this assignment:

1. Teaches students to use bibliographic resources and conduct literature reviews.
2. Introduces students to primary literature in the field.
3. Allows students to gain knowledge of an area of their choosing.
4. Encourages students to recognize & reconcile different points of view within an area of research.
5. Provokes students to think critically.
6. Demonstrates that the progress of an academic career is seldom linear or inevitable.

Galotti, K.M. (1989). Describing the development of a developmental psychologist: An alternative term paper assignment. *Teaching of Psychology, 16*, 8-10.

Adolescent Development in the Classics

For this assignment, students are asked to discuss the psychological development of a fictional adolescent. Students should select one or more areas of psychosocial development (e.g., identity, autonomy, intimacy, sexuality, or achievement) and discuss the development of the character in the context of what we know about adolescent development in this domain. For example:

1. What are the most significant aspects of this character's development during adolescence?
2. What do you find interesting about this character?
3. What seem to be the pressing issues that this character must resolve?
4. How have the specific factors inherent in the context in which this individual lives (or had lived) affected the course of his/her development in adolescence?
5. To what extent is this character's development typical, in the sense that it appears to correspond (or not correspond) to what we learn from scientific research and theory about adolescence?

Be sure to have students briefly introduce the character and the story so that the reader is familiar enough to understand the references to the novel. Encourage students to include direct quotes from the novel for purposes of illustration, but do not let them rely on this as an alternative to providing their own interpretation or opinion. Students should also be encouraged to tie in references and information from the scientific literature that has been presented in the text and in class.

Below are a few classics in which characters encounter issues associated with adolescent development:

Salinger, *The Catcher in the Rye*
Knowles, *A Separate Peace*
Golding, *Lord of the Files*
McCullers, *The Member of the Wedding*
Twain, *The Adventures of Tom Sawyer*

Design a Parenting Class of Parents of Adolescents

This paper allows the student to take an applied approach to the material being presented. Tell students to imagine that the local school in their community has asked them to design a parenting class for parents of adolescents. Their task is to develop one lecture that incorporates both general information and research examples. Have students select a specific topic relating to adolescence (e.g., early vs. late maturation, parenting styles, peer influences) about which that can educate parents. An interesting classroom activity (time permitting) would be to have the students present their lectures orally.

Comic Relief

Comic strips often illustrate myths and/or truths regarding adolescence. Have students identify examples of common stereotypes regarding adolescence that are formed in comic strips or other media. To what extent are these stereotypes support by the literature discusses in class? Instructors may have students bring clippings to class for discussion, or may instead use specific examples in introduce new lecture topic.

Suggestions for Term Paper Format

When you assign a paper to students, it is helpful to give them a set of guidelines. This may include any or all of the following:

1. Due date and consequences for late papers.

2. A list of approved topics, or, if students are allowed to choose their own topic, a statement citing what type of approval is required.

3. Length of paper (e.g., number of words, number of pages).

4. The form of the paper, including whether the paper must be typed, double spaced, or in APA format. If you require APA format, it will probably be necessary to cover thoroughly such things as typing requirements (e.g., margins, running heads) and referencing. The students will need access to the *Publication Manual of the American Psychological Association*.

5. Guidelines on the content of the paper. Students will want to know, for example, whether their own opinions should be included.

6. Sources for finding material, such as *Psychlit*. Also, specify whether you wish students to focus on journal articles, whether textbooks are allowed as references, and how recent cited articles should be.

7. Plagiarism. Most students do not have a good sense of what constitutes plagiarism. Some students may think that rewriting a sentence by transforming the order of two words does not constitute plagiarism. By explaining your policy in advance, you avoid misunderstandings and leave yourself in a better position if issues of plagiarism, in fact, arise.

8. Grading policies. Students should be given some sense of what will be the criteria for grading their papers and what weight will be give to content and format.

Film and Video Distributors

AIMS Media, Inc.
(AIMS)

626 Justin Avenue
Glendale, CA 91201

Ambrose Video
(AV)

1390 Avenue of the Americas
Suite 2245
New York, NY 10104
(800) 526-4663

Annenberg/CPB Collection
(A/CPB)

Department CA95
P.O. Box 2345
South Burlington, VT 05407-2345
(800) 532-7637

Carousel Film and Video
(CF-V)

260 Fifth Avenue, Room 405
New York, NY 10001

CRM/McGraw-Hill Films
(CRM/M-H)

2233 Faraday Avenue
Carlsbad, CA 92008

Davidson Films
(DV)

3701 Buchanan Street
San Francisco, CA 94123

Filmakers Library, Inc.
(FL)

124 East 40th Suite 901
New York, NY 10016
(212) 355-6545

Films for the Humanities and Sciences
(FFHS)

P.O. Box 2053
Princeton, NJ 08543
(800) 257-5126

Florida State University
(FSU)

Instructional Support Center
Film Library, 54 Johnston Bldg.
Tallahassee, FL 32306-1019

Human Relations Media
(HRM)

Room GV
175 Tompkins Avenue
Pleasantville, NY 10570
(800) 431-2050

Indiana University
(IU)

Audio Visual Center
Bloomington, IN 47405

Insight Media
(IM)

121 West 85th Street
New York, NY 10024
(212) 721-6316

Learning Corporation of America (LCA)	108 Wilmot Road Deerfield, IL 60015-9990 (800) 621-2131
Louisiana State University (LSU)	16mm Film Library 118 Hines Hall Instructional Resource Center Baton Rouge, LA 70803
Magna Systems, Inc. (MS)	95 West County Line Road Barrington, IL 60010 (800) 523-5503
Marshfilm/Marshmedia (M/M)	P.O. Box 8082 Shawnee Mission, KS 66208
MTI Teleprograms, Inc. (MTI)	108 Wilmot Road Deerfield, IL 60015
Pennsylvania State University (PSU)	Audio Visual Services Special Services Bldg. University Park, PA 16802 (800) 826-0132
Perennial Education, Inc. (PE)	P.O. Box 855, Ravinia Highland Park, IL 60035
Perspective Films, Education Group (PF)	Simon and Schuster Communications 108 Wilmot Road Deerfield, IL 60015
Riverside Publishing Company (RP)	8420 Bryn Mawr Chicago, IL 60631 (312) 693-0040
RMI Media Productions (RMI)	2807 West 47th Street Shawnee Mission, KS 66205 (800) 745-5840
Syracuse University (SU)	Film Rental Center 1455 E. Colvin St. Syracuse, NY 13210
Time-Life Film and Video (TLF)	100 Eisenhower Drive Paramus, NJ 07652
University of California (U of CA)	Extension Media Center 2176 Shattuck St. Berkeley, CA 94704

University of Connecticut (U of CT)	Center for Instructional Media and Technology 249 Blenbrook Rd. Storrs, CT 06269-2001
University of Illinois (U of IL)	Film Center 1325 South Oak St. Champaign, IL 61820
University of Iowa (U of IA)	Audio-Visual Center C-5 Seashore Hall Iowa City, IA 52242
University of Michigan (U of MI)	Film and Video Library 400 4th Street Ann Arbor, MI 48103-4816
University of Minnesota (U of MN)	University Film and Video 1313 Fifth St., SE Suite 108 Minneapolis, MN 55414
University of Missouri (U of MO)	Academic Support Center Film and Video Library 505 E. Stewart Rd. Columbia, MO 65211
University of Nevada (U of NV)	Film Library Getchell Library Reno, NV 89557
University of New Hampshire (U of NH)	Dept. of Media Services Diamond Library Durham, NH 03824
University of Wisconsin (U of WI)	Bureau of Audio-Visual Instruction 1327 University Ave. P.O. Box 2093 Madison, WI 53701-2093
Wiley and Sons (W&S)	603 Third Avenue New York, NY 10016

Section II:

Chapter Information

CHAPTER 1

❖

Biological Transitions

The Total Teaching Package Outline: Chapter 1 *Biological Transitions*	
Heading	**Resource**
PUBERTY: AN OVERVIEW	Learning Objective 1 Lecture Topics I Video: *Adolescence – Physical Growth and Development (Magna Systems, 1995)*
The Endocrine System	Learning Objective 2 Figure 1.1
What Triggers Puberty?	Learning Objective 2
SOMATIC DEVELOPMENT *Changes in Stature and the Dimensions of the Body*	Learning Objective 3 Figures 1.2, 1.3 Table 1.1 Classroom Activities I

Sexual Maturation
  • *Sexual Maturation in Boys*
  • *Sexual Maturation in Girls*
	Learning Objective 3
	Figures 1.4, 1.5
	Video: *Menstruation – Understanding Your Body (Video Learning Library, 1993); Boy to Man (U. of MN, 1984); Girl to Woman (U. of MN, 1984)*
	Classroom Activities II

TIMING AND TEMPO OF PUBERTY *Variations in the Timing and Tempo of Puberty*	Learning Objective 4 Figure 1.6

Genetic and Environmental Influences
  • *Individual Differences in Pubertal Maturation*
  • *Group Differences in Pubertal Maturation*
	Learning Objective 4
	Figures 1.7, 1.8
	Outside Activities I

THE PSYCHOLOGICAL AND SOCIAL IMPACT OF PUBERTY	Learning Objective 5 Figure 1.9

The Immediate Impact of Puberty
  • *Puberty and Self-esteem*
  • *Adolescent Moodiness*
  • *Changes in Patterns of Sleep*
  • *Puberty and Family Relations*
	Learning Objective 6
	Figure 1.10
	Table 1.2
	Video: *Am I Normal? (FSU, 1979)*
	Outside Activities II

The Impact of Specific Pubertal Events	Learning Objective 5

The Impact of Early or Late Maturation
   • *Early versus Late Maturation among Boys*
   • *Early versus Late Maturation in Girls*
	Learning Objective 5
	The Scientific Study of Adolescence Box: *Early Maturation and Girls' Problem Behavior – Activation or Accentuation?*
	The Sexes Box: *The Effects of Early Maturation*
	Classroom Activities III
	Outside Activities III

EATING DISORDERS *Anorexia Nervosa and Bulimia*	Learning Objective 7 Lecture Topics II Figure 1.11 Video: *Bulimia – The Binge-Purge Obsession (RP); Eating Disorders (FFHS, 1994)* Classroom Activities V Outside Activities IV *Problematic Behaviors[1]: Chapter 9*
PHYSICAL HEALTH AND HEALTH CARE IN ADOLESCENCE	Learning Objective 8

For further information on these and other topics, please check out PowerWeb (packaged with the text), and the Online Learning Center for this edition, located at <u>www.mhhe.com/steinberg6</u>.

[1]Refers to *Problematic Behaviors During Adolescence* by Jeffrey Haugaard (2001, McGraw-Hill).

Learning Objectives

1. Describe the five chief physical manifestations of puberty.

2. Discuss the role of the hypothalamus and pituitary gland in the hormonal feedback loop.

3. List the normal sequence of events in puberty for males and females.

4. Discuss the factors, both biological and environmental, that influence individual variability in pubertal growth and development. Be sure to include a discussion of the secular trend.

5. Explain the adjustments that accompany puberty and comment on the advantages and disadvantages associated with early and late maturation.

6. Describe how physical maturation affects the adolescent's self-image, mood, and relationships with parents.

7. Describe anorexia nervosa, bulimia, and obesity. How do they relate to pubertal development?

8. Discuss the "new morbidity and mortality" of adolescence and the steps being taken to promote adolescent health (particularly the "five A's").

Key Terms

activational role of hormones
adolescent growth spurt
adolescent health care
adrenarche
androgens
anorexia
asynchronicity in growth
basal metabolism rate
bulimia
cross-sectional study
delayed phase preference
disordered eating
endocrine system
estrogens
feedback loop
glands

gonads
health-compromising behaviors
health-enhancing behaviors
hormones
HPG (hypothalamic-pituitary-gonadal) axis
hypothalamus
leptin
longitudinal study
menarche
organizational role of hormones
ovaries
peak height velocity
pheromones
pituitary gland
puberty
school-based health centers

Chapter Overview

I. **PUBERTY: AN OVERVIEW**

A. The physical changes that accompany sexual maturation are called puberty. Although puberty is a universal feature of adolescence, individuals develop physically at different ages and at different rates. For example, in the United States, girls reach menarche (the time of first menstruation) at an average age of 12, but in New Guinea, the average age is 18. Both genetic and environmental factors play a part in determining the onset and duration of puberty.

B. Rapid acceleration in growth, the further development of the gonads, the development of secondary sex characteristics, changes in body composition, and changes in the respiratory and circulatory systems.

C. The Endocrine System: Puberty is a gradual process that begins at conception. The endocrine system produces, circulates, and regulates levels of hormones that are already present since birth. These hormones perform both an organizational role (e.g., organize or program the brain to behave in certain ways) and an activational role (e.g., activate changes in behavior) during adolescent development.

D. During infancy a feedback loop develops involving the pituitary gland (which controls hormone levels), the hypothalamus (the part of the brain that controls the pituitary gland), and the gonads (in males, the testes; in females, the ovaries). At puberty a change occurs in the hypothalamus such that it takes higher and higher levels of androgens and estrogens to trigger the hypothalamus (known as the system's set point). The hypothalamus then stimulates the pituitary gland, which in turn stimulates the gonads to produce more androgens and estrogens.

E. Both sexes produce androgens and estrogens (the sex hormones released by the gonads), however, the average male typically produces more androgens than estrogens while the average female produces more estrogens than androgens.

F. <u>What Triggers Puberty</u>? Although the increased secretion of these sex hormones is one of the most important endocrinological changes to occur at puberty, it is not the only one. The hypothalamus also controls changes in the secretion of hormones that act on the thyroid and the adrenal cortex. These hormonal changes stimulate many of the changes in stature and bodily dimensions characteristic of the period. In addition, recent research indicates early feelings of sexual attraction may be stimulated by adrenarche (the stimulation of the adrenal glands).

II. SOMATIC DEVELOPMENT

A. <u>Changes in Stature and the Dimensions of the Body</u>: Increases in the levels of hormones lead to the adolescent growth spurt, which occurs about 2 years earlier in girls than in boys. During peak height velocity, an adolescent is growing at approximately the same rate as a toddler (about 4 inches per year for boys and 3.5 inches per year for girls).

B. The asynchronicity in growth of body parts during early adolescence often result in a clumsy or gawky appearance. In addition to sheer changes in height and weight, there are changes in the relative proportion of body muscle and body fat, and changes in the circulatory and respiratory systems. Sex differences in these latter areas are especially important, since such differences are minimal prior to adolescence. For example, body fat in boys tends to decrease whereas in girls it tends to increase. Many girls react to the increase in body fat at puberty by dieting unnecessarily.

C. <u>Sexual Maturation</u>: Another important aspect of somatic development at puberty is the emergence of reproductive capability and the development of secondary sex characteristics (changes related to physical appearance). The sequence of changes (often referred to as Tanner stages) is more orderly for males than for females.

D. <u>Sexual Maturation in Boys</u>: In boys, the changes in physical development occur in the following order: rapid growth of testes and scrotum and appearance of pubic hair; the beginning of the growth spurt, enlargement of the penis and thickening of pubic hair; growth of facial and body hair and lowering of the voice. The first ejaculation usually occurs about a year after the beginning of the accelerated growth of the penis.

E. <u>Sexual Maturation in Girls</u>: Girls' development is in a less regular sequence, but usually begins with the development of the breast buds or growth of pubic hair. Later, breasts develop nipples and aerola (the area around the nipple) and enlarge, and pubic hair thickens. Menarche, the first menstrual period, occurs later in puberty, and ovulation and the ability to carry a baby to full term usually follow menarche by several years, although it is possible for a girl to become pregnant at any time following her period.

III. TIMING AND TEMPO OF PUBERTY

A. Variations in the Timing and Tempo of Puberty: There are tremendous variations among individuals in the timing (i.e., age at onset) and tempo (i.e., rate of change) of puberty. Some individuals will have completed pubertal maturation before their same-age peers will have even begun puberty.

B. Genetic and Environment Influences: Generally speaking, studies indicate that individuals who are closely related genetically have similar patterns of pubertal timing and tempo. However, genetic influences on pubertal growth are better thought of as creating a predisposition to mature at a given time and at a given rate rather than as determining a fixed absolute.

C. Individual Differences in Pubertal Maturation: Although the most important influence on the timing of maturation is genetic, adolescents who have been well-nourished and healthy during childhood go through puberty earlier than their less fortunate peers. Recent studies suggest that social factors may also influence the onset of maturation. For example, family conflict and stress may accelerate the pubertal process while living in the proximity of one's biological relatives appears to slow it down.

D. Group Differences in Pubertal Maturation: The age at which adolescents mature physically varies around the world. On average, teenagers in highly industrialized countries, like Japan, mature earlier than their counterparts in developing nations, where health and nutritional problems slow growth. The age at menarche has declined considerably over the past 150 years, a phenomenon known as the secular trend, which may be attributed to improved nutrition, better sanitation, and better control of infectious diseases.

IV. THE PSYCHOLOGICAL AND SOCIAL IMPACT OF PUBERTY

A. Two approaches can be taken to studying the psychological and social consequences of puberty. Longitudinal studies identify a group of subjects of the same pubertal stage and then follow them for a period of time, often over several years. In cross-sectional studies, researchers select groups of individuals who are at different stages of puberty and then compare these groups to one another.

B. The Immediate Impact of Puberty: Regardless of whether puberty occurs early or late, physical maturation has been found to affect the adolescent's self-image, mood, and relationships with parents. Self-esteem has been found to decline among girls who are going through puberty but only when accompanied by other changes that require adaptation (e.g., dating, changing schools). Puberty has also been associated with increases in negative moods but only during the early stages of puberty when hormone levels are fluctuating widely. Furthermore, physical maturation increases distance between parents and adolescents and has been linked to adolescent sleep patterns of staying up late and sleeping in, referred to as the delayed phase preference. More important than puberty itself is how puberty is viewed within the context in which the adolescent matures, and the extent to which the adolescent has been prepared psychologically for the biological changes of puberty.

C. The Impact of Specific Pubertal Events: Most adolescents respond positively to the changes associated with puberty. Girls' attitudes, however, still vary, with those who view menarche negatively experiencing the most discomfort. Far less is known about males' reactions to first ejaculation. In contrast to girls, boys tend not to discuss this experience with either parents or friends.

D. <u>The Impact of Early or Late Maturation</u>: Researchers have also examined the impact of early and late maturation. Generally speaking, early-maturing boys may have some short-term advantages (e.g., during adolescence itself, early maturers are more popular and confident), but some long-term disadvantages (e.g., during adulthood, men who were early maturers are more conventional and conforming). For girls, it may be more advantageous—at least in terms of popularity—in the short run to be either somewhat late or to mature around the same time as one's peers. In the long run, however, early-maturing girls may show some psychological benefits, in that they appear to develop more sophisticated coping skills. For both sexes, however, early physical maturation is associated with more problem behavior, including drug and alcohol use, delinquency, and precocious sexual activity.

V.   EATING DISORDERS

A. Eating attitudes and behaviors that are considered unhealthy are referred to by psychologists as disordered eating. These can range from a preoccupation with weight to a clinical eating disorder. Weight gain during puberty due, in part, to the drop in the body's basal metabolism rate may cause adolescents (especially girls) to become extremely concerned about their weight. Many U.S. adolescents, however, have legitimate concerns about gaining weight, 20% of are overweight; 5% are obese.

B. <u>Anorexia Nervosa and Bulimia</u>: Bulimia is an eating disorder characterized by a cycle of bingeing and purging while anorexia nervosa exhibits symptoms of extremely restrictive self-induced diet. Although the incidence of anorexia and bulimia is small, it is far more common among females than males, and is rarely seen before puberty. Contrary to previous reports, recent research does not exclude any social class or ethnic group from the likelihood of developing an eating disorder. Several theories have been proposed to account for the emergence of eating disorders, ranging from biological to environmental or interplay between the two.

VI.   PHYSICAL HEALTH AND HEALTH CARE IN ADOLESCENCE

A. Adolescent health care has become a salient issue in the last two decades due to the prevalence of risk-taking behaviors in this age group. Although adolescence is characterized as one of the healthiest periods in the life span, the "new morbidity and mortality" of adolescence indicate that adolescent health problems are often psychosocial in nature. Contributors to this new morbidity and mortality include automobile accidents, violence, substance abuse, and unprotected sex.

B. New approaches to adolescent health care emphasize health promotion by reducing health-compromising behaviors (e.g., drinking and driving) and increasing health-enhancing behaviors (e.g., wearing seat belts). Among the most important innovations are school-based health centers.

C. Any successful health promotion program for adolescents should include the "five A's": anticipatory guidance, ask, advise, assist, and arrange.

Lecture Topics and Supplementary Readings

I.   Endocrinological and Physical Changes of Puberty

For students who are interested in the more biological aspects of human growth and development, a lecture on the endocrinological and physical changes of puberty may be an interesting supplement to the material presented in the text. In such a lecture, the instructor may want to provide some additional information on the structure and function of the endocrine system, elaborating on the concept of the feedback loop discussed in the text and having students follow the relevant diagrams and figures included in the text during the lecture. Students are also often curious about the pathways through which specific hormonal changes lead to specific somatic changes. It is one thing simply to list the various somatic changes that occur during puberty, but it is something else actually to explain why they occur when they do. It is an interesting exercise to use an anatomical chart and trace the physiological course of events that begins with changes in the hypothalamus and ends, for example, with the spurt in height and weight.

Brooks-Gunn, J., and Reiter, E. (1990). The role of pubertal processes (pp. 16-23). In S. Feldman & G. Elliott (Eds.), *At the threshold: The developing adolescent.* Cambridge: Harvard University Press.

Grumbach, M., Grave, G., and Mayer, F. (Eds.) (1974). *Control of the onset of puberty.* New York: Wiley.

Marshall, W. (1978). Puberty. In F. Falkner and J. Tanner (Eds.), *Human growth* Vol. 2. New York: Plenum Press.

Tanner, J. (1972). Sequence, tempo, and individual variation in growth and development of boys and girls aged twelve to sixteen. In J. Kagan and R. Coles (Eds.), *Twelve to sixteen: Early adolescence.* New York: Norton.

II.   Eating Disorders

Students invariably find the topic of eating disorders interesting. On many college campuses, of course, anorexia and bulimia are serious health problems, and lecturing on the etiology and treatment of these disorders can do some social as well as intellectual good. Anorexia, a disorder limited almost exclusively to adolescent girls, typically has its onset around the time of puberty, although the connection between anorexia and puberty per se is open to debate. The conventional psychoanalytic view holds that the disorder represents a denial of sexuality and/or a refusal to become an adult. More contemporary theorists, such as those whose works are referenced below, focus instead on multiple determinants, including the role that puberty plays in signifying the adolescent's passage into adulthood, the adolescent's attempt to establish autonomy and independence during this time period, the importance of physical appearance to the adolescent female's self-image, and the historical and cultural factors that shape our current fascination with thinness and no doubt influence the prevalence of anorexia and bulimia. Invite a mental health counselor from your college's health service program to make a presentation in your class on the treatment of eating disorders on college campuses.

Attie, I., & Brooks-Gunn, J. (1989). Development of eating problems in adolescent girls: A longitudinal study. *Developmental Psychology, 25,* 70-79.

Brumberg, J. (1988). *Fasting girls*. Cambridge: Harvard University Press.

Cauffman, E. & Steinberg, L. (1996). Interactive effects of menarcheal status and dating on dieting and disordered eating among adolescent girls. *Developmental Psychology, 32*, 631-635.

Garfinkel, P., & Garner, D. (1982). *Anorexia nervosa: A multidimensional perspective*. New York: Brunner/Mazel.

Levine, M., & Smolak, L. (1992). Toward a developmental psychopathology of eating disorders: The example of early adolescence. In J. Crowther, S. Hobfoll, M. Stephens, & D. Tennenbaum (Eds.), *The etiology of bulimia: The individual and familial context*. Washington, D.C.: Hemisphere.

Polivy, H., & Herman, P. (1985). Dieting and bingeing. *American Psychologist, 40*, 193-201.

Classroom Activities

I.   What You've Always Wanted to Ask the Opposite Gender

It is a widespread belief that adolescents are incredibly naive and uninformed about sexuality and the other gender, but this is not true *only* for adolescents. A large percentage of individuals retain myths about the other gender and are not very knowledgeable. This exercise allows people to ask the opposite gender any questions that they always wanted to ask. The best way to conduct this activity is to divide the class into small groups with approximately equal numbers of males and females. Since many psychology courses have more females than males, try to ensure that each group has at least two or three males. First, each gender should create a list of questions that they have always wanted to ask the opposite gender. This will typically take about 15 minutes. Then, males and female should reconvene and take turns asking their questions. After a short time, feelings of awkwardness will dissipate and everyone will begin having fun. (For some reason, most males want to know why women need to go to the restroom in pairs or groups!) This exercise is informative for the students and increases communication between the genders.

Pyzbla, D.P.J. (1990). *Instructor's manual to accompany Hyde: Understanding human sexuality*. New York: McGraw-Hill.

II.   Menarche and All That Goes with It

The onset of menstruation is typically a vivid memory for most women. This memory may have related negative feelings or positive feelings, or a combination of both. The following simple exercise can be used to highlight a discussion of the subjective side of menarche in adolescence.

During the class period prior to the discussion of menarche, ask the women in your class to write on a piece of paper the age they were when they first began to menstruate and to write briefly (three or four sentences) about their experience. Both the mean age of menarche, and the range, can be tabulated for the class to reinforce the information provided in the text. In addition, several sample "stories" can be read to the class which demonstrate both the negative and positive feelings attached to this significant event.

This activity may also be conducted with the male students by asking them to recall the age of their first ejaculation.

III.   Early Versus Late Maturation

To begin the discussion of early versus late maturation, have students recount some of their own experiences. Students can be divided into small groups of three to five individuals and told to rate their development as early, average, or late. Students should then discuss the advantages and disadvantages of early, average, and late maturation. You may wish to have them focus on one sex and then on the other. Some students may be uncomfortable with parts of this exercise. However, their discomfort can be used as an educational tool. Being able to share feelings about changes occurring during puberty will help an individual understand and support others undergoing puberty (Charlesworth & Slate, 1986). Parents and teachers who are comfortable with, and knowledgeable about, changes occurring during puberty will be better able to educate and help adolescents understand and adjust to changes they are undergoing.

Charlesworth, J.R. & Slate, J.R. (1986). Teaching about puberty: Learning to talk about sensitive topics. *Teaching Psychology, 13*, 215-217.

IV.   Bringing Puberty to Life

Oftentimes students are reluctant or embarrassed to discuss their own pubertal experiences. In order to stimulate discussion on pubertal development, it often helps to use case studies to bring the event to life. Case studies also provide the student with the opportunity to apply what they have learned from the text. Below are several case studies that are both enjoyable and, at times, quite humorous.

Frank, A. (1967). *Anne Frank: The diary of a young girl.* Translated from the Dutch by B. M. Mooyaart-Doubleday; with an introduction by Eleanor Roosevelt. *(See pages 145-146 for Anne Frank's description of her pubertal experience)*

Ephron, N. (1975). Crazy salad: Some things about women. New York: Alfred A. Knopf. *(See chapter on "A few words about breasts")*

V.   Eating Attitudes Test (EAT)

To illustrate the importance of physical development and body image to psychological adjustment, distribute the following questionnaire created by Garfinkel and Garner (1979). The format requires subjects to respond on a six-point scale (ranging from always to never) to how often they agree with a series of 26 statements. The most symptomatic response receives a score of 3, the second most symptomatic response receives a 2, the third a 1, and the rest are scored as zeroes. The total EAT-26 score thus ranges from zero to 78, with higher scores (>26) indicating more disturbed dieting behaviors. After students have completed the questionnaire, have them write only their score and their sex on a piece of paper and pass them forward. Ask them to consider what they think the average score for males and females will be. Divide the piles by sex and then read the scores for the piles (you may with to have a student calculate the means as you read out the scores). Students will probably be surprised, but relieved, at how high the average scores are (particularly among women). This activity often ignites a discussion of the sources of negative self-image. The prevalence of negative self-images about the body is especially interesting because, in most areas of self-assessment, people generally tend to view themselves as "above average" when compared to other people of their own age and sex.

(The EAT appears on the next page)

Eating Attitudes Test

1 - Always
2 - Very Often
3 - Often
4 - Sometimes
5 - Rarely
6 - Never

1. _____ Am terrified about being overweight
2. _____ Avoid eating when I am hungry
3. _____ Find myself preoccupied with food
4. _____ Have gone on eating binges where I feel that I may not be able to stop
5. _____ Cut my food into small pieces
6. _____ Aware of the calorie content of foods that I eat
7. _____ Particularly avoid foods with high carbohydrate content (e.g., bread, rice, potatoes)
8. _____ Feel that others would prefer if I ate more
9. _____ Vomit after I have eaten
10. _____ Feel extremely guilty after eating
11. _____ Am preoccupied with a desire to be thinner
12. _____ Think about burning up calories when I exercise
13. _____ Other people think that I am too thin
14. _____ Am preoccupied with the thought of having fat on my body
15. _____ Take longer than others to eat my meals
16. _____ Avoid foods with sugar in them
17. _____ Eat diet foods
18. _____ Feel that food controls my life
19. _____ Display self-control around food
20. _____ Feel that others pressure me to eat
21. _____ Give too much time and thought to food
22. _____ Feel uncomfortable after eating sweets
23. _____ Engage in dieting behavior
24. _____ Like my stomach to be empty
25. _____ Enjoy trying new, rich foods
26. _____ Have the impulse to vomit after meals

Garner, D. & Garfinkel, P. (1979). The Eating Attitudes Test: An index of the symptoms of anorexia nervosa. *Psychological Medicine, 9,* 1-7.

Web Researcher

A Girl Scout troupe asks you to run a session on feeling good about yourself during the transition to adolescence. You know that sleep and good nutrition are important parts of feeling good about yourself that often get neglected because of busy schedules and worries about their looks. What would you tell the them, and how might you help them take what you have to say to heart? Go to www.mhhe.com/steinberg6 for further information.

Outside Activities

I.   Secular Trend

To examine the secular trend in the age of pubertal onset, have students record the following information. (Some research will, of course, be necessary!) If older students have mature children, their information can be included as well.

Record Age of Puberty for:

Self   _____

Mother   _____

Father   _____

Maternal
         Grandmother   _____
         Grandfather   _____

Paternal
         Grandmother   _____
         Grandfather   _____

The following questions can then be addressed for individual students' data as well as for the data provided by the class as a whole (providing an opportunity to discuss simple statistical concepts).

1. Does the age of onset differ as a function of generation? If so, how?
2. Does the age of onset differ as a function of gender? If so, how?
3. How do these findings on generational and gender differences relate to the trends described in the text? Why might they be similar or different from the findings described in the text?

II.   Dear Son / Dear Daughter

Have students imagine that they are departing on a 10-year voyage, leaving behind their pre-adolescent child. Their task is to compose a letter to help the child cope with the changes that will soon occur.

III.   A Visit to Middle School / Junior High

Have students visit a middle school or junior high school (after obtaining the school administration's permission, of course) and observe groups of young adolescents in order to assess variability in pubertal maturation. As an exercise designed to teach the concept of interrater reliability, students might work with partners and try to classify adolescents as prepubertal, at the pubertal apex, or postpubertal.

IV.   Media Influences on Eating Disorders

To sensitize your students to the subtle and not-so-subtle ways in which the media contributes to the development of eating disorders, have your students engage in a survey of the television and print media. Ask them to select a television program or magazine designed for a teen audience, then tally the number of underweight, average-weight, and overweight (in their opinion) women they see in the show (and the commercials aired during the show) or in the magazine. The students should convert their frequency data to percentages so that the various programs and magazines can be easily compared. Your students should report back to the class the percentages of women viewed who were underweight, average-weight, and overweight. Their data should confirm that the media reinforces an underweight "norm" for attractiveness. This exercise will prepare the students for a discussion of the media influence on the body ideals of adolescent females.

Film and Video List

Adolescence - Physical Growth and Development (Magna Systems, 1995), 30 minutes
Panels of early and middle-adolescents, supplemented by experts in physical development, review all aspects of pubertal development in adolescent males and females.

Am I Normal? (Florida State University; 1979), 24 minutes
Examines psychosocial aspects of male puberty.

Boy to Man (University of Minnesota; 1984), 14 minutes
Examines physiological aspects of male puberty.

Bulimia – The Binge-Purge Obsession (Riverside Publishing, no date), 20 minutes.
Explores the causes and effects of bulimia and the way that this type of behavior is routine for many high school and college students.

Eating Disorders (Films for the Humanities and Sciences, 1994), 19 minutes.
This program covers the personality profiles of those most likely to suffer from anorexia and shows how anorexia develops and can be cured.

Girl to Woman (University of Minnesota; 1984), 17 minutes
Examines physiological aspects of female puberty.

Menstruation – Understanding Your Body (Video Learning Library, 1993), 28 minutes.
Part of an 8-part series which provides clear, concise answers to the health issues facing women of all ages. This program is hosted by Holly Atkinson, MD, NBC News' *Today Show* Medical Correspondent.

CHAPTER 2

❖

Cognitive Transitions

The Total Teaching Package Outline: Chapter 2 *Cognitive Transitions*	
Heading	**Resource**
CHANGES IN COGNITION *Thinking about Possibilities* *Thinking about Abstract Concepts* *Thinking about Thinking* *Thinking in Multiple Dimensions* *Adolescent Relativism*	Learning Objectives 1 & 2 Classroom Activities I, II & III Videos: *Adolescence – Cognitive and Moral Development (Magna Systems, 1995); Cognitive Development (IM, 1990)* Outside Activity I
THEORETICAL PERSPECTIVES ON ADOLESCENT THINKING *The Piagetian View of Adolescent Thinking* <ul><li>*Piaget's Theory of Cognitive Development*</li><li>*The Growth of Formal-Operational Thinking*</li></ul>	Learning Objective 3 Table 2.1 The Scientific Study of Adolescence Box: *Separating Competence and Performance in Studies of Adolescent Reasoning* Videos: *Formal Reasoning Patterns (UM, 1987); Piaget's Developmental Theory - Formal Thought (Davidson, 1971); Piaget's Developmental Theory - An Introduction (Davidson, 1989); Piaget on Piaget (YU, 1978)*
The Information-Processing View of Adolescent Thinking	Learning Objectives 4 & 5 Classroom Activity IV
New Directions for Theories about Adolescent Thinking	Lecture Topic I
THE ADOLESCENT BRAIN	Learning Objective 6 Figure 2.2 Table 2.3
INDIVIDUAL DIFFERENCES IN INTELLIGENCE IN ADOLESCENCE <ul><li>*The Measurement of IQ*</li></ul>	Learning Objective 7 Transparency #99: *The Normal Curve and Stanford-Binet IQ scores;* #100: *Sample Subscales of the WAIS-R* Table 1.1 Video: *The IQ Myth - Sir Cyril Burt Controversy (Carousal, 1977)* Classroom Activities I

• Sternberg's Triarchic Theory • Gardner's Theory of "Multiple Intelligences"	Learning Objective 8
Intelligence Test Performance in Adolescence • The SAT	Learning Objective 9 Figures 2.3, 2.4 & 2.5 The Sexes Box: *Are there Differences in Mental Abilities at Adolescence (Anymore)?* Video: *Menstruation – Understanding Your Body (Video Learning Library, 1993)*; Classroom Activity V
Culture and Intelligence	Learning Objective 9 Video: *Vygotsky's Developmental Theory - An Introduction (Davidson, 1994)*
ADOLESCENT THINKING IN CONTEXT Changes in Social Cognition • *Impression Formation* • *Social Perspective Taking* • *Conceptions of Morality and Social Convention*	Learning Objective 10 Lecture Topic II Table 2.2 Videos: *Adolescence - A Case Study (CRM, 1978)*; *Teenage Mind and Body (IM, 1992)*
Adolescent Risk-Taking	Learning Objective 11 Figure 2.6 *Problematic Behaviors*[1] Chapter 4: *Sensation-Seeking, Risk-Taking, and Reckless Behaviors*
Adolescent Thinking in the Classroom	Learning Objective 12 Outside Activities II

For further information on these and other topics, please check out PowerWeb (packaged with the text), and the Online Learning Center for this edition, located at *www.mhhe.com/steinberg6*.

[1]Refers to *Problematic Behaviors During Adolescence* by Jeffrey Haugaard (2001, McGraw-Hill).

Learning Objectives

1. Describe the changes in thinking that characterize the transition from childhood to adolescence.

2. Provide examples of two different types of adolescent egocentrism.

3. Discuss the Piagetian and information-processing perspectives as they relate to the development of adolescent cognition.

4. Explain how the information-processing approach and Piagetian perspective may be compatible.

5. Describe the five changes in information-processing abilities that occur during adolescence.

6. Describe the aspects of brain maturation that may be linked to behavioral, emotional and cognitive development during adolescence.

7. Describe the measurement of IQ and its stability as well as improvement during adolescence.

8. Explain Sternberg's and Gardner's approach to studying the development of intelligence.

9. Describe the individual, gender, and cultural differences found using the IQ test.

10. Describe the context of adolescent thinking and the changes in social cognition.

11. Examine the role that decision-making plays in adolescent risk-taking and compare it to that of adults.

12. Describe the current educational system's methods and curricula and how they relate to changes in adolescents' cognitive abilities.

Key Terms

automatization
behavioral decision theory
cognitive-developmental view
cohort
competence-performance distinction
concrete operations
critical thinking
culture-fair tests
deductive reasoning
divided attention
formal operations
functional magnetic resonance imaging (fMRI)
imaginary audience
implicit personality theory
inductive reasoning
information-processing perspective
limbic system
long-term memory
metacognition

mutual role taking
myelination
personal fable
Piagetian perspective
Positron Emission Topography (PET)
prefrontal cortex
preoperational period
propositional logic
scaffolding
selective attention
sensation-seeking
sensorimotor period
social cognition
social conventions
social perspective taking
statistical interaction
synaptic pruning
working memory
zone of proximal development

Chapter Overview

I. **CHANGES IN COGNITION**

    A. Adolescents not only know more than children but they are now able to think in ways that are more advanced, efficient, and generally more effective.

    B. There are five chief ways in which adolescents' thinking differs from that of children: Adolescents are better at thinking about the world of the possible; they are better at thinking about abstract concepts; they are able to think about the process of thinking itself; they think multidimensionally; and they are able to think in relative (as opposed to absolute) terms.

    C. <u>Thinking about Possibilities</u>: Whereas children's thinking is oriented to concrete events that they can directly observe, adolescents have the ability to think about what might be. Related to this new ability to think about possibilities is the adolescent's development of hypothetical thinking, or thinking that involves "if-then" statements.

    D. <u>Thinking about Abstract Concepts</u>: A second notable characteristic of adolescent thinking is the ability to understand abstract, conceptually based relationships and concepts. This ability underlies the adolescent's interest in topics such as interpersonal relationships, politics, philosophy, religion, and morality.

    E. <u>Thinking about Thinking</u>: The ability to think about thinking, called **metacognition**, permits teenagers to think about the strategies they use to solve problems and to think about their own thoughts and feelings. A byproduct of metacognition is a kind of egocentrism characterized by an intense preoccupation with the self. According to Elkind, adolescents develop **personal fables**, or beliefs that they are so unique that what happens to others will not happen to them. These personal fables can cause the teen to feel invulnerable and lead to risky behavior based on the belief that bad things only happen to others. Also, adolescents sometimes experience the effect called the **imaginary audience**, which is an extreme self-consciousness and belief that others are constantly watching and evaluating one's actions. These phenomena may not be limited to adolescence; in fact, adults have been found to exhibit these behaviors as well. Some research suggests that adolescents are egocentric for emotional and social reasons, not cognitive ones.

    F. <u>Thinking in Multiple Dimensions</u>: Whereas children tend to think about things one aspect at a time, adolescents can consider several dimensions of a situation at once. This makes possible more sophisticated and complicated relationships with other people. In addition, it helps provide a new understanding and appreciation of things such as: sarcasm, satire, metaphor, and double-entendres.

    G. <u>Adolescent Relativism</u>: Children tend to see things in absolute terms, as either black or white. Adolescent thinking is characterized by relativism, the ability to see that situations are not just good or bad but rather can be interpreted in many different ways.

II. THEORETICAL PERSPECTIVES ON ADOLESCENT THINKING

A. The two theoretical viewpoints about the nature of cognitive development that have been especially important are the **Piagetian perspective** and the **information-processing perspective**.

B. Piaget's View of Adolescent Thinking: Generally, theorists who adhere to the Piagetian approach take a **cognitive-developmental view** of intellectual development and argue that cognitive development proceeds in a stage like fashion (**sensorimotor**; **preoperational**; **concrete operations**; **formal operations**), that adolescent thinking is qualitatively different from the type of thinking employed by children, and that during adolescence individuals develop a special type of thinking—"**formal operational**"—that they use across a variety of situations.

C. The chief feature that differentiates adolescent thinking from the type of thinking employed by children is the abstract system of **propositional logic**. Although young adolescents may demonstrate formal thinking, it has a transient quality and does not become consolidated until middle or even late adolescence. Research in this realm suggests that differentiating between what adolescents are capable of and what they actually do (referred to as the **competence-performance distinction**) may reveal the extent to which formal operations are displayed. Although Piaget thought formal operations developed in a stage-like fashion, more recent research suggests that these skills develop more gradually and continuously.

D. Changes in Information-Processing Abilities during Adolescence: In response to criticisms of the Piagetian perspective, the information-processing approach suggests that a more **componential approach** be taken. This approach divides cognitive processing into its basic components (attention, working memory, processing speed, organization, metacognition) and suggests that the advanced thinking that comes with adolescence is the result of better strategies for the input, storage, manipulation, and use of information. Changes that information-processing theorists observe in adolescents include advances in both **selective** and **divided attention**, increases in **working** and **long-term memory**, an increase in the speed of information processing, improvement in organizational strategies, and improvement in knowledge about their own thinking processes.

E. New Directions for Theories about Adolescent Thinking: Several recent theorists have attempted to integrate elements from the Piagetian perspective and the information-processing approach to explain adolescent cognitive development. A neo-Piagetian approach proposed by Case suggests that cognitive development proceeds in discrete stages, but that differences between stages are due to the cognitive components proposed by the information-processing approach. Thus, **automatization** (where various cognitive processes become automatic or second nature) occurs. Demetriou, on the other hand, argues that there are a series of **specialized structural systems** that are used to solve different types of intellectual problems.

III. THE ADOLESCENT BRAIN

A. What physiological changes in the brain can be linked to changes in the adolescent's thinking and behavior? Recent improvements in the study of brain maturation during adolescence and the use of various imaging techniques, including **fMRI (functional magnetic resonance imaging)** and **PET (positron emission tomography)**, have revealed changes in synapses, neurotransmitters, and the prefrontal cortex that may account for the observed changes in adolescent thinking and behavior.

B. In the cortex, "pruning" of excessive and unnecessary synapses may lead to increased efficiency in information processing.

C. Increased emotionality, increased responses to stress, and decreased responses to rewards during adolescence may be the result of changes in several neurotransmitters, including dopamine and serotonin. These changes in neurotransmitter levels appear to affect most prominently the **limbic system**, the part of the brain that processes emotional stimuli.

D. A great deal of efficiency-enhancing **synaptic pruning** and **myelination** of neurons in the prefrontal cortex occurs during adolescence. The prefrontal cortex is where higher-order cognitive processes like planning, decision-making, goal-setting, and metacognition occur.

IV. INDIVIDUAL DIFFERENCES IN INTELLIGENCE IN ADOLESCENCE

A. Some researchers have focused on the measurement and assessment of individual differences in mental abilities during adolescence -- in particular, differences in intelligence.

B. The Measurement of IQ: Standardized intelligence tests, or IQ tests, are often used to study individual differences in cognitive abilities as compared to the scores of others from the same **cohort** (or group of people born during the same historical era). Initially developed by the French psychologist Alfred Binet, a variety of tests now exist, including the Stanford-Binet, the Wechsler Intelligence Scale for Children, and the Wechsler Adult Intelligence Scale. Critics of such tests argue that they measure just one type of intelligence—"school smarts"—and neglect other equally important skills, such as social intelligence, creativity, and "street smarts."

C. Multiple Intelligences: Sternberg and Gardner propose an alternative approach to studying intelligence. Sternberg has suggested a **triarchic theory of intelligence** which examines three distinct types of intelligence: (1) componential intelligence (similar to what traditional tests measure), (2) experiential intelligence (creativity), and (3) contextual intelligence ("street smarts"). Gardner has proposed that there are seven types of intelligence (verbal, mathematical, spatial, kinesthetic, self-reflective, interpersonal, and musical) in his **theory of multiple intelligences.**

D. Intelligence Test Performance in Adolescence: Research suggests that intelligence is a very stable trait during adolescence. For example, children who score high on IQ tests during early adolescence are likely to score high throughout their adolescent years. Despite the fact that IQ scores remain stable during adolescence, adolescents' mental abilities do increase. Thus, schooling has been found to enhance individuals' performance on standardized tests of intelligence.

E. Recent studies of sex differences in mental abilities have shown that the earlier gender gap in math abilities, favoring boys, has disappeared. Male and female adolescents also score equally well in tests of verbal ability. It appears that the only reliable sex difference in mental abilities is in the area of spatial ability.

F. The SAT: Unlike intelligence tests, aptitude tests, such as the Scholastic Aptitude Test (SAT), are designed to predict a student's future performance in school. The SAT has been found to be correlated with college performance. However, the SAT may be a more valid predictor of college math grades for males than for females.

G. Culture and Intelligence: It has been argued that youth learn best when they are stimulated to "reach" a little further intellectually than they can grasp (which Vygotsky has referred to as their **zone of proximal development**). Additionally, ideal learning situations include a mentor who provides additional support for cognitive performance, a technique known as **scaffolding**. Defining one's cognitive competence or intelligence, however, has been fraught with many challenges. Intelligence tests may be culturally biased against ethnic minorities as they tend to score lower than their white peers. A more **culture-fair test** has been proposed in order to minimize the language differences as well as reduce favoritism of one ethnic group over another.

V. **ADOLESCENT THINKING IN CONTEXT**

A. Psychologists have studied the practical side of adolescent thinking in three domains: in social situations, in risk-taking, and in the classroom

B. Changes in Social Cognition: Changes in **social cognition** refer to how adolescents think about other people, about interpersonal relationships, and about social institutions. Studies of social cognition fall into three categories: impression formation (how individuals form and organize judgments about other people), social perspective taking (how accurately individuals make assessments about the thoughts and feelings of others), and social conventions (concerning individuals' conceptions of justice, social norms, and guidelines that regulate social interaction).

C. Impression Formation: Studies of impression formation examine how individuals form and organize judgments about other people. These impressions mark the development of an **implicit personality theory** and develop in five directions. Specifically, impressions become (1) more differentiated, (2) less egocentric, (3) more abstract, (4) more dependent on the use of inference, and (5) more highly organized.

D. Social Perspective Taking: The development of **social perspective taking** provides the adolescent with the ability to view events from the perspective of others. According to Selman, the young adolescent progresses through the stage of **mutual role taking** which allows the adolescent to be an objective third party who can see how the thoughts or actions of one person can influence another. Later in adolescence, perspective taking develops an in-depth, societal orientation which eventually improves the ability to communicate and reason with others.

E. Conceptions of Morality and Social Convention: Preadolescent thought on **social conventions**, or norms that govern everyday behavior, is based on rules from authorities, whereas adolescents view these conventions as expectations that grow out of social norms. In all three areas, thinking becomes more abstract and more sophisticated during the adolescent years.

F. Adolescent Risk-taking: Research on cognitive development during adolescence has also been aimed at understanding the thought processes behind adolescent risk-taking. One perspective for understanding this behavior comes from the **behavioral decision theory** which suggests that all behaviors can be analyzed as the outcome of a series of 5 steps (from identifying options to creating a decision rule based on those consequences). Contrary to popular wisdom that adolescents are poor decision makers, research suggests that adolescents make decisions in much the same way that adults do. Research also indicates that adolescents are no more likely than adults to suffer from feelings of "invulnerability." The current consensus is that young people sometimes behave in risky ways not because of faulty decision making but because they evaluate the possible consequences of their actions differently than adults do. Additionally, individuals who are high in **sensation seeking** are more likely to engage in various types of risky behaviors than those who are low in this quality.

G. Adolescent Thinking in the Classroom: Research on cognitive development in adolescence suggests a number of ways that schools might change in order to make classroom instruction better matched to the developing capabilities of adolescent students. For example, adolescents require schools to challenge their **critical thinking** skills so that their performance (what they achieve) matches their competence (what they can do). Unfortunately, however, little has been done to change the way that adolescents are taught, and few high school programs are designed to stimulate the development of formal operations or more sophisticated information-processing skills.

Lecture Topics and Supplementary Readings

I.   New Approaches to the Study of Cognitive Development

An examination of new developments in the study of cognition would be useful, especially in a class in which most students had already been exposed to the more conventional Piagetian and psychometric approaches. Especially interesting to students would be a discussion of two new approaches that call into question the assumption that "real" intelligence is limited to the sorts of skills that equip us to do well in school, including the theories of Howard Gardner and Robert Sternberg. For more advanced students, this lecture might also look at some recent attempts to integrate cognitive-developmental and information-processing approaches, such as that by Robbie Case.

- Case, R. (1985). *Intellectual development: Birth to adulthood.* New York: Academic Press.
- Gardner, H. (1983). *Frames of mind.* New York: Basic Books.
- Sternberg, R. (1988). *The triarchic mind.* New York: Viking Penguin.

II.   Cognitive Change and its Impact on Social Cognition

Examining how the cognitive changes of adolescence affect social cognition is an excellent lecture topic. Such a lecture helps students to see how intellectual development has an impact on youngsters' development and behavior outside of academic or test situations and, more importantly, how many of the psychosocial changes of the period can be traced to cognitive ones. Because Kohlberg's perspective on moral development is discussed in detail in another chapter, it might be better to save this widely used illustration for a later lecture. Instead, one might examine Selman's perspective on role taking, Turiel's perspective on social convention (discussed in the article by Smetana), Elkind's discussion of adolescents' sometimes bizarre social behaviors, and/or the growing literature on person perception. In such a lecture, one could begin with the social or psychosocial phenomenon in question (e.g., role taking) and work backward in trying to tie development in this domain to underlying cognitive changes.

Demorest, A., Phelps, E., Gardner, H., & Winner, E. (1984). Words speak louder than actions: Understanding deliberately false remarks. *Child Development*, *55*, 1527-1534.

Elkind, D. (1978). Understanding the young adolescent. *Adolescence*, *13*, 127-134.

Selman, R. (1980). *The growth of interpersonal understanding: Developmental and clinical analyses*. New York: Academic Press.

Smetana, J. (1988). Concepts of self and social convention: Adolescents' and parents' reasoning about hypothetical and actual family conflicts. Pp. 79-122 in M. Gunnar (Ed.), *21st Minnesota symposium on child psychology* . Hillsdale, N.J.: Erlbaum.

Classroom Activities

I.   The Poker Chip Problem

The poker chip example from the textbook is an interesting way to begin the topic of cognitive transitions during adolescence. While students are filing into class, write on the board or have on an overhead the following instructions: "Imagine 4 poker chips (one red, one blue, one yellow, one green). Make as many different combinations of chips, of any number, as you can. Use the notations R, B, Y & G to record your answers." After about 5 minutes, ask for volunteers to describe how they tackled this problem and what strategies they employed. For example, did they need poker chips to solve this problem? Did they approach the probably haphazardly or did they generate an abstract system? This exercise not only settles the class down quickly, but allows for an immediate discussion of the cognitive differences between children and adolescents.

II.   Imaginary Audience Versus Personal Fable

In order to illustrate Elkind's theory of adolescent egocentrism, provide students with a scenario and ask them to determine whether it falls under the category of imaginary audience or personal fable and why. For example:

- Sally is going on a date and has a pimple on the end of her nose. *(imaginary audience)*
- John is arguing with his parents at a restaurant when the girl he likes walks in. *(imaginary audience)*
- Sylvia and Gerald decided to have sex even though they didn't have any birth control. *(personal fable)*
- Molly is having her class picture taken and she just got braces the day before. *(imaginary audience)*
- Elise broke up with her boyfriend, and when Mom tries to comfort her, Elise screams that she just doesn't understand. *(personal fable)*
- Even though Cheryl is known for her reckless driving, Gordon decides to take a ride from her anyway. *(personal fable)*

You may also wish to have students generate their own examples of the imaginary audience phenomenon and personal fable. In addition, students should try to find examples that are common to both adolescents and adults in order to illustrate that these phenomenon are not unique to adolescents.

III.   The Development of Humor and Sarcasm

Yalisove (1978) has noted that the cognitive differences between individuals of various ages should be reflected in the sorts of humor they appreciate most. Riddles popular among young children tend to involve conceptual tricks, while language ambiguity is most frequently observed in adolescent humor, and absurdity is most appreciated by adults. As a classroom activity, read a variety of jokes to your class.

Those used by Yalisove include:
- What's black and white and read (red) all over? Answer: A newspaper.
- You call suicide prevention, and they put you on hold.
- Can you jump higher than a ten-foot fence? Answer: Yes, a fence cannot jump.
- What table has no legs but never falls? Answer: The multiplication table.

Ask students to identify cognitive skills required to understand the humor in the different punchlines (e.g., realizing that words can have two meanings, understanding hypothetical ideas) and to predict the age groups that would find each joke most amusing.

Yalisove, D. (1978). The effect of riddle structure on children's comprehension of riddles. *Developmental Psychology, 14*, 173-180.

IV.   Changes in Information-Processing

In order to clarify for your students the five information-processing abilities covered in the text that change during adolescence, have your students reflect of their own information-processing abilities and how they have changed from high school to the present. To facilitate this exercise, have students complete the handout that appears on the next page. This handout can be completed in class or as a homework assignment in preparation for coverage of this material in class. If used as a class exercise, students may benefit from small group discussions of the general changes that occur in each area prior to completing the exercise.

Changes in Information-Processing

Directions: Think back to your freshman or sophomore year in high school and list examples of your information-processing abilities in each of the areas indicated in the table below. When finished with these reflections, list the information-processing abilities you currently employ. Are the changes in your thinking similar to those changes experienced by most adolescents? How so?

Information-Processing Ability	High School Processing	College Processing
Attention (selective & divided)		
Memory (working & long-term)		
Speed of information processing		
Organizational strategies		
Knowledge about own thinking		

V.   Predicting Grade Point Average with SAT Scores

Collect anonymous information about SAT scores and grade point averages. Compute correlations for overall SAT and overall GPA. You could also compute correlations between each subsection score and GPA to see if subsections differ in their predictive abilities. Follow up this demonstration with a discussion of factors that might influence performance on standardized tests and GPA, and discuss why they might not always be strongly correlated.

Web Researcher

Pick a risky behavior that teenagers are believed to engage in and find out whether they really do take more risks than adults. How might behavioral decision theory explain these differences? Do you think changes in their cognitive abilities make them more or less vulnerable to risk? Go to *www.mhhe.com/steinberg6* for further information.

Outside Activities

I.   Developmental Shifts in Understanding Humor and Metaphor

This activity may be used to prepare students for a lecture (or the classroom activity) on developmental changes in humor. Have students collect jokes from children of various ages (e.g., first graders, fifth graders, eighth graders, twelfth graders) and have them ask why the joke is funny. The results can be used as the basis of a class discussion, as outlined previously.

II.   Witnessing Critical Thinking in a College Classroom

A good way for your students to witness the teaching of critical thinking skills is to have them visit an introductory psychology class (after obtaining permission from the instructor, of course), and observe any attempts on the part of the instructor to have the introductory psychology students engage in critical thinking. Introductory psychology courses tend to share a course objective of fostering critical thinking, so this course provides greater opportunity than many other courses to witness the practice of critical thinking. Your students should record the strategies that the instructor employed to try to foster critical thinking in the students enrolled in the introductory psychology course, then your students can share their observations with the rest of your class.

If classroom visits are not feasible, ask your students to make an appointment with an introductory psychology instructor to discuss the strategies the instructor uses to foster critical thinking.

Film and Video List

Adolescence: A Case Study (CRM/McGraw-Hill Films, 1978), 20 minutes.
Shows the relationship between improved mental abilities and changes in adolescent psychosocial development.

Cognitive Development (Insight Media, 1990), 30 minutes.
Focuses on Piaget's theory and criticisms of that theory to describe stages of cognitive development. Looks at development of thought, reasoning, memory, and language.

Formal Reasoning Patterns (University of Michigan, 1987), 32 minutes.
Illustrates tasks that invoke formal reasoning.

Piaget's Developmental Theory: An Introduction (Davidson Films, 1989), 25 minutes.
Using both archival photographs of Dr. Piaget and newly shot footage of Dr. Elkind conducting interviews with children of varying ages, this film presents an overview of Piaget's developmental theory, its scope, and content.

Piaget's Developmental Theory: Formal Thought (Davidson Films, 1971), 32 minutes.
Differences between concrete and formal operations are clarified as students aged 12 to 17 address Piagetian tasks.

Piaget on Piaget (YU, 1978), 42 minutes.
Piaget discusses his theory and illustrates some key concepts of his theory.

Teenage Mind and Body (Insight Media, 1992), 30 minutes.
Focuses on the cognitive and physical development of adolescence. This program probes the differences between teenagers' abilities and parents' expectations.

The IQ Myth (Sir Cyril Burt Controversy) (Carousal Films, 1977), 15 minutes.
Critical examination of the heritability controversy and of ethnic differences in IQ. Explores the political and social abuses of the tests.

CHAPTER 3

❖

Social Transitions

The Total Teaching Package Outline: Chapter 3 *Social Transitions*	
Heading	**Resource**
SOCIAL REDEFINITION and PSYCHOSOCIAL DEVELOPMENT	Learning Objective 1
ADOLESCENCE AS A SOCIAL INVENTION	Learning Objective 2 Lecture Topic I Video: *The Invention of Adolescence (PE, 1968); Adolescence - The Prolonged Transition (IM, 1992)*
CHANGE IN STATUS *Changes in Interpersonal Status* *Changes in Political Status* *Changes in Economic Status* *Changes in Legal Status*	Learning Objective 3 Table 3.1 Classroom Activity I
THE PROCESS OF SOCIAL REDEFINITION *Common Practices in the Process of Social Redefinition*	Learning Objective 3 Classroom Activity II Videos: *World Culture and Youth Series (U of MO, 1983); Teenagers (TLF, undated)*
VARIATIONS IN SOCIAL TRANSITIONS *Variations in Clarity* • *The Clarity of Social Redefinition in Contemporary Society* • *The Clarity of Social Redefinition in Traditional Cultures* • *The Clarity of Social Redefinition in Previous Eras*	Learning Objective 4 Figures 3.1, 3.2, 3.3 Video: *A Rite of Passage (PSU, 1966)*
Variations in Continuity • *The Continuity of the Adolescent Passage in Contemporary Society* • *The Continuity of the Adolescent Passage in Traditional Cultures* • *The Continuity of the Adolescent Passage in Previous Eras*	Learning Objective 4 Classroom Activity III The Sexes Box: *Similarities and Differences in the Transition into Adulthood* Figure 3.4 The Scientific Study of Adolescence Box: *Does Leaving Home Too Early Cause Problems for Adolescents?*

THE TRANSITION INTO ADULTHOOD IN CONTEMPORARY SOCIETY
Special Transition Problems of Poor and Minority Youth
  • *The Effects of Poverty on the Transition into Adulthood*
  • *The Effects of Growing Up in a Poor Neighborhood*
What Can Be Done to Ease the Transition?
	Learning Objectives 5 & 6
	Lecture Topic II
	Figures 3.6 & 3.7

For further information on these and other topics, please check out **PowerWeb** (packaged with the text), and the **Online Learning Center** for this edition, located at *www.mhhe.com/steinberg6*.

Learning Objectives

1. Understand how society redefines individuals as they enter adulthood.

2. Understand how the period we call "adolescence" is a socially-constructed phase of life.

3. Understand the experiences of adolescents as they are redefined by society.

4. Understand how cultures and societies differ in terms of how clear and how continuous they make the process of redefinition for adolescents.

5. Understand the impact of social redefinition on adolescent development.

6. Understand how the transition to adulthood is experienced differently by different adolescents in contemporary American society.

Key Terms

age of majority
Bar (Bas) Mitzvah
brother-sister avoidance
child protectionists
collective efficacy
continuous transitions
discontinuous transitions
extrusion
initiation ceremony
inventionists
juvenile justice system

marginal man
median
quinceañera
scarification
school-to-work transition
social redefinition
status offense
teenager
youth
youth apprenticeship

Chapter Overview

I. **SOCIAL REDEFINITION AND PSYCHOSOCIAL DEVELOPMENT**

   A. In all societies, adolescence is a time of change in individuals' social roles and status. The **social redefinition** of adolescence, however, can vary from one society to another. In addition, earlier maturation and increased schooling have lengthened adolescence and made the social passage to adulthood more vague and tumultuous.

   B. The social redefinition of individuals during adolescence has important implications for their behavior and psychosocial development. As adolescents reach the **age of majority** (legal age for adult status), they begin to act and see themselves in different ways and are treated differently by others. For example, adolescents experience changes in identity, autonomy, intimacy, sexuality, and achievement.

II. **ADOLESCENCE AS A SOCIAL INVENTION**

   A. **Inventionists** have argued that adolescence is more a social invention than a biological or cognitive phenomenon. According to this view, the origins of adolescence are closely linked to the industrial revolution of the 19th century.

   B. Prior to the 19th century, children were treated as miniature adults, and adolescents served as an important source of labor for their families. The primary distinction between children and adults was based on property ownership rather than age or ability.

   C. With industrialization, however, came new patterns of work and family life. Changes in the economy led to a shortage of jobs and an increase in crime. As a result, **child protectionists**, as well as adults concerned about their own employment, removed adolescents from the labor force and placed them in formal schooling.

   D. It was not until the late 19th century that adolescence came to be seen as a lengthy period of preparation for adulthood, in which young people remain economically dependent on their elders. With these changes came the rise of new terminology and ideas. Adolescents were now considered **teenagers**, a term popularized fifty years ago to connote a more frivolous and lighthearted image. **Youth**, once used to refer to individuals between the ages of 12 and 24, is now a term generally used to refer to individuals between the ages of 18 and 22.

III. **CHANGE IN STATUS**

   A. Social redefinition at adolescence typically involves a dual-sided change in status. On the one hand, adolescents are given privileges and rights that have been reserved for society's adult members. On the other hand, this increased power and freedom is accompanied by increased expectations and obligations. Status changes of this sort occur in the interpersonal, political, economic, and legal domains.

B. <u>Interpersonal, Political, and Economic Status</u>: Individuals who have been recognized as adults usually are addressed with adult titles, are allowed to engage in community decision making (e.g., voting), and are expected to enter the work force.

C. <u>Changes in Legal Status</u>: Changes in legal status also distinguish adolescents from adults. In contemporary society, driving, purchasing alcohol, and gambling are just a few of the many privileges reserved for individuals who have reached a "legal" age. Adolescents who engage in behaviors that are considered illegal for their age but not for adults are said to be committing **status offenses**. In addition, a separate **juvenile justice system** has been created to handle adolescent crime and delinquency. Several issues surrounding the legal status of adolescents, however, remain vague and confusing. For example, one study found that American jurors were more likely to recommend the death penalty for adolescents aged 16 years or older than for adolescents aged 15 years or younger.

D. In general, the law tends to restrict the behavior of adolescents when the behavior is viewed as potentially dangerous (e.g., buying cigarettes) but have supported adolescent autonomy when the behavior is viewed as having potential benefit (e.g., using contraceptives).

IV. THE PROCESS OF SOCIAL REDEFINITION

A. The process of social redefinition usually occurs over a period of years. In many societies, the social redefinition of young people occurs in groups. Although there is a good deal of cross-cultural variability in specific practices, three general themes are usually found: the real or symbolic separation of the young person from his or her parents (**extrusion**); the accentuation of physical and social differences between males and females (in traditional societies referred to as **brother-sister avoidance**); and the passing on of cultural, historical, and practical information. Many initation ceremonies also include **scarification**, the intential creation of scars on some parts of the body.

B. Two important dimensions along which societies differ in the process of social redefinition are in the clarity (or explicitness) and continuity (or smoothness) of the adolescent's passage into adulthood. In traditional societies, the **initiation ceremony** of the young person into adulthood provides a clear delineation between childhood and adolescence. Contemporary societies have few formal ceremonies marking the transition from childhood into adolescence. However, some contemporary ceremonies are still practiced, such as the **quinceañera** and the **Bar/Bas Mitzvah**.

V. VARIATIONS IN SOCIAL TRANSITIONS

A. <u>Variations in Clarity</u>: The adolescent has been referred to as the **marginal man** caught in the transitional space between childhood and adulthood. In fact, research suggests that the adolescent transition may have been even cloudier 100 years ago.

B. In addition to the clarity of the adolescent passage, societies also vary in the extent to which the passage is a **continuous** or **discontinuous transition**. In a continuous transition, characteristic of more traditional societies, the adolescent assumes the roles and status of adulthood bit by bit, with a good deal of preparation and training along the way. In a discontinuous transition, characteristic of contemporary societies, the adolescent is thrust into adulthood abruptly, with little prior preparation.

C. The continuity of the adolescent passage in previous eras suggests that today's adolescents experience even more discontinuity than previous generations. Furthermore, historical events have been found to alter the adolescent passage temporarily. For example, the Great Depression of the early 1930's forced disadvantaged adolescents to engage in adult activities earlier than their privileged peers. Policy-makers have proposed to reduce the discontinuity by implementing a **school-to-work transition**, similar to the **youth apprenticeships** of other industrialized nations (e.g., Germany).

VI. THE TRANSITION INTO ADULTHOOD IN CONTEMPORARY SOCIETY

A. Many social commentators have argued that the vague and discontinuous nature of the transition through adolescence in contemporary society has contributed to numerous psychological and behavioral problems among today's youth. These difficulties are more severe among adolescents who are not bound for college, and especially among minority youth living in the inner city.

B. African-American, Hispanic-American, and American Indian youth have more trouble negotiating the transition into adulthood than do their white and Asian-American counterparts. The effects of poverty on the transition into adulthood include increased likelihood of failure in school, unemployment, and out-of-wedlock pregnancy.

C. Due to growing numbers of poor families in economically and racially segregated communities, researchers have begun to explore whether neighborhood poverty, in addition to family poverty, is predictive of adolescents' transition difficulties. Preliminary results indicate that adolescents growing up in impoverished communities are more likely than their peers from equally poor households, but better neighborhoods, to drop out of high school and to become pregnant. It appears to be the absence of affluent neighbors, rather than the presence of poor neighbors, that places adolescents who live in impoverished communities at greater risk.

D. A number of commissions have recommended that we reexamine the structure of schools and expand work and service opportunities for young people as a means of addressing these problems.

Lecture Topics and Supplementary Readings

I.   The History of Adolescence

Many instructors find that one or more lectures on the history of adolescence will help students gain a better perspective on the nature of adolescence in contemporary society. During the last fifteen years, many excellent sources on the history of childhood and adolescence have become available, and there is a wealth of information from which to draw. Additionally, one might incorporate examples from art and literature to illustrate changing views of adolescence. In such a lecture on the history of adolescence, one might examine historical changes in the conceptualization of adolescence, discuss the notion that adolescence was "invented" as a byproduct of the industrial revolution, or contrast adolescence today with adolescence in one or more previous eras. In each case, it would be helpful to show how economic and social changes influence the nature of the life span and, in so doing, shape the period of adolescence. Assign teams of students to prepare brief reports on the nature of adolescence in different historical eras, and organize a class discussion around contrasts and comparisons of the various periods.

Bakan, D. (1972). Adolescence in America: From idea to social fact. In J. Kagan and R. Coles (Eds.), *Twelve to sixteen: Early adolescence*. New York: Norton.

Gillis, J. (1981). *Youth and history*. New York: Academic Press.

Kett, J. (1977). *Rites of passage: Adolescence in America, 1790 to the present*. New York: Basic Books.

Lapsley, D., Enright, R., and Serlin, R. (1985). Toward a theoretical perspective on the legislation of adolescence. *Journal of Early Adolescence, 5*, 441-466.

Modell, J., and Goodman, M. (1990). Historical perspectives. Pp. 93-122 in S. Feldman and G. Elliott (Eds.), *At the threshold: The developing adolescent* . Cambridge: Harvard University Press.

II.   How to Handle the "Forgotten Half"

One of the liveliest debates in the study of adolescence concerns the nature of young people's transition into adulthood. An interesting lecture might discuss the "transition" problems of young people, especially disadvantaged and minority youth, and examine the viability of various proposals made to address these difficulties. One proposal that always sparks heated discussion is that of mandatory youth service. It would be interesting to present arguments for and against this proposal, either in a lecture or in a more debate-like format.

Children's Defense Fund. (1989). *Service opportunities for youths*. Washington, D.C.: Children's Defense Fund.

Nightingale, E., & Wolverton, L. (1988). *Adolescent rolelessness in modern society*. Washington: Carnegie Council on Adolescent Development.

William T. Grant Foundation, Commission on Work, Family, and Citizenship. (1988). *The forgotten half: non-college youth in America*. Washington, D.C.: William T. Grant Foundation.

Wilson, W. (1987). *The truly disadvantaged: The inner city, the underclass, and public policy.* Chicago: University of Chicago Press.

Classroom Activities

I. When Should an Adolescent be Treated as an Adult?

Over the past several decades, adolescents have become increasingly involved in what historically have been considered "adult" activities, including violent crime, sexual activity, and substance use. This trend has forced lawmakers to determine, with increasing frequency, whether or not adolescents who engage in these "adult" activities should be treated as minors (who are deemed incompetent and unaccountable) or adults (who are deemed competent and responsible for their own actions) The ability to evaluate a minor's level of maturity has thus become very important. For example, does a teenage murderer understand the consequences of his actions? If so, should he be held accountable and punished as an adult? Should a sixteen-year-old be allowed to seek treatment for a venereal disease? To make an abortion decision? When is a minor competent enough to be allowed to waive his right to counsel during police questioning? These questions tend to spark a lively debate among students and provide an excellent way to tie together the three fundamental changes of adolescence (biological, cognitive, and social). Have students generate guidelines that determine when an adolescent should be treated as an adult.

II. Coming of Age - The Initiation Rites of Traditional and Contemporary Societies

In some cultures, the passage from childhood to adulthood occurs gradually. In America, for example, teenagers progress from being allowed to drive to being allowed to vote and then to being allowed to drink alcohol. In other cultures, the social transition to adulthood occurs through a specific ritual of passage. For example:

1. In the Mandan Tribe of Native Americans, young men must endure a series of trials to become a warrior. First, the initiate must live for four days without food, water, or sleep. Next, the chief medicine man cuts slices from the initiate's chest and shoulders and places wooden skewers through the muscles. Leather straps are then attached to these skewers and secured to the hut's rafters. The initiate is hoisted from the floor, with weights attached to his legs, and is twirled about until unconscious. Upon recovery, the initiate must remove the little finger of his left hand with a hatchet. Finally, ropes are tied to his wrists and he runs in a circle until he drops unconscious from exhaustion. Survivors become full-fledged warriors.

    Source: *Strange Stories, Amazing Facts.* (1976). Pleasantville, New York: The Reader's Digest Association, Inc. p. 311.

2. In Mali, Sudan and Somalia, females undergo a radical form of circumcision as part of the ceremonial transition to adulthood. All or part of the clitoris, and sometimes the internal vaginal lips, are removed. The outer lips are then sewn shut, leaving a small opening through which urine and menstrual discharge can pass. One of the main goals of the operation is to ensure that sex is linked with procreation rather than enjoyment. Throughout Africa, more than 75 million females are circumcised, but increasing numbers are trying to eliminate this tradition. In Sudan, for example, 96% of female students surveyed had been circumcised, but 70% strongly believed that other girls should not be circumcised.

Sources: Sommer, B. (1978). *Puberty and adolescence*. New York: Oxford University Press.
           Pugh, D. (1983). Bringing an end to mutilation. *New Statesman, 11*, 8-9.
           Taylor, D. (1985). *Women: A world report*. New York: Oxford University Press.

3.   In remote regions of Australia, 16-year-old male Aborigines must face a rite of passage called the walkabout. The youth must leave the village and live for six months on his own. This estrangement is designed not only to test his survival skills, but also to develop patience and self-confidence. Upon his return, the youth is accepted as an adult member of the tribe.

Source: Gibbons, M. (1974). Walkabout. *Phi Delta Kappan*, 596-602.

After describing the various initiation rites of different cultures, ask the class to generate a list of initiation ceremonies that contemporary adolescents may experience. Do these rights help an adolescent become an adult? Here are a list of the types and some examples of each:

Religious
Bar mitzvah or Bas mitzvah
Confirmation

Sexual
Menarche
Nocturnal Emissions
Losing one's virginity

Economic
Getting a checking account or credit card
Buying a car
Getting one's first job

Educational
Getting a driver's license
Graduating from high school
Going away to college

Social
Sweet Sixteen
Going to the senior prom
Turning 21 & buying your first drink
Joining a gang, fraternity, sorority
Joining the armed forces
Getting married
Becoming a parent

Dacey, J. & Kenny, M. (1994). *Adolescent development*. Madison, WI: Brown & Benchmark Publishers.

III.   Easing the School-to-Work Transition

During the early 1990's, with the enthusiastic backing of President Clinton, many educators and policy-makers have called for changes in our educational system in order to improve the school-to-work transition. Many individuals have difficulty making this transition successfully because, at present, there really exists only one acceptable way of making this passage — through higher education — and not all individuals can, or want to, make the transition via this route. Is possible to create a route from high school to adult work that doesn't involve college? Divide the class into small groups and have them generate a program that attempts to address this question. Provide the class with general guidelines and then have them present their program at the end of class. This activity is an excellent way to demonstrate how research can influence policy.

Web Researcher

Photographs can sometimes startle us by violating our expectations about how people should behave. Find 10 or 20 photographs of adolescents from different historical periods. In what ways does it seem as if adolescents made a faster transition from childhood to adulthood than they do now? In what ways does it seem that their transition was slower? Can you draw any conclusions? Go to *www.mhhe.com/steinberg6* for further information.

Outside Activities

I.   Adolescents Today and Yesterday

Schwanenflugel (1987) suggests that interviews are an effective tool for teaching adolescent development. Have students interview adolescents on the specific topic(s) of development to be covered during the following week's lectures, and have them write summaries of their findings. These reports can serve as the basis for class discussions, with the instructor pointing out ways in which the data are (or are not) consistent with findings discussed in the text. Since students will be in direct contact with adolescents of different ages, they are likely to gain a better understanding of the developmental changes about which they read in the text. Students will also become familiar with interview procedures, an important component of psychological research.

Schwanenflugel's structured interviews are designed to cover specific aspects of adolescent psychology, but students should not be afraid to deviate somewhat from the prepared questions. Also, remind students that parental permission must be obtained before interviewing an adolescent. Interviews rarely require more than 20 minutes.

<u>Sample Interview Assignment</u>

Next week, we will be discussing how perceptions of adolescence have changed in recent history. In preparation, you must interview an adolescent (between the ages of 12 and 18), and someone who is over 70. Find out about his or her adolescence and how it differed from that of today's adolescent. A list of suggested questions is provided below. However, you may also develop your own.

Interview of Senior Citizen:

1. Did you attend high school? Did you want to? What kinds of subjects did you study? What kind of homework did you get? Did most of the adolescents in your neighborhood go to high school?
2. How many hours per week did you work (not including school-related work)? How much did you contribute to the family income? Did you want to go to work?
3. What were your clothes like? Were you concerned about fashion?
4. Did you date in high school? At what age were you allowed to date? What did you typically do on a date?
5. How did you and your friends spend your free time?
6. What was your most nagging problem as a teenager?
7. What do you see as the main difference between the teenagers of today and yourself as a teenager? What do you think of today's teenagers?

Interview of Adolescent:

1. How do you feel about school? How much time do you spend doing homework? What do you plan to do when you graduate?
2. Do you have a part-time job? If so, how many hours a week do you work? Do you want to work?
3. What kind of clothes do your friends wear? How important is fashion to you?
4. Do you have a boyfriend/girlfriend? If so, how old were you when you began dating? If not, why? When are you allowed to go on a date? What do you do on a date?
5. How do you spend your free time?
6. When you get together with your friends, what do you do?
7. What is your biggest problem in life right now?
8. What do you see as the main difference between the yourself and teenagers 50 years ago? What do you think of today's teenagers?

Schwanenflugel, P. (1987). An interview method for teaching adolescent psychology. *Teaching of Psychology, 14*, 167-168.

II. The Age Limits of Adolescence

Our society determines ability by age. This demarcation, however, is inconsistent with the definition of development, since development is "change over time" and age does not determine change. Have students determine the age limits for the following activities in the state where they grew up: (1) Drive a car, (2) Consent to health care, (3) Vote, (4) Hold a part-time & full-time job, (5) Leave school. After students have gathered this information, have them share with the class the age limits for their state. Based on the diversity of the student population, many will be surprised to learn of the different ages at which their peers were allowed to engage in certain activities. For example, the age of majority is 18 in all but three states (Alaska, Nebraska, and Wyoming, where the age is 19). Adolescents are able to work part time at age 14 and full time at age 16, according to the Fair Labor Standards Act of 1938. Adolescents are able to leave school at age 16 in most states (in Mississippi adolescents are permitted to leave school at age 14). Adolescents are typically allowed to drive by age 16 (although some states allow driving at age 14, while Idaho, Nevada and New Jersey do not allow an adolescent to drive until age 17). Five states (Alabama, Kansas, Rhode Island, South Carolina, and Oregon) have enacted statutes that specifically authorize minors who have reached a designated age (ranging from 14 to 16) to consent to health care.

Hechinger, F. M. (1992). *Fateful choices: Healthy youth for the 21st Century.* New York: Hill and Wang.

Film and Video List

A Rite of Passage (Penn State University, 1966), 14 minutes.
Examines rites of passage among the !Kung people.

Adolescence: The Prolonged Transition (Insight Media, 1992), 30 minutes.
Uses historical and cross-cultural comparisons to question the view of adolescence as a social construction.

The Invention of Adolescence (Perennial Education, 1968), 28 minutes.
The film traces the history of the concept of adolescence.

Teenagers (Time Life Films, undated), 45 minutes.
Explores differences among adolescents in different cultures.

World Cultures and Youth Series (University of Missouri - Columbia, 1983), 26 films, 25 minutes each.
Each film focuses on an adolescent in a different culture.

Lecture Topics and Supplementary Readings

I. The Process of Socialization and the Role of Peers

Margaret Mead's distinction among postfigurative, configurative, and prefigurative cultures is fundamental to understanding the changing role of peer groups in contemporary society. A lecture on social change and the role of peers in adolescent development will help expand upon many of the ideas presented in the text. In this lecture, it would be helpful to discuss the process of socialization and the various roles played in different societies by different socializing agents. In so doing, one can illustrate how and why peers have come to play such a crucial role in modern societies – that is, because of increased age grading, rapid social change, and the general prevalence of universalistic norms for individual behavior. Discussing socialization in prefigurative, cofigurative, and postfigurative cultures, with frequent illustrations of life in each, will enable students to understand why the rise of peer groups is not necessarily a "bad" thing – as it is usually presented – and why they will become increasingly important in the future.

Brown, B. (1990). Peer groups (pp. 171-196). In S. Feldman and G. Elliott (Eds.), *At the threshold: The developing adolescent.* Cambridge: Harvard University Press.

Eisenstadt, S. N. (1956). *From generation to generation.* Glencoe, IL: Free Press.

Hartup, W. (1977). Adolescent peer relations: A look to the future. In J. Hill and F. Monks (Eds.), *Adolescence and youth in prospect.* Surrey, England: IPC Press.

Mead, M. (1978). *Culture and commitment.* Garden City, NY: Doubleday/Anchor.

II. The Adolescent Society

Many college students enjoy hearing more about the nature and structure of peer crowds. A lecture focusing on the heterogeneity of peer groups within schools and reexamining the findings of *The Adolescent Society* would be an excellent addition to the material presented in the text. In this lecture, one might begin by asking whether there is indeed an "adolescent society" and then discuss the multidimensionality of adolescent peer culture. Students will often be able to provide lively examples of the crowds they remember from their own adolescent years.

Brown, B., Eicher, S., & Petrie, S. (1986). The importance of peer group ("crowd") affiliation in adolescence. *Journal of Adolescence, 9,* 73-96.

Brown, B. B., Lohr, M. J., & Trujillo, C. (1990). Multiple crowds and multiple lifestyles: Adolescents' perceptions of peer group stereotypes (pp. 30-36). In. R. E. Muuss (Ed.), *Adolescent behavior and society.* New York: McGraw-Hill.

Coleman, J. (1962). *The adolescent society.* Glencoe, Ill: Free Press.

Epstein, J. (1983). Selecting friends in contrasting secondary school environments. In J. Epstein and N. Karweit (Eds.), *Friends in school.* New York: Academic Press.

Classroom Activities

I.   Revenge of the Nerds

A lively way to introduce the topic on peer groups is to have each student report on the crowd structure of the high school he or she attended and, if willing, the group to which he or she belonged (it is helpful to ask students to name the group that most of his or her classmates would have said he or she belonged to). It's amazing how many "brains" and "nerds" from high school are some of the more "popular" students in class.

II.   My Best Friend

A poignant memory for many people is that of their best friend from childhood. Divide the students into small groups and have them recall everything they can remember about their best friend from freshman year in high school. Who was that person? Why do they think they were friends with that person? What types of activities did they do together? What happened to that person? Are they still friends? If they are not friends today, why and when did the friendship dissolve? How does the evolution of that particular friendship compare with theories of peer relationships described in the text?

Web Researcher

Popular media – especially advertising – is designed to influence behavior. Look at websites aimed at teenagers. What methods do advertisers and wed designers use to influence their audiences? Look for subtle techniques such as product placements as well as more blatant bids for attention. What parallels do you see between these techniques and the kinds of peer influences adolescents experience in real life? If you found differences between the behaviors of adolescents who spent time on these different sites, would you conclude that they result from the sites' influence, or might other processes be operating as well? Go to *www.mhhe.com/steinberg6* for further information.

Outside Activities

I.   Cliques and Crowds

This activity is most effective for classes at traditional residential colleges. On such campuses, there are a large number of cliques (exclusive social circles of friends) and crowds (loosely formed groups organized chiefly on the basis of shared activities). These groups will dramatically differ in composition across campuses. Some schools have groups of "hippies" and others a large number of "punks." In towns and cities with several colleges and universities, the differences that exist within the same few square miles can be astounding. Students can easily make observations and study the different cliques and crowds that exist on their own and other campuses. The students can identify categories of individuals, as well as specific cliques and crowds. As a classroom activity, have students compare their conclusions. An attempt to describe the dominant crowds and understand their composition can then be made.

II.   Adolescence and Conformity

Adolescence is a period marked by conformity. Conformity begins to be directed away from parents, but steers instead toward peers. An good place to observe conformity in teenagers is at a local mall or video arcade. Students can observe different behavioral norms to which adolescents conform. These aspects may include activities, music, attire, body language, vocabulary, and speech patterns. An interesting way to conduct this activity is to assign individuals or groups to different cliques (e.g., jocks, punks, nerds—or whatever groups exist for your local area). Then have the group report the details of their observations, such as what the observed individuals were wearing and saying.

Film and Video List

Adolescence: Social and Emotional Development (Magna Systems, 1995). Looks at how parents, peers and values influence adolescents' search for identity. Includes a panel of teens that discuss peer pressure.

Coping with Peer Pressure (Films for the Humanities and Sciences, 1994), 15 minutes.
Viewers learn to cope with peer pressure by looking ahead to the consequences of their actions and being honest with themselves.

Coping with Peer Pressure: Getting Along without Going Along (University of Missouri, 1986), 25 minutes.
Adolescents discuss how they have handled peer pressure.

Culture, Time, and Place (Insight Media, 1992), 30 minutes.
Shows how language, school and relationships bring about acculturation about attitudes, values, and beliefs.

How's Your New Friend? (University of Minnesota, 1975), 12 minutes.
Examines social relations in an adolescent clique.

It's a Thought (University of Wisconsin, 1980), 23 minutes.
Examines social rejection and popularity in early adolescence.

Peer Stress (Marshfilm/Marshmedia, 1988), 45 minutes.
Shows some of the ways that peer pressure can cause stress in adolescents.

Peers in Development (Insight Media, 1991), 60 minutes.
This video provides a thorough overview of the important functions peers serve during child and adolescent development. Includes information about how peer groups and friendships change, and examines the effects of conflict, sexual development, and inadequate peer relationships.

Teenager Relationships (Insight Media, 1991), 60 minutes.
Examines social development during early and late adolescence, differentiating peer and family influences.

Understanding Aggression (Prentice Hall Media, undated), 29 minutes.
Examines and explains aggression from a learning theory perspective.

II.   Who Was Your Favorite Teacher and Who Wasn't?

An enjoyable, and educational, activity for students is to have them discuss in small groups who was their favorite high school teacher and who was their least favorite teacher. In addition, now that they have a somewhat broader perspective, the students should attempt to analyze why they liked a certain teacher and not another. For example, did the student's personality and the teacher's style clash? Why? What teaching styles proved most (or least) popular?

III.   Violence in the Schools

In a 1992 poll of high school students, 24% responded that they had feared for their physical safety while at school. Seven percent had been physically assaulted at school, while 15% reported having money stolen. Minorities and teens under age 16 were the most concerned about physical safety. Ask students how big a problem each of the following was at their school:

Fighting?

Theft of personal property?

Vandalism?

Students bringing weapons to school?

Did the student ever fear for his or her physical safety at school?

After stimulating a discussion on school violence, ask students what methods are currently being taken to reduce these problems. Are these methods working? Why or why not? What would they suggest to reduce these problems? Also, how does fear of violence affect the school climate and teacher-student relations?

Bezilla, R. (1993). *America's youth in the 1990s*. Princeton, NJ: George H. Gallup International Institute.

Web Researcher

What is the average class size in elementary schools, high schools, liberal arts colleges, and large universities? How many students do teachers in each of these institutions see in a week? How much time do they spend with each student? How might these differences relate to the goals and means of instruction, the types of assignments teachers give, and students' experience in the classroom? Go to *www.mhhe.com/steinberg6* for further information.

Outside Activities

I.   Interview Your High School Teacher

Students may gain additional insight regarding the issues that face educators by returning to (or calling) their alma mater and interviewing their favorite (or perhaps their least favorite) teacher. Questions to ask might include:

> What problems and challenges are associated with the teaching of adolescents?
> What are their views on the purpose of high school today?
> What are the most effective teaching strategies, classroom climates, and teacher qualities?
> What are the major advantages and disadvantages of their jobs?
> If they could start over again, would they go into teaching as a vocation?

Film and Video List

High School (University of Michigan, 1969), 75 minutes.
Dated but still interesting documentary about an urban high school.

Schools (University of Wisconsin – Madison, 1985), 29 minutes.
Investigates what messages children really receive in school.

Shortchanging Girls, Shortchanging America (Insight Media, 1992), 19 minutes.
This program interviews educators and business leaders to illuminate the devastating effects of gender bias in schools. It calls upon educators to encourage girls to develop math and science skills.

CHAPTER 7

❖

Work and Leisure

The Total Teaching Package Outline: Chapter 7 *Work and Leisure*	
Heading	**Resource**
WORK AND LEISURE IN CONTEMPORARY SOCIETY .	Learning Objective 1 Lecture Topic I Figure 7.1
ADOLESCENTS AND WORK *School and Work in the Early Twentieth Century* *The Emergence of the Student-Worker*	Learning Objective 2 Lecture Topic I Classroom Activity I Figure 7.2
Teenage Employment in America and in Other Nations	Learning Objective 3 Lecture Topic II Figure 6.2 Video: *Three Apprentices (U of NH, 1963)*

The Adolescent Workplace Today
  • *Common Adolescent Jobs*
  • *The Adolescent Work Environment*
Working and Adolescent Development
  • *The Development of Responsibility*
  • *Money and Its Management*
  • *Work and Deviance*
  • *Work and Its impact on School*
	Learning Objective 4
	The Sexes Box: *Leisure, Work, and Sex-Role Socialization*
	Video: *Foxfire (U of MI, 1974)*

Youth Unemployment	Learning Objective 5 Figure 7.4
ADOLESCENTS AND LEISURE *Participation in Extracurricular Activities* *After-School Activities and Adolescent Development*	Learning Objective 6 Figures 7.5, 7.6 & 7.7 The Scientific Study of Adolescence Box: *The Experience Sampling Method* Classroom Activities II & III Outside Activity I Video: *Gotta Have It (FFHS, 1988)*
Leisure and Mass Media *Leisure and the Economy*	Learning Objective 7 Figure 7.8

For further information on these and other topics, please check out PowerWeb (packaged with the text), and the Online Learning Center for this edition, located at *www.mhhe.com/steinberg6*.

Learning Objectives

1. Understand the two primary factors that contributed to the rise of adolescents in the work force.

2. Understand how younger and older adolescents spend their time.

3. Understand the roles of school and work during the early twentieth century and how they have changed over the years.

4. Understand how adolescent involvement in the American workplace compares with that of adolescents in other industrialized countries.

5. Understand the primary jobs obtained by adolescents and the impact of part-time work on their development.

6. Understand youth unemployment and its impact on the "Forgotten Half."

7. Understand the impact of leisure activities on adolescent socialization.

8. Understand the mass media's influence on younger versus older adolescents.

Key Terms

community service   premature affluence
curvilinear pattern   service learning
Experience Sampling Method (ESM)   youth employment

Chapter Overview

I. **WORK AND LEISURE IN CONTEMPORARY SOCIETY**

   A. The rise of compulsory schooling and the affluence of the adolescent population have contributed to the increased importance both of part-time employment and of leisure activities in the lives of contemporary adolescents. Adolescents spend 29% of their time in "productive" activities (e.g., school), 31% of their time in "maintenance" activities (e.g., grooming, eating), and 40% of their time in "leisure" activities (e.g., socializing).

   B. The average American high school student spends fewer than five hours per week on homework, whereas in Japan the average is close to five hours per day. Having large amounts of free time is one hallmark of adolescence in modern American society.

II.   ADOLESCENTS AND WORK

A. <u>School and Work in the Twentieth Century</u>: Before 1925, adolescents were either students or workers, but not both. Today, more than 80% of high school students will have worked before graduating. The student-worker, however, is a relatively new phenomenon that has become prevalent only in recent years.

B. <u>The Emergence of the Student Worker</u>: The expansion of part-time employment opportunities in retail and service industries following 1945 drew youngsters back into the labor force. Also, the cost of living for the American teenager increased dramatically over the last thirty years, so adolescents who were looking for spending money were drawn into the world of work. Today, the typical high school student works more than fifteen hours each week, although working during high school is slightly more common for middle and upper class white students than among poor youth. Many young people, however, have worked prior to this age, either around their houses on assigned chores, or on an informal basis in their neighborhood, in activities such as baby-sitting or yard work.

C. <u>Teenage Employment in America and in Other Nations</u>: Although the student-worker has become a more common phenomenon in other industrialized countries, it is still far less prevalent abroad than in the United States. This is due to the fact that part-time work is not as readily available elsewhere as it is in America. Also, the scheduling of part-time work does not match the schedule of students in other countries, since school in other countries demands more "out-of-school" time (e.g., homework). Furthermore, in other countries, employment of children is associated with being poor, and students are more likely to gain work experience through structured apprenticeship programs in career-related jobs. Consequently, the **school-to-work transition** is more systematic and effective.

D. <u>The Adolescent Workplace Today</u>: Adolescents are typically employed in service and retail positions and it is only recently that researchers have begun to study the work environments of young people. These studies challenge many widely held assumptions about the value of early work experience. Far from being conducive to learning and psychological development, many adolescents' jobs are monotonous, unchallenging, and stressful. Meaningful contact with adults is limited, and opportunities for developing responsibility or using school-taught skills are scarce.

E. <u>Working and Adolescent Development</u>: The notion that holding a job makes an adolescent more responsible has not been supported by the research. In fact, today's working teenagers may have more income than they can manage maturely, otherwise known as **premature affluence**. For example, studies show that adolescents spend most of their earnings on their own needs and activities, rather than on their education or their family's household needs. As a result, part-time employment often leads to cynicism about the value of hard work.

F. Recent studies indicate that working long hours may increase occupational deviance in the adolescent workplace and take a toll on youngsters' schooling. Teenagers who work in excess of fifteen to twenty hours weekly are more likely to use drugs and alcohol, are less engaged in school, and are more likely to "protect" their grades by taking easier classes and expending less effort on their schoolwork.

G. Youth Unemployment: There remains a good deal of controversy over the nature and causes of **youth unemployment**. Unemployment appears to be a problem for only a small minority of teenagers, and these teenagers are more typically minority youngsters who have dropped out of high school and are living in depressed inner-city areas. But even among these youngsters, unemployment is usually short-lived and the long-term consequences are not great. Many social commentators have called for improving the transition between school and full-time work, especially among non-college-bound students. Among the suggestions offered are increasing adolescents' opportunities for **community service**, strengthening counseling and career service for high school students, and encouraging the development of apprenticeship programs like those found in Europe.

III. **ADOLESCENTS AND LEISURE**

A. Adolescents spend more time in leisure than they do in school and work combined. Although adults are prone to see leisure as "wasted" time, leisure serves a number of important functions during adolescence. It socializes adolescents for adult roles, exposes them to elements of the popular culture, and helps support certain segments of the economy.

B. Participation in Extracurricular Activities: School sponsored extracurricular activities, such as athletics, provide the context for much of the adolescent's leisure activity. Furthermore, whereas employment tends to decrease school performance, increase delinquency, and heighten drug and alcohol use, participating in school-sponsored activities seems to have the reverse effect.

C. After-School Activities and Adolescent Development: Many leisure activities are structured to socialize adolescents into adult roles. For example, athletics were found to be a chief route to popularity and status for boys, whereas cheerleading was the main route to popularity for girls. The culture of boys' athletics emphasizes achievement, toughness, and competition. In contrast, girls were socialized to focus on their appearance and "bubbliness". In addition, leading magazines aimed at girls focus on dating and heterosexual relationships and emphasize the importance of physical attractiveness.

D. Leisure and the Mass Media: Much of adolescents' leisure time involves one or more of the mass media. Whereas television viewing declines during adolescence, use of music media, movies, and print media all increase. The average adolescent is exposed to the mass media about eight hours daily. Although adults have worried about the corrupting influence of media such as television or rock music, it has been difficult to document such alleged effects.

E. Leisure and the Economy: The power of adolescents as consumers has increased in recent decades. The average adolescent has nearly $400 per month in spending money, which makes this group an attractive target for a variety of businesses.

Lecture Topics and Supplementary Readings

I.   The History of Child Labor

A lecture on the history of child labor would supplement the material covered in the text. Such a lecture could trace the uses and abuses of adolescents in the workplace, placing the current immersion of young people in part-time jobs in social and historical context. One might begin by looking at the role of adolescent workers in preindustrialized societies (where they helped in farming, gathering, and domestic work), turn to a discussion of youth work during the 18th century and early stages of industrialization and the rise of the child protection movement (it was during this time that young workers were employed in "sweatshops"), and finally, discuss the employment of teenagers today in the retail and service economy.

Elder, G. (1974). *Children of the great depression*. Chicago: University of Chicago Press.

Greenberger, E., & Steinberg, L. (1986). *When teenagers work: The psychological and social costs of adolescent employment*. New York: Basic Books.

Kett, J. (1977). *Rites of passage: Adolescence in America, 1790 to the present*. New York: Basic Books.

II.   I Want My MTV

Students would certainly enjoy a lecture or presentation on the mass media and its influence on adolescent development. Of particular interest are issues regarding the "corrupting" influences of music, film, and television. Rather than spend a lot of time presenting material through formal lectures, one might choose to bring in (or have students bring in) examples of music and video toward which teenagers gravitate, and then discuss what teenagers may be learning from them. Musical preference is one of the most obvious areas in which teenagers separate themselves from adults. You can engage the class by playing tapes of popular songs from the past several decades, as well as from the current teenage rage. Have students analyze these songs in terms of (1) sexual themes, (2) conflict or rebellion, and (3) adolescent preoccupations (e.g., love, cars, surfing, etc.). Below are several song suggestions for this exercise; you may wish to use others.

1950s
Elvis Presley
"Hound Dog"
"Burning Love"

1960s
Beatles
"I Saw Her Standing There"
"I Wanna Hold Your Hand"
"Hard Days Night"

1970s

Kiss
"Rock-n-Roll All Night"

Queen
"Fat Bottom Girls"
"Another One Bites the Dust"

Led Zeppelin
"Whole Lotta Love"

1980s

Madonna
"Like a Virgin"
"Material Girl"
"Papa Don't Preach"

Prince
"I Would Die 4 You"
"Little Red Corvette"

George Michael
"I Want Your Sex"

1990s

Nirvana
"Smells Like Teen Spirit"
"Lithium"

Ice T
"Cop Killer"

Walraven, M. (1993). *Adolescence: An Introduction.* Madison, WI: Brown & Benchmark Publishers.

Classroom Activities

I.   Should High School Students Be Allowed to Work?

Many parents encourage their adolescent children to obtain part-time jobs, believing that even if this work is not challenging, it will nevertheless build character and develop useful skills, such as management of time and money, dealing with people, and self-presentation. In addition, some families may rely on the additional income provided, while some adolescents are able to attend college only because of the money the earned during high school. Many believe that an adolescent has the right to seek employment if he or she chooses.

Recent research, however, has questioned the idea that, generally, teenage employment is advantageous. The jobs adolescents fill are often menial, with little potential for advancement, or even for the acquisition of skills that will be useful in adult careers. Most teenage jobs do not teach money management or personal skills beyond the scope of making change for customers. The money earned by most teens is most often spent on personal entertainment, rather than on family needs or on college tuition. As one might expect, working for more than 20 hours a week also tends to result in poorer school performance, as well. Finally, some argue that jobs filled by adolescents should be given instead to unemployed adults who must support themselves and their families.

After providing this background material, divide the class into panels and have them debate whether adolescents should be encouraged to seek part-time employment, or whether they should be forbidden to work during school.

Lennings, C. (1993). The role of activity in adolescent development: A study of employment. *Adolescence, 28,* 701-710.

Sibereisen, R. & Todt, E. (1994). *Adolescence in context: The interplay of family, school, peers, and work in adjustment.* New York: Springer, Verlag.

Steinberg, L. & Cauffman, E. (1995). The impact of employment on adolescent development. *Annals of Child Development, 11,* 131-166.

II.   What Do You Want to Be When You Grow Up?

The value of adolescent employment can also be addressed by having each student write down what his or her career goals were at the following points in his or her development:

(1) in elementary school
(2) in junior high/middle school
(3) in high school
(4) starting college
(5) now

Next, have them list the jobs they have held during these periods. How many were related to their career goals? What skills did they learn from these jobs? Did actual employment and career goals converge as students progressed through school? How might students' lives or plans have been different if they had not worked, or if they had worked elsewhere?

Web Researcher

Financially strapped school districts are being forced to make tough decisions about how their budgets are spent. Some people argue that extracurricular activities are a "frill" that should be cut. Build a case for making extracurricular activities a central part of the educational experience. What do they do for adolescents? Whom do they benefit? How would you structure them to best support the school's academic program? Go to *www.mhhe.com/steinberg6* for further information.

Outside Activities

I.   Career Development

Have students interview two people in careers of their choice. One should be new to the career (a young adult), while the other should have ten or fifteen years of experience. Students should ask each person about the prerequisites for jobs in that field, the knowledge required, the duties involved, and the opportunities for advancement. Also, are they satisfied with their careers? Do they plan to change fields in the future? Would they recommend the field?

II.   Adolescents at Work

Assign students different work settings in which to observe teenagers at work (e.g., fast-food restaurants, retail stores, construction jobs, yard work). Have them report back to the class about what actually takes place on these jobs. Students may also wish to interview adolescents who hold part-time jobs. Possible questions include:

How long has the adolescent worked at this part-time job?
What are major advantages and disadvantages of working?
Why did they choose their present job?

What potentially beneficial experiences does their job provide?
If they didn't need the money, would they still work? Why or why not?
Where does the bulk of their income go?

Film and Video List

Three Apprentices (U of NH, 1963), 28 minutes.
Profiles of three adolescent apprentices in different cultures.

Foxfire (U of MI, 1974), 22 minutes.
Illustrates the positive impact of a work experience program.

Gotta Have It (Films for the Humanities and Sciences, 1988), 26 minutes.
Looks at today's teen fads, fashions, and foibles; light-heartedly examines teen concerns over physical appearance, rock music, dating rituals, and peer pressure, then turns the clock back to look at teen "musts" of the 1950's.

CHAPTER 10

❖

Intimacy

The Total Teaching Package Outline: Chapter 10 *Intimacy*	
Heading	**Resource**
INTIMACY AS AN ADOLESCENT ISSUE	Learning Objectives 1 & 2
THEORETICAL PERSPECTIVES ON ADOLESCENT INTIMACY *Sullivan's Theory of Interpersonal Development* • *Sullivan's View of Interpersonal Development During Adolescence* *Erikson's View of Intimacy* • *Erikson and Sullivan: Conflicting Views?*	Learning Objective 3 Table 10.1 Video: *Everybody Rides the Carousel (PF, 1975)*
..tachment in Adolescence	Learning Objective 4 Lecture Topic I The Scientific Study of Adolescence Bo⌐ *Characterizing Adolescent attachmຜ ..ng the Q-Sort Procedure* Figure 10.1 Outside Activity I
THE DEVELOPMENT OF INTIMACY IN ADOLESCENCE *Changes in the Nature of Friendship* *Changes in the Display of Intimacy*	Learning Objective 5 Figure 10.2 Classroom Activity I The Sexes Box: *Are There Sex Differences in Intimacy?* Video: *Snowbound (U of MI, 1977)*
Changes in the "Targets" of Intimacy • *Parents and Peers as Target of Intimacy* • *Other Individuals as Targets of Intimacy*	Learning Objective 6 Figures 10.3, 10.4, 10.5 Video: *Teenage Relationships (IM, 1991)*
Friendships with the Other Sex	Learning Objective 7 Outside Activity II Video: *Peers in Development (IM, 1991)*
DATING AND ROMANCE	Learning Objective 8 Lecture Topic II Classroom Activities II & III Video: *The Dating Scene (U of WI, 1972); Learning to Love (IM, 1988)*

INTIMACY AND ADOLESCENT PSYCHOSOCIAL DEVELOPMENT	Learning Objective 9

For further information on these and other topics, please check out PowerWeb (packaged with the text), and the Online Learning Center for this edition, located at *www.mhhe.com/steinberg6*.

Learning Objectives

1. Understand the difference between intimacy and sexuality.

2. Understand the differences between the friendships of children and those of adolescents.

3. Understand the similarities and differences between Sullivan's theory of interpersonal development and Erikson's view of intimacy.

4. Understand the perspective of attachment theory and how it pertains to the development of intimacy during adolescence.

5. Understand the changes in the level of intimacy and its expression/display in adolescent friendships.

6. Understand the relative changes in parent and peer targets of intimacy, as well as changes in other targets of intimacy.

7. Understand the dynamics underlying friendships with the other sex and the age-related changes in cross-sex friendships.

8. Understand the function of dating during adolescence.

9. Understand the possible negative effects of intimate relationships.

Key Terms

Adult Attachment Interview
anxious-resistant attachment
anxious-avoidant attachment
attachment
homophobia
internal working model
intimacy

intimacy versus isolation
need for intimacy
need for integration into adult society
need for sexual contact
need for intimacy with a peer of the opposite sex
Q-Sort
secure attachment

Chapter Overview

I. **INTIMACY AS AN ADOLESCENT ISSUE**

   A. During adolescence, remarkable changes take place in our capacity to form close relationships with other people, and, consequently, in the types of relationships we form. Most researchers draw a distinction between **intimacy** and sexuality. Intimacy refers to the development of relationships characterized by self-disclosure, trust, and concern.

   B. The growth of intimacy, a central feature of adolescent psychosocial development, can be traced to the fundamental biological, cognitive, and social changes of the era.

II. **THEORETICAL PERSPECTIVES ON ADOLESCENT INTIMACY**

   A. The three main theoretical approaches to the study of intimacy in adolescence are those of Sullivan, Erikson, and the attachment theorists.

   B. Sullivan's Theory of Interpersonal Development: According to Sullivan, the **need for intimacy** emerges in preadolescence and is typically satisfied through same-sex friendships. During adolescence, this need is integrated with sexual impulses and desires, and the focus of the adolescents' interpersonal concerns is redirected toward opposite-sex peers.

   C. Erikson's View of Intimacy: In Erikson's theory, the psychosocial crisis of late adolescence is labeled "**intimacy versus isolation**." According to this viewpoint, individuals must first develop a coherent sense of identity before they are able to develop genuinely intimate relationships with others. This position contrasts somewhat with that of Sullivan, who argues that the development of intimacy precedes the development of a coherent sense of self. There is some evidence that Erikson's model may be more true for males than females, and that for females, the tasks of identity and intimacy may be somewhat merged. However, most researchers view the development of identity and intimacy as complementary, not competing tasks.

   D. Attachment in Adolescence: According to **attachment** theorists, intimacy during adolescence must be examined in relation to the individual's history of close relationships, and in particular, the individual's infant-caregiver attachments. There is evidence that individuals who enjoyed a **secure attachment** to their caregiver during infancy develop more healthy ideas about relationships and more advanced social competencies as opposed **anxious-avoidant** or **anxious-resistant**. Some theorists have argued that the initial attachment relationship forms the basis for a more general model of interpersonal relationships that we employ throughout our life, known as the **internal working model**. A secure internal working model permits the individual to enter more satisfying intimate relationships in adolescence and adulthood. Research has attempted to understand the parent-adolescent relationship by using a retrospective measure called the **Adult Attachment Interview**.

III. THE DEVELOPMENT OF INTIMACY IN ADOLESCENCE

A. Research on the development of intimacy in adolescence points to changes in individuals' conceptions about friendship, changes in the display of intimacy, and changes in the "targets" of intimacy.

B. <u>Changes in the Nature of Friendship</u>: With development, adolescents become more concerned about trust and loyalty as defining features of friendship, more self-disclosing in their relationships, and more responsive to their friends.

C. <u>Changes in the Display of Intimacy</u>: Numerous studies have revealed that adolescents become increasingly sensitive to the feelings and needs of their friends, provide more comfort to their friends when their friends are having problems, and are less controlling and more tolerant of their friends' individuality.

D. <u>Changes in the "Targets" of Intimacy</u>: Adolescence is also a time during which teenagers broaden their circle of confidants. In general, new types of relationships are added to the adolescent's social world without replacing previous ones. Whereas in childhood, the primary targets of intimacy are parents, and to a lesser extent, siblings, beginning in preadolescence, the network of intimates widens to include peers, family members, and mentors.

E. <u>Friendships with the Other Sex</u>: It is not until relatively late in adolescence, however, that intimacy with opposite-sex peers develops. Cross-sex friendships are relatively rare before adolescents begin to date. The emotional assistance from others, or social support, aids the adolescent in making this transition.

IV. DATING AND ROMANCE

A. Despite the fact that almost all adolescents date by the time they are 16, far less is known about the nature and consequences of romantic relationships during adolescence than about adolescent friendships. Sullivan's theory of interpersonal development suggests that adolescents begin establishing intimate relationships through same-sex friendships, then transition into expressing intimacy in romantic relationships. This model is more accurate for females than for males.

B. Recent research has indicated that the evolution of romance for adolescents proceeds through four stages: the infatuation phase, the status phase, the intimate phase, and the bonding phase. The level of intimacy and commitment to the relationship increase across these phases.

C. In general, social activities with the opposite sex begin in early adolescence as group activities, proceed to casual dating in couples, and, later in adolescence, progress to serious involvement with a steady romantic partner. A moderate degree of dating, without serious involvement until late adolescence, is associated with better mental health and well-being than either early, intense dating or no dating at all.

D. Models of romantic relationships may be less applicable to **sexual-minority youth** – adolescents who are not exclusively heterosexual. Stigmas and stereotypes make the development of intimate relationships of all kinds far more complicated for sexual-minority youth than for their straight peers.

E. Because the age at which individuals marry has become considerably later over the past half-century, dating during adolescence has lost its courtship significance.

V.   INTIMACY AND ADOLESCENT PSYCHOSOCIAL DEVELOPMENT

A. Adolescents who have intimate friendships typically have better mental health than their peers who do not. We do not know which comes first, however, intimacy or psychological health. Intimacy, and the social support it provides, enhances adolescents' well-being.

B. Intimate friendships can also have negative effects resulting from frequent conversations with friends about personal problems and difficulties. These conversations may lead to too much introspection and self-consciousness. Also, while good friendships serve many positive functions, they also provide opportunities for insecurity, conflict, jealousy, and mistrust. Nevertheless, experts agree that close peer relationships are an essential part of healthy social development during adolescence.

Lecture Topics and Supplementary Readings

I.   Attachment Theory

In recent years, the study of attachment, once limited to the research on social and emotional development during infancy, has been extended to the study of close relationships during later periods of development, including adolescence. It may be useful in a course on adolescence, therefore, to discuss the notion of attachment, review what is known about differences in early attachment relationships, and describe how early relationships may affect the development of intimate and romantic relationships later in life. In such a lecture, one would discuss the attachment theories of Bowlby and Ainsworth, describe differences among securely and insecurely attached infants, and present research findings on the later social relationships of insecure and secure infants as well as on "attachments" during adolescence. It is interesting for students to see how attachment is measured by developmental psychologists. (The procedure is described in many of the articles presented below.) If a video camera is available, it is possible to record an infant's behavior during an attachment procedure (called the "Strange Situation") and replay this for the class, pointing out aspects of the infant's behavior during separation and reunion that are important markers.

Ainsworth, M., Blehar, M., Waters, E., & Wall, S. (1978). *Patterns of attachment*. Hillsdale, N.J.: Erlbaum.

Armsden, G., & Greenberg, M. (1987). The inventory of parent and peer attachment: Individual differences and their relationship to psychological well-being in adolescence. *Journal of Youth and Adolescence, 16*, 427-43.

Bowlby, J. (1969). *Attachment and loss*, Vol. 1: *Attachment*. New York: Basic Books.

Kobak, R., & Sceery, A. (1988). Attachment in late adolescence: Working models, affect regulation, and representations of self and others. *Child Development, 59*, 135-146.

Main, M., & Kaplan, N. (1985). Security in infancy, childhood, and adulthood: A move to the level of representations. In I. Bretherton and E. Waters (Eds.), Growing points of attachment theory and research. *Monographs of the Society for Research in Child Development, 50 (1-2)* (Serial No. 209).

II.   Dating and Marriage

Most students would find a lecture on dating and romantic relationships during adolescence interesting. Such a lecture might begin with some work by Sullivan on the development of intimacy, examine some survey research on the prevalence of dating, discuss the functions of dating during adolescence, and examine the different "scripts" for males and females in the dating relationship.

Gordon, M., & Miller, R. (1984). Going steady in the 1980s: Exclusive relationships in six Connecticut high schools. *Sociology and Social Research, 68*, 463-479.

Long, B. (1989). Heterosexual involvement of unmarried undergraduate females in relation to self-evaluations. *Journal of Youth and Adolescence, 18*, 489-500.

Miller, R., & Gordon, M. (1986). The decline in formal dating: A study in six Connecticut high schools. *Marriage and Family Review, 10*, 139-156.

Savin-Williams, R., & Berndt, T. (1990). Friendship and peer relations (pp. 277-307). In S. Feldman and G. Elliott (Eds.), *At the threshold: The developing adolescent*. Cambridge: Harvard University Press.

Classroom Activities

I.   Friendships Past and Present

The textbook traces the path from childhood friendships to late adolescent romantic relationships. One poignant way to illustrate this path is to have students write down who their close friends were in 6th-, 8th-, 10th-, 12th grade, and now. Are any of the friends mentioned in 6th grade also mentioned now? What characterized their friendships during 6th grade and what characterizes their friendships now? Also, what do they look for in a friend now? Are these qualities different from the qualities of their earlier friendships (e.g., maybe they learned that trust was something very important after one of their friends blabbed)? This activity will help illustrate how early friendships are characterized by activities while friendships later in life center on trust and loyalty.

II.   My First Date

A funny way to discuss intimacy in adolescence is to have students recall their first date. If students have difficulty recalling their first date, ask them to remember their first boyfriend or girlfriend. How old were they? How did they approach a girl or boy that they liked? Where did they go? Did they go in groups or did they go out alone? What was the date like? (Could they share their intimate feelings? Were they secure in their relationship?) Now have students evaluate their current romantic relationships. How is it different from their first one? What "pick up" line do they use, and has it changed since their first date? By recalling their first intimate experiences, and then evaluating their current ones, students will be better able to see how intimacy develops over the course of adolescence.

III.   Letting Your Child Date

After students recall their first date, it's interesting to watch them respond to the hypothetical issue of letting THEIR child date. You may even have older students in the class who have teenage children and can relate what it is like to watch their child form intimate relationships with members of the opposite sex. At what age would they allow their child to date? What rules or limits would they set? (Do they need to meet the girl or boy before they go out? Could they go out alone or would they need to go in groups?) To make this even livelier, students could role-play a teenage daughter (or son) asking to go on his or her first date.

Web Researcher

Intimacy and autonomy are both important adolescent needs. But they sound like they are antithetical to one another. Examine several websites that give adolescents advice about handling close personal relationships. How do these two themes play themselves out in this context? Is the same advice given to boys as to girls? About same-sex and opposite-sex relationships? Go to *www.mhhe.com/steinberg6* for further information.

Outside Activities

I.   Attachment and the Student

Students can begin to explore the issue of attachment in their own lives. For most students this exercise will be applicable, however be aware that this exercise may not be for everyone. You may wish to make this activity optional or one of a choice of several options.

Each student should be asked to write a short essay on his or her mother and father (or for just one parent). The focus of the paper should be on their parents' behavior toward them when they were very young and its consequences in terms of attachment across the life span. For example, students can consider such questions as: Who was their primary caretaker in the household? What percentage of child care was each parent responsible for? Was each parent responsible for different things (e.g., mother, discipline; father, schoolwork)? How does their parents' behavior then reflect on their relationship with their parents now? (Do they now go to their father when making school or job decisions? Do they tend to approach their mother when asking about how to discipline their own child?) Also, how does their attachment to their parents affect their current romantic relationship? (Are there similarities between their parents' marriage and their romantic relationship? What qualities do they look for in a partner and why?)

II.   Advice Columns on Intimacy

Since establishing intimacy, especially within cross-sex friendships, is challenging for most adolescents, ask your class to investigate the kinds of advice that adolescents are receiving from the print media or internet. Divide your class into small groups and ask some groups to search through teen-oriented magazines while others will search the internet for columns/sites offering advice for teens. Each group should provide copies of the advice columns they found, share brief, oral summaries of the advice, and also provide an oral evaluation of the advice regarding its accuracy, as compared to the research-based information reviewed in the text.

Film and Video List

The Dating Scene (University of Wisconsin – Madison, 1972), 16 minutes.
Explores dating attitudes and concerns.

Everybody Rides the Carousel (Perspective Films, 1975), 73 minutes.
A carousel and its riders provide metaphors to describe Erikson's eight stages of development.

Learning to Love (Insight Media, 1988), 30 minutes.
Looks at the concepts of love and falling in love, detailing three stages of the process. Discusses the importance of strong self-concept to a relationship.

Peers in Development (Insight Media, 1991), 60 minutes.
This video provides a thorough overview of the important functions peers serve during childhood and adolescence, focusing on issues of friendship, conflict, sexual development, and inadequate peer relations.

Snowbound (University of Michigan, 1977), 50 minutes.
Examines development of friendship and interpersonal understanding.

Teenage Relationships (Insight Media, 1991), 60 minutes.
Examines social development during early and late adolescence, differentiating between peer and family influences.

CHAPTER 11

❖

Sexuality

The Total Teaching Package Outline: Chapter 11 *Sexuality*	
Heading	**Resource**
SEXUALITY AS AN ADOLESCENT ISSUE	Learning Objectives 1 & 2
HOW SEXUALLY PERMISSIVE IS CONTEMPORARY SOCIETY? *Sexual Socialization in Restrictive Societies* *Sexual Socialization in Semirestrictive Societies* *Sexual Socialization in Permissive Societies*	Learning Objective 3 Classroom Activity I
SEXUAL ATTITUDES AMONG ADOLESCENTS	Learning Objective 4 Outside Activities I & II
TRENDS IN SEXUAL ACTIVITY DURING ADOLESCENCE *Stages of Sexual Activity* *Premarital Intercourse during Adolescence* *Changes in Patterns of Adolescent Premarital Intercourse over Time*	Learning Objective 5 Figures 11.1, 11.2 & 11.3 Video: *Taking Charge (Teen Sexuality) (U of MN, 1986)*
THE SEXUALLY ACTIVE ADOLESCENT *Psychological and Social Characteristics of Sexually Active Adolescents* *Parental and Peer Influences on Adolescents' Sexual Behavior*	Learning Objective 6 The Scientific Study of Adolescence Box: *Risk Factors for Sexual Activity*
Sex Differences in the Meaning of Sex	Learning Objective 7 The Sexes Box: *The Influences of Hormones and Friends on Adolescent Sexual Behavior*
Homosexuality During Adolescence	Learning Objective 8 Lecture Topic I Figure 11.4 Video: *Michael, A Gay Son (U of MN, 1980); Teenage Homosexuality (IU, 1980)*
Sexual Harassment, Rape, and Sexual Abuse During Adolescence	Learning Objective 9 Figure 11.5 Video: *Date Rate: No Means No! (U of CA, 1985)* *Problematic Behaviors*[1]: Chapter 11

Contraceptive Use	Learning Objective 10 Lecture Topic II Figure 11.6 Videos: *Hope is Not a Method (PF, 1984);* *Ignoring the Risks: Teenage Pregnancy and AIDS* *(FFHS, 1994)* *Problematic Behaviors[1]:* Chapter 4
AIDS and Other Sexually Transmitted Infections	Learning Objective 11 Classroom Activity II Videos: *AIDS, Teens and Latinos (FFHS, 1994);* *Teens, Sex and AIDS (FFHS, 1994)*
TEENAGE PREGNANCY AND **CHILDBEARING** *The Nature and Extent of the Problem* *Contributing Factors* *The Role of the Father* *Consequences for Mother and Child*	Learning Objective 12 Videos: *And Baby Makes Two: A Look at* *Teenage Single Parenting (U of MN, 1986);* *Children of Children (SU, 1988); Daddy is 17 (U* *of WI, 1987); Educating Pregnant Teens (FFHS,* *1994); Schoolboy Father (LCA, undated)*
Teenage Pregnancy Prevention and Intervention *Programs*	Learning Objective 13 Classroom Activities III & IV

For further information on these and other topics, please check out PowerWeb (packaged with the text), and the Online Learning Center for this edition, located at *www.mhhe.com/steinberg6*.

[1]Refers to *Problematic Behaviors During Adolescence* by Jeffrey Haugaard (2001, McGraw-Hill).

Learning Objectives

1. Understand the role puberty, cognition, and social context play in the development of sexuality during adolescence.

2. Understand the four developmental challenges concerning sexuality during adolescence.

3. Understand the process of sexual socialization in restrictive, semi-restrictive, and permissive societies and the effect this has on sexual behavior.

4. Understand adolescents' attitudes toward sex.

5. Understand the stages of sexual activity and the changes in patterns of adolescent premarital intercourse over time.

6. Understand the changes in psychological and social characteristics of sexually active adolescents over time.

7. Understand the differences between boys' and girls' responses to their first sexual encounter.

8. Understand the development of homosexuality and the difference between sexual preference and sex-role development.

9. Understand the prevalence as well as the psychological effects of rape and sexual abuse during adolescence.

10. Understand the contraceptive behavior of adolescents and be aware of the most commonly used methods of birth control.

11. Understand which sexually transmitted diseases most common during adolescence and the prevalence of AIDS among the teenage population.

12. Understand the problem of teenage pregnancy and childbearing as well as the role of the father.

13. Understand the effectiveness of sex education programs during adolescence.

Key Terms

AIDS (Acquired Immune Deficiency Syndrome)
androgens
autoerotic behavior
chlamydia
date rate
estrogens
gender identity
gonorrhea
herpes
human ecology
nocturnal orgasms

permissive societies
restrictive societies
risk factor
semirestrictive societies
serial monogamy
sex-role behavior
sexual preference
sexual socialization
sexually transmitted infections (STIs)
sociosexual behavior
testosterone

Chapter Overview

I.   **SEXUALITY AS AN ADOLESCENT ISSUE**

   A. Sexuality becomes an important issue during adolescence due to the physical changes of puberty, the increased capacity for the individual to think about sexual feelings, and the new social meaning given to sexual behavior by society.

   B. The four developmental challenges of adolescence during this time are: (1) accepting one's changing body, (2) accepting one's feelings of sexual arousal, (3) understanding that sexual activity is voluntary, and (4) practicing safe sex.

II. **HOW SEXUALLY PERMISSIVE IS CONTEMPORARY SOCIETY?**

   A. In the most extensive study to date on sexual behavior in different cultures, Ford and Beach categorized the **sexual socialization** of adolescents into three distinct societies: (1) **restrictive** (where adolescents are pressured to refrain from sex), (2) **semirestricitve** (where sexual activity is frowned upon but abstinence is not enforced), and (3) **permissive** (where attitudes towards sex are lenient).

B. <u>Sexual Socialization in Restrictive Societies</u>: Adolescents are pressured to refrain from sexual activity until they have undergone a formal rite of passage or have married.

C. <u>Sexual Socialization in Semirestrictive Societies</u>: Contrary to popular stereotypes of American society as being excessively permissive when it comes to matters of sex, especially in comparison with many other cultures, American society typically has followed either a restrictive or semirestrictive pattern.

D. <u>Sexual Socialization in Permissive Societies</u>: The transition of young people into adult sexual activity is highly continuous and usually begins in childhood.

III. SEXUAL ATTITUDES AMONG ADOLESCENTS

A. Attitudes toward sex have changed during the past four decades among American youth. Most teenagers today believe that it is acceptable to have intercourse before marriage as long as it takes place within the context of a loving, intimate relationship. Although an adolescent may have a series of sexual partners over time, he or she is likely to be monogamous within each relationship, a pattern known as **serial monogamy**.

B. An important trend in young peoples changing attitudes toward sex has been the decline in acceptance of the double standard for men and women. Most importantly, there has been a shift away from conformity to institutionalized norms and toward a perspective that places greater emphasis on individual judgment.

IV. TRENDS IN SEXUAL ACTIVITY DURING ADOLESCENCE

A. <u>Stages of Sexual Activity</u>: The developmental progression of sexual behaviors has not changed very much over the last forty years. Both boys and girls follow a similar sequence of behavior beginning with **autoerotic behavior** (i.e., masturbation or **nocturnal orgasms**) and moving toward **sociosexual behavior**.

B. <u>Premarital Intercourse During Adolescence</u>: Sexual intercourse, once delayed until early adulthood, is now a part of the typical adolescent's experience. Approximately two-thirds of all teenagers have sexual intercourse before graduating from high school, although there are wide ethnic and regional differences in the age of onset of sexual activity. African-American adolescents are more likely to begin sexual activity earlier than other adolescents and to progress toward intercourse more quickly. The most dramatic change during the past two decades in the incidence of premarital sex has been among white females, however. Over the past twenty-five years, rates of premarital intercourse in different sub-groups of American adolescents have converged.

C. <u>Changes in Patterns of Adolescent Premarital Intercourse Over Time</u>: Rates of premarital sex accelerated rapidly in the early 1970s, stabilized until the late 1980s where the rates escalated again, stabilizing in the 1990s at over 50 percent of adolescents reporting being sexually active. Rates of early sexual activity are quite high, and since the 1960s, rates of premarital sex for males and females are nearly the same.

V.   THE SEXUALLY ACTIVE ADOLESCENT

A. Early sexual activity does not carry the psychological risks that many adults associate with it. In general, adolescents who are sexually active have psychological profiles that are similar to those of their peers. There is evidence, however, that early sexual activity is more common among teenagers growing up in single-parent households and is associated with higher rates of problem behaviors. Adolescent sexual behavior is influenced not only by the family but also by peers, siblings, and forces in the broader community.

B. Parental and Peer Influences on Adolescents' Sexual Activity: Parent-child communication about sex has only a small effect on the sexual activity of the adolescent. Permissive parental attitudes is associated with more sexual activity, but the adolescents' opportunity to have sex, having sexually active friends, and their use of alcohol and drugs are far more important predictors of sexual activity than are family factors. One important family factor is family composition; girls from single-parent households are more likely to be sexually active than their peers. Peers influence the sexual behavior of adolescents in two ways: (1) if an adolescent's peers are sexually active, the peers establish a norm that sex is acceptable, and (2) peers or potential sex partners may exert direct influence through comments they make to the less sexually experienced adolescents.

C. Sex Differences in the Meaning of Sex: Any discussion of the psychological aspects of adolescent sexuality must differentiate between the experiences of males and females. Early sexuality for males is tinged with elements of recreation, whereas for females it is more linked to feelings of intimacy and closeness. Because of the risks of pregnancy, adolescent girls are more likely than boys to be socialized to view sex with caution and are therefore more likely to feel ambivalent, rather than uniformly positive, about engaging in sex.

D. Homosexuality During Adolescence: Approximately 8 percent of the adolescent and young adult population is either partially or exclusively gay or lesbian. **Sexual preference** (the extent to which someone prefers heterosexual, homosexual or both types of activities) is not connected to an individual's **sex-role behavior** (the extent to which an individual behaves in masculine, feminine, or androgynous ways) or **gender identity** (which gender an individual believes he or she is psychologically). Current theories of the origins of homosexuality suggest a complex interaction of genetic and environmental influences. Experts agree that homosexuality is not a form of psychopathology. In addition, many of the difficulties experienced by gay and lesbian youth result from their being harassed by peers and adults.

E. Sexual Harassment, Rape, and Sexual Abuse During Adolescence: The majority of teenagers report having been sexually harassed at school and a significant minority of youth, mainly females, are forced to have sex against their will. Date rape continues to be a problem on many college campuses, as well. Living apart from one's parents, having physical or psychological problems, being raised in poverty, and having parents who abuse drugs and/or alcohol are all risk factors for sexual abuse. Adolescents who have been sexually abused show higher than average rates of poor self-esteem, anxiety, fear, and depression; are more likely to engage in risky behavior; and are more likely to become pregnant as teenagers.

F. Contraceptive Use: Adolescents are infamously poor users of contraception, especially in the United States. Most experts agree that the reason so few adolescents use birth control regularly is that contraceptives are not as accessible as they might be, that adolescents seldom anticipate having intercourse until they become sexually active on a regular basis, and that using birth control requires the sort of long-term planning that many young people are reluctant or unable to engage in.

G. AIDS and Other Sexually Transmitted Infections: Previously referred to as "venereal diseases," **sexually transmitted infections** (STIs) affect 1 in 4 teenagers. Some of the most common forms of STIs are **gonorrhea** and **chlamydia** (both caused by a bacterium), and **herpes** and **human papilloma** (both caused by a virus). Acquired Immune Deficiency Syndrome (**AIDS**) has come to the forefront in the past ten years as one of the more serious STIs. AIDS is transmitted through bodily fluids—typically semen and blood. The human immunodeficiency virus (**HIV**) attacks the body's immune system, interfering with the body's ability to defend itself against life-threatening diseases like pneumonia. Although AIDS was initially concentrated within two groups, gay men and drug users, the incidence of AIDS is increasing among the heterosexual population, and the number of HIV-infected adolescents is doubling almost every year.

VI. TEENAGE PREGNANCY AND CHILDBEARING

A. The Nature and Extent of the Problem: Preventing teenage pregnancy has been extremely difficult, and most sex education programs developed during the last two decades have failed in this respect. There are approximately one million teenage pregnancies each year in the United States, about half of which are carried to term.

B. Contributing Factors: Sporadic and inadequate use of contraception is the primary cause of teenage pregnancies. Among minority youth, ambivalence about childbearing may also be a contributing factor. Research shows that teenagers are not harmed psychologically by aborting their pregnancy or by placing their infant up for adoption, but each of these options is influenced by the S.E.S. of the adolescent's family.

C. The Role of the Father: Adolescent males who become fathers are distinguished from their peers who do not by problems with self-esteem, school, work, drugs and alcohol, and the law. The higher rates of problem behavior among teenage fathers suggest that marriage may not be the best response to pregnancy for teenage women. Fathering a child as a teenager hurts educational achievement and mental health, effects that are more pronounced among white and Hispanic males than among African-American males.

D. Consequences for Mother and Child: It is nearly impossible to know whether the problems that teenage mothers and their children face are the result of the mother's young age, or are the result of poverty and other factors associated with poverty. Recent research suggests that it is poverty more than the mother's young age that is responsible for most of the problems that teen mothers and their children experience. One factor that is associated with the age of the mother is that teen mothers are more likely than older mothers to see their infants as difficult and, therefore, spend less time with them. This decreased contact may be responsible for the increased likelihood of school problems, misbehavior and delinquency, and early sexual activity that the child of the teen mother faces. While poverty and teen motherhood usually go together, motherhood adds additional challenges to the already significant problems posed by poverty. Disruptions in education and career development result from teen motherhood, and the likelihood of remaining in poverty is higher among teen mothers than their poor peers who do not have children.

E. Teenage Pregnancy Prevention and Intervention Programs: To date, few programs designed to prevent teenage pregnancy and childbearing have proven effective on a large scale. Most programs administered through schools have helped to increase students' knowledge about sexuality, but these programs rarely alter behavior, with the exception of a small increase in contraceptive use. Programs involving a combination of school-based education and community-based health clinics to provide information about sex and access to contraceptives have diminished the rate of teen pregnancy, but such programs often face objections from parents for fear that they will stimulate sexual activity. While research results suggest that these fears are unwarranted, the benefits of such programs are limited to those teens who actually take advantage of the services. Adolescent mothers who have social support from family or friends and who are able to complete high school fare better than those who do not.

Lecture Topics and Supplementary Readings

I.   The Development of Homosexuality

Many students are misinformed about the development of homosexuality during adolescence, and a lecture on the subject would be a valuable addition to the material presented in the text. A lecture might include information on theories of the development of homosexuality as well as on the expression of homosexuality in adolescence and young adulthood. On most campuses there are gay and lesbian groups that can provide speakers and additional information. A presentation from one or more of these groups can be an informative use of class time.

Bell, A., Weinberg, M., & Hammersmith, S. (1981). *Sexual preference: Its development in man and woman*. Bloomington: Indiana University Press.

Ellis, L. & Ames, M. (1987). Neurohormonal functioning and sexual orientation: A theory of homosexuality–heterosexuality. *Psychological Bulletin, 101*, 233-258.

Green, R. (1980). Homosexuality. In H. Kaplan, A. Freedman, and B. Sadock (Eds.), *Comprehensive textbook of psychiatry* (Vol. 2, 3rd ed.). Baltimore: Williams and Wilkins.

Green, R. (1987). *The "Sissy Boy" syndrome and the development of homosexuality*. New Haven: Yale University Press.

Savin-Williams, R. (1988). Theoretical perspectives accounting for adolescent homosexuality. *Journal of Adolescent Health Care, 9*, 95-104.

II. Adolescent Contraceptive Use

A lecture on adolescent contraceptive behavior provides a good context within which to integrate information on adolescent sexuality, cognitive development, social relations, sex roles, and the impact of broader sociocultural factors on the adolescent experience. One might begin by discussing rates of adolescent contraceptive use, and then turn to a discussion of the reasons for young people's infrequent and sporadic contraceptive behavior. Most scholars now reject the idea that many pregnancies occur because young women unconsciously "want" to have children. Instead, writers have turned their attention to the cognitive limitations of early adolescence, the limited availability of contraceptives to young people, adolescents' lack of accurate information about sex and pregnancy, young people's difficulty in acknowledging—to themselves and others—that they are sexually active, and society's ambivalent attitude toward teenage sexuality.

Cvetkovich, G., Grote, B., Bjorseth, A., & Sarkissian, J. (1975). On the psychology of adolescents' use of contraceptives. *Journal of Sex Research, 1*, 256-270.

Hayes, C. (Ed.). (1987). *Risking the future: Adolescent sexuality, pregnancy, and childbearing* (Vol. 1). Washington, D.C.: National Academy Press.

Jones, E., et al. (1987). *Teenage pregnancy in industrialized countries*. New Haven: Yale University Press.

Westoff, C. (1988). Unintended pregnancy in America and abroad. *Family Planning Perspectives, 20*, 254-261.

Classroom Activities

I. Penis and Vagina

Before beginning the topic on sexuality, have students turn to the person on their right and say "penis." Then, have students turn to the person on their left and say the word "vagina." Some prodding may be necessary and they may need to say these words in unison before they can say them to their neighbor. This activity will generate a lot of giggles and will illustrate the awkwardness people feel about sex. This exercise is a nice prelude into the different ways societies socialize adolescents on sex. At the end of the discussion, ask students to determine whether the United States is a restrictive, semi-restrictive, or permissive society.

As an alternative to the above exercise, you may want to ask your class to think about the last time they talked with their parents or a friend about their own sexuality. Have they had many discussions about sexuality? When sex is a subject of conversation, is it discussed seriously or is it cloaked in humor? If they were to count the number of sexual encounters they viewed on television this past week, would that number be greater than the number of serious discussions they have had about sex during their lifetime? The lack of frequency with which sex is seriously discussed, when compared to the frequency with which we are exposed to sexual content in various media, serves as an indicator of the semi-restrictive status of American society.

II.   Guest Speaker

Invite a guest speaker to give a presentation on STIs/AIDS. You can usually find health educators from the campus health office who would not only be able to present the causes, symptoms, cures, and/or methods of prevention for STIs/AIDS, but also the current rates of STIs and AIDS on *your* campus. This would not only provide educational information for the class, but also a touch of reality. If your campus does not offer a health education program, Planned Parenthood is also an excellent resource.

III.   Develop a Sex Education Program for Teens

Simon and Garfunkel sang, "The words of prophets are written on the subway walls" – not the best place to receive one's sex education. Divide students into small groups and have them devise a sex education program for adolescents. Below are some questions students should address when creating their program:

1. What is the goal of their program (e.g., to increase contraceptive use, to improve knowledge about STIs)?
2. Who is their target population (e.g. what grade will they start their program in)?
3. How will they respond to parental concern/objection?
4. What criterion will be used to measure the success of their program?
5. How will they present the information?

Some groups will focus on STIs, some on AIDS, others on teen pregnancy. More specific information (and visual aids) can be included in their presentations if students have an opportunity to research the subject material outside of class. Have students present their programs to the class. This exercise gives students a chance to "teach" the course for a while – and gives you a nice reprieve!

IV.   Media Messages

In an attempt to prevent the problems of teenage pregnancy, The Children's Defense Fund has created posters of adolescent mothers and their babies. These posters have captions such as, "It's like being grounded for eighteen years." The latest campaign has focused on abstinence. Divide the students into small groups and have them devise a media message that they feel would be effective in changing adolescents' sexual behavior. Students should first identify what type of behavior they wish to modify, and then devise a campaign. Have students present their ideas to the class and evaluate each other's promotions.

Web Researcher

Check out one or more websites aimed at gay, lesbian, or bisexual teenagers. What seem to be the dominant issues and concerns? Go to *www.mhhe.com/steinberg6* for further information.

Outside Activities

I.   Where Do Babies Come From?

Asking young children the above question (and ones related to it) can yield interesting and humorous responses. Have students ask children of various ages "where babies come from." (Students should try to pose the question in a more "mature" way when asking older children.) Students should be sure to attain permission from children's parents before asking such questions, since this topic is controversial in nature. You may wish to make this exercise extra credit, rather than a required class assignment, since access to subjects may vary from student to student. After students gather their responses, discuss them in class. For instance, some young children might think if a boy kisses a girl using his tongue, she can get pregnant, or that you have to eat a rabbit, or that eating green M&M's makes you horny, or that you get pregnant because of marriage, or.... After students share the responses they have found, they can also share some of the sex myths that they heard or believed when they were kids. This is sometimes difficult, since students may be embarrassed to share their misconceptions about sex, although you'd be surprised to learn how many misconceptions they still have! (Tip: Having students write their misconceptions anonymously on blank notecards that you collect and read to the class can help overcome the embarrassment the students might feel about this subject.)

II.   "Everything I Needed to Know about Sex I Learned from Television"

As a homework assignment, have your students keep a log of the sexual content they were exposed to during the course of a week (or a few nights) of viewing their favorite television programs. Ask your students to develop a set of "rules about sex" that they learned from their viewing. For example, "One should expect sexual intercourse to occur after just one or two dates." "Lust at first sight happens frequently, and often results in sexual intercourse." "After sex, one's hair and makeup remain perfect." Students should share their "rules" with the class, followed by a discussion of the perceptions of romance and sexuality that the media may be conveying to child and adolescent viewers.

Film and Video List

AIDS, Teens, and Latinos (Films for the Humanities and Sciences, 1994), 28 minutes.
This program profiles a Cuban-American teenager with AIDS who is dedicating his life to public awareness efforts and the education of Miami Latinos.

And Baby Makes Two: A Look at Teenage Single Parenting (University of Minnesota, 1986), 25 minutes.
Explores approaches for preventing and dealing with teenage single parenthood.

Children of Children (Syracuse University, 1988), 30 minutes.
Social and economic effects of teenage pregnancy are addressed. The cultural and psychological reasons for the occurrence of teenage pregnancy are also discussed.

Daddy is 17 (University of Wisconsin – Madison, 1987), 30 minutes.
Perspective on teenage boys who father children.

Date Rape: No Means No! (University of California, 1985), 25 minutes.
Dramatically illustrates the prevalence and consequences of "date rape." Student misconceptions of sex resulting in trauma, and ways to prevent date rape are discussed.

Educating Pregnant Teens (Films for the Humanities and Sciences, 1994), 28 minutes.
Takes a candid look at teenage pregnancy and attitudes toward it through the forthright views of a young group of women.

Hope Is Not a Method (Perspective Films, Education Group, 1984), 20 minutes.
Overview of birth control methods and discussion of possible methods for the future.

Ignoring the Risks: Teenage Pregnancy and AIDS (Films for the Humanities and Sciences, 1994), 28 minutes.
In this specially adapted Phil Donahue program, teens themselves explain why they ignore the warning that unprotected sex can cost them their lives.

Michael, a Gay Son (University of Minnesota, 1980), 27 minutes.
An adolescent male "comes out."

Schoolboy Father (Learning Corporation of America, undated), 30 minutes.
Presents a 16-year-old male living with his divorced mother who assumes custody of his baby boy and copes with raising the boy.

Taking Charge (Teen Sexuality) (University of Minnesota, 1986), 22 minutes.
Looks at the myths and misconceptions that influence adolescent use of birth control.

Teenage Homosexuality (Indiana University, 1980), 10 minutes.
Five teenagers discuss their homosexuality.

Teens, Sex, and AIDS (Films for the Humanities and Sciences, 1994), 28 minutes.
Combines an open discussion among teens about their AIDS concerns, with dramatizations of teens dealing with decisions about sex.

CHAPTER 12

❖

Achievement

The Total Teaching Package Outline: Chapter 12 *Achievement*	
Heading	**Resource**
ACHIEVEMENT AS AN ADOLESCENT ISSUE	
ACHIEVEMENT MOTIVES AND BELIEFS *The Motive to Achieve* *The Importance of Beliefs*	Learning Objectives 1, 2 & 3 Lecture Topic I Classroom Activities I & II The Sexes Box: *Patterns of Achievement in Adolescent Boys and Girls* Table 12.1
Environmental Influences on Achievement *The Influence of the Home Environment* *The Influence of Friends*	Learning Objectives 4 & 5 The Scientific Study of Adolescence Box: *Stress as the Link Between Socioeconomic Status and Achievement* Outside Activities
Educational Achievement *The Importance of Socioeconomic Status* *Ethnic Differences in Educational Achievement*	Learning Objective 6 Figure 12.1 Video: *Adventures of Teenage Scientists (TLF, 1982)*
Changes in Educational Achievement over Time	Learning Objective 7 Classroom Activity III Figures 12.2, 12.3, 12.4, & 12.5
Dropping Out of High School	Learning Objective 8 Video: *Dropout (U of IL, 1985); Specific Learning Disabilities in Adolescence (UC-Berkeley, 1987).*
OCCUPATIONAL ACHIEVEMENT *The Development of Occupational Plans*	Learning Objective 9 Lecture Topic II Video: *Career Education (U of MI, 1972)*
Influences on Occupational Choices • *The Role of Personality* • *The Influence of Parents and Peers* • *The Broader Context of Occupational Choice*	Learning Objective 10 Outside Activity I

For further information on the preceding and other topics, please check out PowerWeb (packaged with the text), and the Online Learning Center for this edition, located at *www.mhhe.com/steinberg6*.

Learning Objectives

1. Understand the importance of need for achievement during adolescence and its relation to the fear of failure.

2. Understand the distinction between intrinsic and extrinsic motivation and their influence on adolescents' need for achievement.

3. Understand the effect of learned helplessness on achievement during adolescence.

4. Understand the role of authoritative parenting on academic performance as well as the influence of cultural capital.

5. Understand how adolescents' peers may influence the level of achievement attained.

6. Understand the influence of socioeconomic status and ethnicity on educational attainment.

7. Understand the changes in educational achievement over time.

8. Understand the risk factors associated with dropping out of school, and the effect of dropping out on occupational achievement.

9. Understand the development of occupational plans according to Super.

10. Understand the influences on occupational choice, especially the role of personality.

Key Terms

academic achievement
achievement attributions
achievement
crystallization
cultural capital
educational attainment
extrinsic motivation
fear of failure
fear of success
intrinsic motivation

learned helplessness
mediating variable
need for achievement
occupational attainment
school performance
Self-Directed Search
social capital
specification
stressful life events
underachievers

Chapter Overview

I. ACHIEVEMENT AS AN ADOLESCENT ISSUE

    A. **Achievement** is an important issue during adolescence because society typically designates adolescence as a time of preparation for adult work roles, because individuals now can understand the long-term implications of their educational and career decisions, and because during adolescence, schools begin making distinctions among individuals that potentially have profound effects on their long-term occupational development.

    B. Because educational and occupational achievement are cumulative, during adolescence the "rich" tend to get richer, while the "poor" tend to get poorer.

II. ACHIEVEMENT MOTIVES AND BELIEFS

    A. The Motive to Achieve: Early theories of the development of achievement stressed individual differences in achievement motivation – some individuals were believed to have a stronger **"need for achievement"** than others.

    B. An adolescent's need for achievement and his or her **fear of failure** work together simultaneously to pull the individual toward, and repel the individual from, achievement situations. For example, many students who have trouble persisting at tasks and who fear failure become **underachievers** – students' whose grades are far lower than one would expect based on their intellectual ability.

    C. The Importance of Beliefs: Contemporary theories, however, stress the interaction of motives, beliefs, **achievement attributions**, and goals as influencing adolescents' achievement orientation. Adolescents who believe that ability is malleable, who are motivated by **intrinsic** (rather than **extrinsic**) rewards, who are confident about their abilities, (e.g., who have a strong sense of **self-efficacy**), and who attribute their successes and failures to effort (rather than to ability or luck) achieve more in school than their peers.

    D. Students who are led to believe that their efforts do not make a difference develop the belief that failure is inevitable, also known as **learned helplessness**.

III. ENVIRONMENTAL INFLUENCES ON ACHIEVEMENT

    A. Some writers have examined differences in adolescents' opportunities for success and the roles of significant adults and peers in influencing achievement goals and behaviors. Rather than attributing differences in achievement to psychological factors, these writers note that access to educational and occupational opportunities varies across socioeconomic and racial groups, and that actual achievement is influenced by a number of environmental and situational factors as well as by psychological ones.

    B. The Influence of the Home Environment: A good deal of research indicates that adolescents perform better and are more engaged in school when they come from authoritative homes in which their parents are highly involved in their education or families that are high in **social capital**. A number of researchers have also shown the extent to which the adolescent's parents provide the youngster with **cultural capital** – by exposing the adolescent to art, music, literature, and so forth – exerts a positive impact on achievement.

C. <u>The Influence of Friends</u>: In addition, adolescents whose friends support academic achievement perform better in school than do peers whose friends disparage academic achievements.

D. <u>Educational Achievement</u>: Educational achievement is usually defined in one of three ways: **school performance**, **academic achievement**, or **educational attainment**. Educational and occupational achievement are highly interconnected. Doing well in school generally leads to higher levels of educational attainment, which, in turn, leads to more prestigious and better-paying employment. In general, there are strong socioeconomic and ethnic differences in educational and occupational attainment.

E. <u>The Importance of Socioeconomic Status</u>: Socioeconomic status is an extremely important influence on educational achievement. Generally, adolescents from high social classes perform better in school and complete more years of schooling than do their less advantaged counterparts. One reason for this difference is that the home environment of more affluent adolescents is more supportive of school success: Middle-class adolescents are better nourished, more consistently encouraged, and less exposed to stress than are their less affluent peers.

F. <u>Ethnic Differences in Educational Achievement</u>: Recent studies indicate that there are ethnic differences in educational achievement above and beyond those attributable to socioeconomic status. In general, Asian-American adolescents outperform Anglo-American students, who in turn do better in school than African-American or Hispanic-American students. One reason for the superior performance of Asian-students is that they are more likely to hold beliefs about achievement that are predictive of success in school. In contrast, parents and teachers in African-American and Hispanic-American communities are more likely to communicate the message that, although education is important, there is little that minority individuals can do to succeed within a discriminatory society. These different messages may lead students from different backgrounds to devote different degrees of effort to their studies.

G. <u>Changes in Educational Achievement over Time</u>: The low level of educational achievement among American youth has been a national concern for some time now. Although some gains in scores on standardized tests of achievement were reported during the mid-1980s, test scores have not improved since that time, and the ground that was lost in the late 1960s and early 1970s has not been recovered. Among the reasons given for this pattern are that teachers are not spending enough time on basic instruction, that students are not taking advanced courses when they are offered, that parents are not encouraging academic pursuits at home, that adolescents are not spending sufficient time on their studies outside of school, and they know that can earn good grades without working very hard.

H. <u>Dropping Out of High School</u>: Dropping out of high school is associated with an array of individual and social costs. Adolescents who drop out of high school are more likely than their peers to come from socioeconomically disadvantaged backgrounds and to have had a history of poor school performance, low school involvement, and poor performance on standardized tests of achievement and intelligence. In addition, there are wide ethnic and regional differences in dropout rates and dropping out of school is an especially serious problem among Hispanic youth. Studies also suggest that the schools from which students drop out are larger, more disorderly, and less focused on academics than other schools. About 25 percent of adolescents leave high school before graduating, although a fair number return to school in young adulthood to earn their diploma. Dropping out is not so much a decision that is made during adolescence as it is the culmination of a long process that begins early on.

IV. OCCUPATIONAL ACHIEVEMENT

A. <u>The Development of Occupational Plans</u>: As suggested by Donald Super, occupational plans do not begin to **crystallize** until middle adolescence. Following this period is the need to **specify** the adolescent's vocational interest. Even so, the process of choosing a career is a long one for most individuals, one that may last well through the final years of college. Occupational plans are influenced by a complex array of personality (as suggested by Holland's **Self-Directed Search**), individual, and environmental factors.

B. <u>Influences on Occupational Choices</u>: Theorists interested in patterns of occupational choice have examined personality factors, the influences of parents and peers, and the impact of the broader social and economic context. As is the case with educational achievement, occupational attainment is strongly influenced by socioeconomic status.

Lecture Topics and Supplementary Readings

I. Attributional Theory

Although the study of achievement motives has a long history in the field of psychology, in more recent years writers have turned away from examining youngsters' motives and focused their attention instead on youngsters' beliefs about, and attributions for, success and failure. A lecture on attributional theory and its uses in understanding achievement behavior would be a valuable supplement to the material presented in the text. In such a lecture, one might begin by over viewing attributional theory. Then one could discuss Weiner's four-factor attribution model, bringing in illustrations of how the model might be applied in studying youngsters' school performance. Finally, one could turn to the interesting work of Dweck and her colleagues linking achievement attributions—and especially sex differences in achievement attributions—to the concept of "learned helplessness."

   Ames, C., & Archer, J. (1988). Achievement goals in the classroom: Students' learning strategies and motivation processes. *Journal of Educational Psychology, 80*, 260-267.

   Dweck, C., & Light, B. (1980). Learned helplessness and intellectual achievement. In J. Garber and M. Seligman (Eds.), *Human helplessness*. New York: Academic Press.

   Henderson, V., & Dweck, C. (1990). Motivation and achievement (pp. 308-329). In S. Feldman and G. Elliott (Eds.), *At the threshold: The developing adolescent*. Cambridge: Harvard University Press.

Stipek, D., & Weisz, J. (1981). Perceived personal control and academic achievement. *Review of Educational Research*, *51*, 101-137.

Weiner, B. (1974). *Achievement motivation and attribution theory*. Morristown, N.J.: General Learning Press.

II.   Career Plans

Given the fact that many college students are in the process of making and reevaluating career decisions, one could fashion an interesting and useful lecture on theories of career choice. In such a lecture one could begin with theories that attempt to relate individuals' personalities and preferences to occupational choices (e.g., Holland) and examine some of the many tests used to help individuals clarify career goals. It would be useful, perhaps, to use a Strong Vocational Interest Test or a Kuder Preference Test as an example. One might then turn to more developmental theories (e.g., Super) and explore how the process of career choice in many ways parallels the process of identity development as outlined by Erikson. One could then discuss the usefulness of programs such as career education, which are designed to provide opportunities for youngsters to engage in work-role experimentation. Most college campuses have offices that provide career counseling and placement. Invite a representative from the office on your campus to give a presentation on how career interest inventories are used to help individuals make occupational decisions.

Crites, H. (1989). Career differentiation in adolescence. In D. Stern and D. Eichorn (Eds.), *Adolescence and work*. Hillsdale, N.J.: Erlbaum.

Holland, J. (1985). *Making vocational choice: A theory of careers* (2nd ed.). Englewood Cliffs, N.J.: Prentice-Hall.

Super, D. (1967). *The psychology of careers*. New York: Harper and Row.

Classroom Activities

I.   Achievement Motivation Versus Mastery Motivation

To help students differentiate between achievement motivation and mastery motivation, present a large number of examples in which the class must choose between the two. Some examples you may wish to use include:
1. An amateur skier tries to perfect her slalom technique in order to qualify for the U.S. Olympic team. *(achievement motivation)*
2. A college student goes skiing for the first time with his friends and sets as his goal to make it down the "bunny slope" without falling by the end of the day. *(mastery motivation)*
3. A 15-year-old keeps practicing his batting at home in hopes of being chosen for the baseball team at school. *(achievement motivation)*
4. A 2-year-old keeps struggling to climb out of her crib. *(mastery motivation)*
5. A high school student spends endless hours each day at the skating rink trying to perfect a double-axle jump. *(mastery motivation)*
6. A 7-year-old is on his third attempt at making the "perfect" birthday card for his mother. *(achievement motivation)*

II. Giving a Sense of Learned Helplessness

Learned helplessness is the belief that one cannot control forces in one's environment. This is a simple demonstration that can be done in the classroom to give students the sense of learned helplessness. First, present the students with a "pop" quiz that involves several extremely difficult questions (essays will work best). (You might instead have them try to solve a series of complex logic puzzles, telling them that their performance will give an indication of their IQ.) While students are taking the quiz, have an accomplice outside the classroom begin making a great deal of noise outside the classroom, or introduce some other noxious stimulant. The students should soon begin to become frustrated. Appear to try to get the noise stopped (unsuccessfully of course), and inform the class that the noise is unavoidable. Several minutes later, admit your deception and discuss feelings of learned helplessness.

III. "Selling a College Education"

Divide students into groups and have them design a brochure advertising your college. Students should determine the particular adolescent population they intend to target (e.g., gifted, reentering, minority, underprivileged). The final products should include the benefits of college education and the advantages of your particular institution, and should be tailored to the audience for which it is intended. When the groups are finished, you might compare their work with the brochures and materials used by your admissions office.

Web Researcher

On average, people who complete more years of schooling earn more money. However, the relationship between education and income differs for men and women and for people of different ethnic backgrounds. Summarize the major patterns you see. Are these differences becoming smaller over time, staying the same, or increasing? Is the pattern the same for people with more and less education? Discuss the implications of your findings in terms of their potential effects on adolescents' decisions to remain in school. Go to *www.mhhe.com/steinberg6* for further information.

Outside Activities

I. Career Development – Occupational Achievement

Have students interview two people in a career of their choice. One should be new to the career (a young adult), while the other should have ten or fifteen years of experience. Students should ask each person about their reasons for pursuing a career in that field, what their goals were when they started, whether they have achieved any of those goals, and whether their aspirations have changed since they started the job. What qualities are necessary for advancement? Can the rate of advancement be controlled, or is it determined by external factors? Interviewers may get a sense of the subjects' beliefs about success and of whether their motivations are intrinsic or extrinsic, in addition to learning about advancement opportunities in a career of interest to the student!

Film and Video List

Career Education (University of Michigan, 1972), 24 minutes.
Examines career education programs and their impact on occupational growth.

Adventures of Teenage Scientists (Time-Life Film and Video, 1982), 57 minutes.
Shows the development of mathematically gifted young people and provides examples of their work. Good for discussion regarding what qualities define "gifted" individuals and how schools can encourage their development.

Dropout (University of Illinois, 1985), 59 minutes.
Explores causes and consequences of dropping out.

Specific Learning Disabilities in Adolescence (University of California – Berkeley, 1987), 33 minutes.
Research findings on learning disabilities in high school students are shown. Their relations to dropping out, delinquency, and social isolation are discussed.

Section III

Test Item File

Overview of Test Item File

◆

Adolescence

This Test File has been developed to accompany the text *Adolescence*. It includes a set of seventy-five multiple-choice test items and five essay items for each of the thirteen chapters in the text. Test bank items draw on the Learning Objectives for each chapter, which are listed in the Instructor's Manual section of this supplement.

Analyzing Your Test Results

You may be interested in finding out how the items you select from the test bank work in your classes. The following sections explain how to evaluate the quality of your test items according to their level of difficulty and their ability to discriminate between good and poor students.

Purpose of an Item Analysis

The purpose of a typical classroom test is to determine, with as little error as possible, each student's relative level of content mastery. To the extent that a test question contributes to this overall goal, it is considered a good question. The method for evaluating the contribution of each individual item to the performance of the test is called an *item analysis*.

Actually, an item analysis is a set of statistical calculations that yields two indices related to the quality of each test item—the discrimination index and the difficulty index. By calculating and interpreting these indices, you can determine which test items are contributing to the test's ability to pinpoint which students have mastered more of the assigned content.

Calculating the Discrimination Index

A discrimination index can be thought of as a correlation coefficient measuring the degree of relationship between responses to a particular item and students' overall scores on the exam. The possible range of the discrimination coefficient is from -1 to $+1$.

There are several acceptable methods for calculating the discrimination index. One method is to calculate the biserial correlation between students' responses to items and their total test scores. Although this method is often used in computer scoring of tests, it is a time-consuming procedure if you do not use an item analysis computer program.

Another type of discrimination index can, however, be easily calculated without a computer. The following steps describe a procedure you can use to determine the discrimination index for the questions on your tests.

Step 1. Arrange your students' tests in order of their scores, from highest to lowest.

Step 2. Separate the tests into three groups—the top 27 percent, the middle 46 percent, and the bottom 27 percent. If for example, your have 50 students in your class, you should select the 14 (50 x .27 = 13.5) best exams and the 14 worst exams, leaving 22 exams in the middle.

Step 3. Set aside the exams in the middle group. They are not needed to calculate the discrimination index.

Step 4. Choose one of the test items, and count and record the number of students in the top 27 percent who answered the question correctly. Then count and record the number of students in the bottom 27 percent who answered correctly.

Step. 5 Divide the number of tests with the correct answer in the top group by the total number of tests in that group. If for example, there are 14 tests in the top group, and if 12 of those tests have the correct answer, 12/14 = 0.86.

Step 6. Do the same for the bottom 27 percent. If for example, 5 of the 14 tests in this group have the correct answer, 5/14 = 0.36.

Step 7. Subtract the ratio of the bottom group from the ratio of the top group (86 – 0.36 = 0.50). This is the discrimination index for this question (+0.50 in our example).

Step 8. Repeat the above procedure (steps 4-7) for each question on the exam.

You may find the form following this section to be useful in calculating the discrimination indices for the items on a test.

Interpreting the Discrimination Index

Any question that has a positive discrimination coefficient is contributing to the test's ability to measure students' relative content knowledge; the higher the coefficient, the greater the contribution of that item to the overall quality of the test. Generally speaking, any item that has a discrimination coefficient higher that +0.40 should be considered very good. If the discrimination coefficient ranges from 0.20 to 0.39, the item is still reasonably good but might be improved through revision. If you plan to reuse an item in this range on another test, you may wish to examine the item to see if the distractors could be improved or the question could otherwise be revised to increase its discrimination power. Items with discrimination coefficients between 0.00 and 0.19 probably should be examined to see if they can be improved or perhaps replaced with better items.

A negative discrimination coefficient indicates that students who did well overall on the test were less likely than poor performers to answer a given item correctly. This situation, of course, should be avoided, and questions with negative discrimination indices should definitely be revised or eliminated from future tests.

Generally, test items should have high discrimination indices, but in some cases it is advisable to retain an item even if the discrimination coefficient is quite low. Item discrimination indices are directly related to the heterogeneity of the test scores, so that when this variability is low (for whatever reason), the discrimination coefficients will inevitably be lower. Consider, for instance, the difference between two classes of students: the students in class A vary widely in their abilities and, consequently, in their test scores; whereas the students in class B are closely matched in ability and all tend to get about the same scores. The discrimination indices for identical test questions will be much higher for class A's tests than for class B's tests. If your classes are rather homogeneous (like class B), you may want to relax the standards on high discrimination indices. Also, in some cases, you may believe that a particular area of content is so important that you wish to include an item testing knowledge of that contest even though past testing has shown that the items contributes little to the test and cannot be revised. Finally, discrimination indices are maximized when items are of intermediate difficulty. In other words, if nearly all students answer an item correctly (or incorrectly), the discrimination coefficient will necessarily be reduced.

DISCRIMINATION INDEX FORM

Question Number	Number of Tests with correct answer in Top 27%	Number of Tests with Correct answer in Bottom 27%	Ratio of Correct to Total Number in top 27%	Ratio of Correct to Total Number in Bottom 27%	Difference between Top and Bottom Ratios (Discrimination Index)
Sample	12	5	12/14=0.86	5/14=0.36	0.86-0.36=0.50
1					
2					
3					
4					
5					
6					
7					
8					
9					
10					
11					
12					
13					
14					
15					
16					
17					
18					
19					
20					
21					
22					

Calculating the Difficulty Index

The difficulty index is simply the percentage (expressed in decimal form) of students taking a given test who answer a particular test item correctly. Thus, it is much simpler to calculate than the discrimination index. To perform the calculation, you count the number of students who answered the test question correctly and divide this number by the total number of students taking the test. If for example, 92 students take a test and 49 of them answer Question 1 correctly, the difficulty index for Question 1 is $49/92 = 0.53$. this simply means that 53 percent of the students taking the test got this question right. As with the discrimination index, a separate difficulty index is calculated for each item on the test.

Interpreting the Difficulty Index

If all students answer an item correctly (or if no student answers correctly), then that item gives no information about which students know more of the content and which know less. From this perspective, items of intermediate difficulty are likely to contribute the most information regarding the relative levels of achievement among the students taking a particular test.

The ideal level of difficulty is the midway point between the chance level of response (25 percent for items with four possible answer choices) and zero difficulty (100 percent). Thus for the items in this test file, the optimal difficulty level is 62.5 percent. It is at this level of difficulty that the variability among students, the reliability of the test, and the test's power to discriminate between good and poor students are maximized. A test performs better overall when all of its items have difficulty indices close to this optimal value of 0.625.

One cannot easily predict the difficulty level of an item because this is in large part determined by classroom instruction. If for example, the instructor announces that the information tested by a particular question will be on the test, the difficulty index will probably be close to 1, with almost 100 percent of the students responding correctly. Should the instructor not make the announcement, quite a different index Will probably result. For this reason, the difficulty index is less informative about the quality of an item than the discrimination index is. It is best used to understand why a question is discriminating the way it is. When the difficulty index approaches 1 or 0, the discrimination coefficient must approach 0.

Although most (about 70 to 80 percent) of the questions in this test file are intended to be of intermediate difficulty, a few (about 10 to 15 percent) are more basic and a few (about 10 to 15 percent) are more advanced. The basic items are included either to serve as "warm-up" items that will build students' confidence or to be used in classes in which the student ability level is relatively low. On the other end, the advanced items should challenge even the best students and can be used to discriminate among the very best students.

Sources of Error in Item Analysis Statistics

There are two major sources of error in interpreting difficulty and discrimination indices. The first is sampling error. Sampling error can be thought of as the difference between an item's true difficulty and discrimination (if it were tested in an infinite number of cases) and the indices calculated on a limited number of responses. Just as it is possible to obtain ten "heads" when tossing coins, it is possible for the responses of a given group of students to yield unrepresentative statistics in an item analysis. Of course, sampling error increases as sample size decreases. Consequently, you should use item analysis statistics as indicators of difficulty and discrimination, not as firm measures of these properties, and be especially careful about drawing conclusions about items when the class size is small.

The other major source of error in item analysis results from not knowing what kind of instruction students have received on the content represented by the test questions. If an instructor emphasizes a particular piece of information, all students may do well on the item, whereas without emphasis, the item may be of intermediate or high difficulty. Discrimination indices can be skewed in a similar fashion. Also, in one class the students may have a higher ability level than those in another class, and this will affect item analysis statistics. Therefore, you should use caution when generalizing from item statistics based on data collected in one classroom to the performance expected for another class.

In addition to sampling error and content exposure, other factors may affect the value of item analysis statistics. As was already mentioned, restricting the variability of students' scores will reduce the discrimination indices, as will giving the exam to a group that does unusually well or unusually poorly on the test. Moreover, the error in the discrimination index estimate will increase if an item is included in a short test, as compared with a long test.

In discussing error in estimating the discrimination and difficulty indices, we are emphasizing that these numbers are not absolute properties of a test item but rather vary from one setting to another. Generally, however, in a fairly typical classroom situation, they provide reasonably accurate and useful information about how each question on the test is performing.

Using the Data Interpretation

We have already indicated the optimal values for discrimination (high positive) and difficulty indices (near 0.62). The real value in calculating these indices lies in their use in item selection and revision. Item analysis statistics give you a basis for deciding whether to include a given item on a second test, discard it from your item pool, replace it with another item from the Test File that measures the same material, or revise it so its ability to measure student performance in your classes increases. Should you decide to revise some of the items in the test file, you might consider the following suggestions.

1. If an item is too easy, try replacing the distractors with responses closer to the correct answer. This revision should make it more difficult for students with partial information to answer correctly.

2. If an item is too difficult, try replacing the distractors with responses that are more obviously wrong.

3. If an item has a low, positive discrimination coefficient (0.00 to 0.20), check first to see if it is either too easy or too difficult. If this is the case, try replacing the distractors as indicated above. If the item is of optimal difficulty and measures a concept you wish to test, you can attempt to revise it or leave it as is.

4. If an item has a negative discrimination coefficient, check to make sure you've scored the item correctly. If scoring is not the problem, try to determine why good students are more likely to miss the question than poor students. Is the stem confusing? Does the question contradict something discussed in class? Does knowing detailed information make the question harder to answer than knowing only the basic facts? If you suspect any of these problems, try to fix them by rewriting the stem or the wrong answers.

We should mention that it is sometimes impossible to determine why a question is not working optimally. In such cases, it may be wise simply to discard the item when testing similar students under similar conditions.

The Frequency Distribution

In revising questions, it is often useful to examine the frequency distribution of responses for each of the question's responses. You can collect these data by counting how many students choose each foil (a, b, c, or d) as the correct response. If few students are choosing one of the foils, you can improve the discrimination of the item by replacing the distractor with a more plausible one. If too many students are choosing a particular wrong answer and the discrimination index is low, try substituting an easier distinction.

References

Anastasi, A. (1988). *Psychological testing* (6th ed.). New York: MacMillan.

Ebel, R.L. (1975). *Essentials of educational measurement*. Englewood Cliffs, NJ: Prentice-Hall.

Tyler, L.E. (1979). *Tests and measurements* (3rd ed.) Englewood Cliffs, NJ: Prentice-Hall.

CHAPTER 1
TEST ITEMS

◆

Biological Transitions

Multiple Choice Items

1. Janet notices a little blood on her underpants and believes that she has begun her first menstrual period. This event is called _____.
   A. menarche
   B. the adolescent growth spurt
   C. puberty
   D. secular trend

   Answer: A

2. The physical transformation from child to adult is called _____.
   A. puberty
   B. early adolescence
   C. middle adolescence
   D. late adolescence

   Answer: A

3. The term puberty refers to the period during which
   A. an individual is between the ages of 12 and 15.
   B. an individual's endocrine system creates new hormones.
   C. an individual becomes capable of sexual reproduction.
   D. an individual stops growing.

   Answer: C

4. According to the text, puberty involves changes in all of the following characteristics _except_

   _____.
   A. development of the gonads
   B. distribution of fat and muscle in the body
   C. the circulatory and respiratory systems
   D. intelligence

   Answer: D

5. Which of the following statements about the production of hormones at puberty is <u>false</u>?
    A. At puberty, the body begins to produce several hormones which have not been present in the body up until this time.
    B. At puberty, there is an increase in the production of certain hormones.
    C. At puberty, boys bodies produce more testosterone and girls bodies produce more estrogen.
    D. At puberty, both boys' and girls' bodies produce more growth hormone.

    Answer: A

6. The endocrine system receives its instructions to increase or decrease levels of particular hormones from _____.
    A. the central nervous system
    B. the autonomic nervous system
    C. the thyroid gland
    D. the gonads

    Answer: A

7. The presence or absence of certain hormones early in life may "program" the brain and the nervous system to develop in certain ways later on. These hormones are considered _____.
    A. androgens
    B. estrogens
    C. organizational
    D. activational

    Answer: C

8. Hormones play two very different roles in adolescence. _____ hormones program the brain to behave in certain ways, while _____ hormones are thought to stimulate development of the secondary sex characteristics.
    A. Activational; organizational
    B. Organizational; activational
    C. Testosterone; endocrine
    D. Endocrine; testosterone

    Answer: B

9. The _____ has been equated to a thermostat with a set point for regulating and circulating your hormones. Right before puberty, the _____ loses its sensitivity to the sex hormones and permits these hormones to rise (similar to turning up the thermostat).
    A. growth spurt; pituitary gland
    B. growth spurt; hypothalamus
    C. endocrine system; pituitary gland
    D. endocrine system; hypothalamus

    Answer: D

10.	Two of the hormones that are especially important for producing sex hormones are _____ and

	_____.
	A. luteinizing hormone; follicle-stimulating hormone
	B. luteinizing hormone; adrenaline hormone
	C. adrenaline hormone; follicle-stimulating hormone
	D. releasing factors; luteinizing hormone

	Answer: A

11.	The chief mechanism in initiating the onset of puberty is _____.
	A. the pituitary secretes hormones that act on the thyroid and adrenal cortex
	B. hormones stimulate overall bodily growth
	C. the hypothalamus begins to lose sensitivity to sex hormones and permits levels of these
	    hormones to rise
	D. the thyroid and adrenal cortex secrete hormones that cause somatic changes

	Answer: C

12.	The loss of sensitivity to sex hormones by the _____ is thought to be related to the onset of
	puberty.
	A. thyroid gland
	B. gonads
	C. pituitary gland
	D. hypothalamus

	Answer: D

13.	Which of the following is not part of the feedback loop?
	A. gonads
	B. hypothalamus
	C. pituitary gland
	D. thyroid hormones

	Answer: D

14.	The onset of the hormonal changes that cause puberty is triggered by a signal from the

	_____.
	A. pituitary gland
	B. adrenal gland
	C. thyroid gland
	D. lacrimal gland

	Answer: A

15. The hormonally-induced increase in the rate of growth in height and weight is referred to as _____.
   A. the adolescent growth spurt
   B. epiphyses
   C. secular trend
   D. delayed phase preference

   Answer: A

16. The hormonally-induced increase in the rate of growth in weight and height is referred to as _____.
   A. the adolescent growth spurt
   B. the delayed phase preference
   C. progeria
   D. all of the above

   Answer: A

17. Which of the following may stimulate early feelings of sexual attraction to others?
   A. menarche
   B. adrenarche
   C. the growth spurt
   D. peak height velocity

   Answer: B

18. The simultaneous release of growth hormones, thyroid hormones, and _____ stimulates rapid acceleration in height and weight during puberty.
   A. pituitary glands
   B. estrogens
   C. androgens
   D. thyroid glands

   Answer: C

19. During the peak of the adolescent growth spurt, adolescents grow at about the same rate as _____.
   A. newborns
   B. infants
   C. toddlers
   D. elementary school children

   Answer: D

20. One reason for the difference in the body shapes of the sexes is _____.
   A. the timing of the growth spurt
   B. that females tend to be more "left-brained" and males more "right-brained"
   C. differences in the size of the hypothalamus
   D. the difference in the amount and distribution of body fat

   Answer: D

21. Dwayne's arms are growing faster than his legs, and his feet are disproportionate to the rest of his body. The awkwardness John is experiencing may be attributed to puberty's _____.
   A. secular trend
   B. asynchronicity in growth
   C. peak height velocity
   D. delayed phase preference

   Answer: B

22. Although both sexes experience changes in muscle tissue and body fat, the ratio of muscle to body fat is:
   A. greater in boys than girls
   B. greater in girls than boys
   C. about the same in both genders
   D. greater in early maturing girls than in late-maturing boys

   Answer: A

23. Alexis has noticed that as she started puberty, she has become a better basketball player. She can run faster and longer than before. This is due to _____.
   A. asynchronicity of growth
   B. increases in the size and capacity of the heart and lungs
   C. a decline in body fat
   D. muscle tissue grows faster in girls than in boys

   Answer: B

24. Dr. Harper is studying the development of secondary sex characteristics among junior high school girls. In order to most accurately assess the onset of these characteristics, Dr. Harper should _____.
   A. determine if ovulation is occurring regularly
   B. see if subjects have reached peak height velocity
   C. ask subjects if they have begun to menstruate
   D. compare subjects with Tanner's five stages of pubertal development

   Answer: D

25.   Which of the following sex characteristics is the first to develop in boys?
        A. production of sperm
        B. appearance of facial hair
        C. growth of testes and scrotum
        D. growth of penis

Answer: C

26.   About a year after penis growth begins _____.
        A. the scrotum and testes grow
        B. facial hair begins to appear
        C. the first ejaculation of sperm occurs
        D. pubic hair begins to grow

Answer: C

27.   The first sign of puberty in girls is generally _____.
        A. budding of the breasts
        B. underarm hair
        C. menarche
        D. acne

Answer: A

28.   Molly's breasts are beginning to develop, she is beginning to grow pubic hair, and her body is growing rapidly. This change is brought about by the secretion of _____ by the _____.
        A. estrogen; testes
        B. androgens; ovaries
        C. estrogen; ovaries
        D. androgens; testes

Answer: C

29.   Which of the following female sex characteristics is usually the last to develop?
        A. menarche
        B. regular ovulation
        C. development of the nipples of the breasts
        D. growth of pubic hair

Answer: B

30. Which of the following statements about puberty in girls is _false_?
    A. Regular ovulation and the ability to carry a baby to term usually follow menarche by several years.
    B. The development of the areola and nipple are far better indicators of sexual maturation than is breast size.
    C. Menarche occurs very early in the process of sexual development.
    D. The changes in the nipple and areola occur regardless of the size to which the breast finally develops.

Answer: C

31. Which of the following statements about timing of sexual maturation is true?
    A. In the United States, and in all other countries, menarche typically occurs around age 12.
    B. The duration of puberty varies widely - from 1 1/2 to 6 years in girls and 2 to 5 years in boys.
    C. Adolescents who begin puberty early are also those who complete it early.
    D. Adolescents who begin puberty earlier usually grow to be taller adults.

Answer: B

32. Which of the following can delay the onset of puberty?
    A. stress
    B. nutritional deficiencies
    C. excessive exercise
    D. all of the above

Answer: D

33. Differences in the timing and rate of puberty among individuals growing up in the same general environment are largely due to _____.
    A. hormonal factors
    B. genetic factors
    C. environmental factors
    D. none of the above

Answer: B

34. Although the precise trigger for puberty is unknown, it is suspected that an important factor is _____.
    A. reaching the age of 11
    B. achieving the correct body temperature
    C. reaching a certain proportion of body fat
    D. the onset of progesterone production

Answer: C

35.   Which of the following factors have *not* been found to influence the onset of maturation?
      A. father absence
      B. good nutrition
      C. family conflict
      D. peer pressure

      Answer: D

36.   Studies have shown that girls from affluent homes are more likely than economically
      disadvantaged girls to _____.
      A. reach menarche first
      B. begin dating earlier
      C. hang out with older kids
      D. adopt health-compromising behaviors

      Answer: A

37.   Over the past century, the onset of puberty has been coming at an earlier age. This has been
      referred to as the _____.
      A. cross-sectional trend
      B. endocrine trend
      C. menarche trend
      D. secular trend

      Answer: D

38.   Puberty began for Nancy when she was 9 years old. Her mother began puberty at 11 years. For
      her grandmother, the onset was at 13 years of age. These changes in the age of onset of puberty
      over time are referred to as _____.
      A. cross-sectional trend
      B. secular trend
      C. longitudinal trend
      D. physiologic trend

      Answer: B

39.   Wendy was born in 1850. Keisha was born in 1975. If both girls were to meet today at age 16,
      all of the following statements would probably be true *except* _____.
      A. Wendy would be shorter than Keisha
      B. Wendy would weigh less than Keisha
      C. Wendy would experience menarche before Keisha
      D. none of the above

      Answer: C

40. Dr. Davis is interested in how puberty affects adjustment. He studies a group of 100 junior high school students over the course of three years. He is conducting what kind of study?
    A. longitudinal
    B. cross-sectional
    C. cross-sequential
    D. secular

    Answer: A

41. A research design in which subjects of different ages are assessed simultaneously is called a
    _____.
    A. longitudinal study
    B. cross-sectional study
    C. cross-sequential study
    D. correlational study

    Answer: B

42. Compared to their later-maturing friends, girls who start to menstruate, date, and change to junior high school all in the same year tend to _____.
    A. suffer a decline in self-esteem
    B. move through puberty at a faster pace
    C. be more popular with girls but not with boys
    D. do worse in school for the next year, but then compensate, becoming above average students

    Answer: A

43. Which of the following statements about adolescent mood swings is <u>false</u>?
    A. The effect of hormones on adolescent mood swings is strongest early in puberty.
    B. Adolescents' moods fluctuate during the course of the day more than the moods of adults.
    C. Adolescent mood swings parallel their changes in activities.
    D. Hormones play a greater role in the development of depression than do stressful life events.

    Answer: D

44. Given a choice, Mike would rather stay up until 1:00 a.m. and sleep until 10:00 a.m. This pattern is called the _____.
    A. secular trend
    B. delayed phase preference
    C. longitudinal design
    D. adolescent growth spurt

    Answer : B

45. Which of the following plays the greatest role in the development of depression?
     A. rapid increases in hormones
     B. early maturation
     C. stressful life events
     D. the delayed phase preference

     Answer: C

46. Studies show that adolescent mood swings parallel their changes in:
     A. hormone levels
     B. family relationships
     C. nutrition
     D. activities

     Answer: D

47. The delayed phase preference suggests that _____.
     A. adolescents should not be taught sex education until high school
     B. school should be held year round
     C. school should begin later in the morning
     D. school should begin earlier in the morning

     Answer: C

48. Joe is extremely moody. His mother attributes his mood swings to being an adolescent. Based on your understanding of adolescent mood swings, what would you tell Joe's mom?
     A. Joe is a victim of raging hormones.
     B. Moodiness is a genetic trait that Joe inherited from his parents.
     C. Joe's moods are most likely linked to his daily activities
     D. Moodiness during adolescence is rare and Joe should seek psychiatric help.

     Answer: C

49. Studies on mood swings suggest that mood swings _____.
     A. parallel changes in activities
     B. are genetically determined
     C. are hormonally driven
     D. none of the above

     Answer: A

50. Which of the following statements about puberty's impact on family relationships is true?
     A. Puberty appears to increase distance between parents and children.
     B. Other species do not experience distance during the pubertal transition.
     C. Being an early maturing adolescent has more impact on family tension than being a late maturing adolescent.
     D. Puberty does not interfere with family relations.

     Answer: A

51. Which of the following girls will experience the greatest menstrual discomfort _____.
   A. Sarita, who is prepared for the physical changes
   B. Alison, who is a late maturer
   C. Loryn, who has negative attitude toward menarche
   D. Janet, who is unpopular among her classmates

Answer: C

52. Studies have shown that prepubertal girls who expect menstruation to be uncomfortable report _____.
   A. milder menstrual symptoms than their peers
   B. more severe menstrual symptoms than their peers
   C. about the same level of menstrual symptoms as their peers
   D. experiencing menarche sooner than their peers

Answer: B

53. Which of the following conditions is most likely to produce the most favorable and easiest adjustment to menarche?
   A. When the girl's mother prepares her by describing the unpleasant aspects of menarche.
   B. When the girl reaches menarche early.
   D. When menarche occurs before the girl has been told about the physical changes which will Occur.
   D. When the girl knows the facts about the physical changes her body will undergo.

Answer: D

54. Suzanne and Greg are the first members of their class to begin the pubertal transition. Based on what you know about early maturing adolescents, Suzanne and Greg are more likely to _____.
   A. become involved in deviant activities
   B. do better in school
   C. be ostracized by their classmates
   D. get along with their parents

Answer: A

55. Which of the following characteristics is not associated with being an early-maturing boy?
   A. a lower likelihood of developing problem behavior like minor delinquency and trouble at school
   B. greater popularity
   C. a more positive self-concept
   D. greater confidence in one's self

Answer: A

56. Early-maturing boys are _____.
   A. likely to have low self-esteem
   B. often expected to be more mature than they are
   C. better prepared to deal with changes of adolescence
   D. more childish than their later-maturing peers

   Answer: B

57. Follow-up studies of men who had been late maturers as adolescents revealed that as adults they are _____.
   A. more conforming
   B. less creative and insightful
   C. more conventional
   D. more assertive and creative

   Answer: D

58. Which of the following characteristics is _not_ typically associated with being an early-maturing girl?
   A. feelings of awkwardness and self-consciousness
   B. being less popular, especially with boys
   C. being more likely to become involved in juvenile delinquency
   D. being less likely to pursue advanced education and a demanding career

   Answer: B

59. In America, early-maturing girls are more likely than their late-maturing peers to _____.
   A. be unpopular
   B. have a lower self-image
   C. succeed in school
   D. perceive themselves as attractive

   Answer: B

60. Nadia is an adolescent who tends to be shy and introverted, has low self-esteem, and feels unhappy about her menstrual periods. According to the text, Nadia is probably _____.
   A. sexually active
   B. underweight
   C. an early-maturing girl
   D. a late-maturing girl

   Answer: C

61.   Generalizing from the text, the children who are most likely to think of themselves as being "off schedule" with respect to their physical development are girls who mature _____ and boys who mature _____.
       A. late; early
       B. early; late
       C. late; late
       D. early; early

       Answer: B

62.   Follow-up studies of women who had been early maturers found that as adults they are _____.
       A. unable to develop coping skills
       B. less likely to continue their education beyond high school
       C. more likely to continue their education beyond high school
       D. indistinguishable from those who had been late maturers

       Answer: B

63.   The _____ is the minimal amount of energy one uses when resting.
       A. basal metabolism rate
       B. delayed phase preference
       C. secular trend
       D. feedback loop

       Answer: A

64.   Both Beth and Janet are 5'2". Beth, however, weighs 95 pounds and eats all the time, while Janet weighs 125 pounds and needs to watch her diet. Their difference in weight is probably due to their _____.
       A. activational hormones
       B. epidemiology
       C. energy level
       D. basal metabolism rates

       Answer: D

65.   Nearly _____ of the adolescents in the United States are overweight and about _____ are obese.
       A. 20 percent; 5 percent
       B. 5 percent; 20 percent
       C. 40 percent; 25 percent
       D. 5 percent; 5 percent

       Answer: A

66.   Which of the following is the most common type of eating disorder?
      A. anorexia
      B. bulimia
      C. obesity
      D. purging

      Answer: C

67.   John has been labeled obese by his doctor. According to the definition of obesity, John is at least
      _____ over the maximum recommended weight for his height.
      A. 10 percent
      B. 20 percent
      C. 30 percent
      D. 40 percent

      Answer: B

68.   Theresa has been known to go on eating binges and then purge afterwards. Theresa is probably
      suffering from _____.
      A. anorexia nervosa
      B. bulimia
      C. oral fixation
      D. obesity

      Answer: B

69.   Karen has been known to exercise excessively, count calories, and diet obsessively. She is
      currently depriving herself of food even though she is 20 pounds underweight. Karen is probably
      suffering from _____.
      A. anorexia nervosa
      B. bulimia
      C. oral fixation
      D. deprivation syndrome

      Answer: A

70.   The potentially fatal disorder in which young women actually starve themselves is called
      _____.
      A. bulimia
      B. anorexia nervosa
      C. obesity nervosa
      D. purging

      Answer: B

71. Which of the following statements about anorexia and bulimia is <u>false</u>?
    A. Anorexia and bulimia are more common among women than men.
    B. The prevalence of anorexia and bulimia is higher among the affluent and better educated.
    C. The incidence of anorexia and bulimia is small.
    D. Anorexia and bulimia usually occur before puberty.

    Answer: D

72. Which of the following is <u>not</u> associated with the "new morbidity and mortality" of adolescence
    _____?
    A. accidents
    B. suicide
    C. homicide
    D. cancer

    Answer: D

73. Which of the following statements about health in adolescence is <u>not</u> true?
    A. Adolescents have low rates of disabling or chronic illness.
    B. Adolescents have high rates of accidents, homicide, and suicide.
    C. The majority of health problems during adolescence are preventable.
    D. The new approach to adolescent health care is a return to traditional medicine.

    Answer: D

74. Which of the following is <u>not</u> a component of Charles Irwin's "five A's"?
    A. ask
    B. advise
    C. arrange
    D. act

    Answer: D

75. School-based health centers have been found to _____.
    A. increase health-compromising behaviors
    B. reduce health-compromising behaviors
    C. increase knowledge about health risks
    D. reduce school attendance

    Answer: C

Essay Questions

76. Dr. Brown believes that adolescence is a time of storm and stress due to the production of new hormones. Do you agree or disagree with his conclusion? Be sure to support your answer with what you know about the physiological changes of adolescence. (HINT: What do we know about the endocrine system?)

Sample Answer:
I disagree with Dr. Brown's belief that adolescence is a time of storm and stress. All of our hormones are present at birth; the only change is in the amount that they are secreted as we grow. Our endocrine system produces, regulates, and controls the hormones in our body. The endocrine system can be equated to a thermostat - the sex hormones are set at a certain set point that is controlled by the hypothalamus stimulating the pituitary gland to trigger the gonads, which will secrete androgens in males and estrogens in females (males and females have both, just but in different amounts). The onset of puberty is triggered by a desensitization of the hypothalamus to the level of hormones it needs to keep it at the set point. When this happens, a higher level is needed to get the hypothalamus at its new "temperature" - this is the feedback loop system that occurs in puberty. It is not the result of new hormones, just a change in the amounts.

Key Points
a) Adolescence is not a time of storm and stress.
b) Description of the endocrine system and feedback loop
c) Mention of the desensitization of the hypothalamus

77. What factors determine the timing and tempo of an individual's pubertal maturation?

Sample Answer:
Both genetic and environmental factors play important roles. Within a population of individuals growing up under similar environmental conditions, genetic differences account for most of the variability in pubertal timing and tempo. However, this genetic influence is better thought of as a predisposition than a fixed absolute. The environment plays an important role in influencing the expression of this predisposition. Of chief importance among environmental variables are nutrition and health: better-nourished and healthier adolescents mature earlier and faster. This can be illustrated through comparisons of adolescents from different countries, from different social classes within the same country, and from different historical epochs. Recent studies have also suggested that some social factors, such as presence or absence of the father within the home, may also influence the onset of maturation, especially among girls.

Key Points
a) Mention of the genetic contribution (inherited factors)
b) The role of the environment (nutrition, health)
c) Social influences (presence/absence of father)

78. Maria and John are the first two students in their class to begin the transition into adolescence. Based on what you know about the timing of puberty during adolescence, what effect, if any, will this have on Maria and John's development?

> *Sample Answer:*
> *Maria, an early maturer, will probably have a significant weight gain, be shorter than other girls, and be more likely to suffer from low self-esteem and depression. She might receive more attention from older boys and in turn start participating in deviant activities. However, she will probably have better coping skills because she has had to deal with more early on in life. John, on the other hand, will probably be popular and athletic. He is also more likely to participate in deviant activities. In John's case, however, he will not develop the coping skills because he has not had as many challenges to deal with*

> Key Points
> a) Early maturation is more negative for girls and more positive for boys.
> b) Early maturing adolescents tend to engage in more delinquent activities.
> c) Early maturing girls develop better coping skills compared to late maturing girls.

79. Suzanne and Raul are the last two students in their class to begin the transition into adolescence. Based on what you about the timing of puberty during adolescence, what effect, if any, will this have on Suzanne and Raul's development?

> *Sample Answer:*
> *For Suzanne, the advantages of late maturation are: she is more likely to be the thin, "leggy" American ideal, and she will have more time to prepare for puberty. She will have less coping skills because puberty won't be a very difficult experience. For Raul, there are greater disadvantages: he will be seen as childish and have trouble being noticed by his peers, especially girls; he will have a negative self-concept, less responsibility, less self-assurance, and a greater need for autonomy. Some advantages are that he will develop better coping skills as an adult and will be seen as more intellectually curious.*

> Key Points
> a) Late maturation is more negative for boys and more positive for girls.
> b) Late maturing adolescents tend to engage in less delinquent activities.
> c) Late maturing boys develop better coping skills compared to early maturing boys.

80.   You are giving a presentation on puberty and eating disorders to parents at a junior high school. What would you say so that they understood the relation between puberty and eating disorders?

Sample Answer:
Although a variety of nutritional and behavioral factors can lead to weight gains during adolescence, gaining weight can sometimes result directly from the physical changes of puberty. Not only does the ratio of body fat to muscle increase markedly during puberty, but the body's basal metabolism rate also drops. Normal weight gain and change in body composition which accompanies puberty leads many adolescents, especially girls, to become extremely concerned about their weight. Girls who go through puberty earlier than their peers have an increased likelihood of developing disordered eating patterns. Eating disorders, such as anorexia and bulimia, which promote starvation and dieting can affect hormone levels that initiate puberty. A consequence of starvation during early adolescence is that pubertal development is severely delayed.

Key Points
a) Mention physical changes that could relate to eating disordered behavior (e.g., weight gain due to drop in basal metabolism rate, ratio of muscle to fat).
b) Early maturing girls are at greater risk.
c) Anorexia nervosa and bulimia can delay pubertal development.

81.   Design a school-based health center by addressing the following questions: What are the most pressing problems in adolescent health care? How do these problems relate to the "five A's" developed by adolescent medicine expert Charles Irwin?

Sample Answer:
School-based health centers are medical service centers located in or near schools. The clinics provide services such as physical examinations, treatment of minor injuries, health education programs, dental care, and counseling related to substance abuse, sexuality, and mental health. Since most adolescent health problems are preventable, the center should develop health enhancing behaviors and reduce health compromising behaviors. Most importantly, the center should provide medical services which are confidential, an issue important to many adolescents who have grown more distant from their parents throughout puberty. As argued by Charles Irwin, these centers should focus on the "five A's": anticipatory guidance (establish a trusting relationship), ask (directly inquire about health), advise (give advice about health promotion), assist (encourage adolescent to participate in programs that promote health), arrange (help with follow-up visits or consultations to monitor progress). These guidelines develop a friendly atmosphere to that services are not underutilized, disseminate information to help prevent problems, and build trust so that adolescents know their questions will remain confidential

Key Points
a) Develop health enhancing behaviors and reduce health compromising behaviors.
b) Most adolescent problems are preventable yet adolescents tend to underutilize conventional medical services. Thus, services need to be confidential.
c) Five A's: anticipatory guidance, ask, advise, assist, and arrange.

CHAPTER 2
TEST ITEMS

◈

Cognitive Transitions

Multiple Choice Items

1.   Which of the following is _not_ one of the five chief changes in cognition during adolescence?
        A. multidimensional thought
        B. metacognition
        C. abstract reasoning
        D. increased imagination

        Answer: D

2.   Bickering and squabbling between teenagers and their parents is largely due to _____.
        A. the generation gap
        B. hormonal changes in adolescents
        C. adolescents' ability to formulate counter arguments
        D. adolescents' anti-social tendencies

        Answer: C

3.   As Joyce was getting ready for a blind date she thought, "What if my date is a nerd?" This type of reasoning may be referred to as _____.
        A. hypothetical thinking
        B. social cognition
        C. mutual perspective taking
        D. impression formation

        Answer: A

4.   Joey enjoys playing the devil's advocate and is always stirring up discussions with his contrary positions. This ability may be referred to as _____.
        A. hypothetical thinking
        B. social cognition
        C. mutual perspective taking
        D. impression formation

        Answer: A

5.	Which of the following terms applies more to adolescent thought than to childhood thought?
	A.	conservation, reversibility, structure
	B.	assimilation, accommodation, complexity
	C.	preoperational, egocentric, scheme
	D.	flexible, speculative, abstract

	Answer: D

6.	The ability to see beyond what is directly observable and reason in terms of what might be possible is called _____.
	A.	social perspective taking
	B.	hypothetical thinking
	C.	imaginary audience
	D.	formal operations

	Answer: B

7.	Mai can understand the metaphor, "My heart is an open book," because she is able to focus on the _____.
	A.	concrete and familiar associations
	B.	semantic structure of the sentence
	C.	abstract and conceptual relations
	D.	observable features of the objects

	Answer: C

8.	Children tend to view things in _____ terms, whereas adolescents tend to view things in ____ terms.
	A.	spatial; concrete
	B.	critical; simple
	C.	absolute; relative
	D.	concrete; absolute

	Answer: C

9.	Leticia is asked by her teacher to solve a problem. The task requires that she turn the problem around in her head, considering many variations before finding a solution. Leticia's ability to solve this would most likely demonstrate her ability to _____.
	A.	think concretely
	B.	think hypothetically
	C.	think with sensorimotor skills
	D.	think preoperationally

	Answer: B

10. Common conversations among adolescents involve the "I think that he thinks that I think..." phenomenon. The technical term for this type of thinking about thinking is _____.
   A. impression formation
   B. social cognition
   C. automatization
   D. metacognition

   Answer: D

11. The ability to think about one's own thoughts is called _____.
   A. hypothetical think
   B. propositional logic
   C. metacognition
   D. social cognition

   Answer: C

12. Teenagers often become self-conscious because they believe that people are talking about them. Which characteristic are they exhibiting?
   A. an imaginary audience
   B. a personal fable
   C. propositional logic
   D. metacognition

   Answer: A

13. The erroneous belief that one's thoughts, feelings, and experiences are unique is called _____.
   A. an imaginary audience
   B. a personal fable
   C. propositional logic
   D. metacognition

   Answer: B

14. Dave knows that kids who drink and drive sometimes get killed, but he believes that he is somehow immune to having such a terrible thing happen to him. Dave's belief is an example of _____.
   A. the imaginary audience
   B. a personal fable
   C. social cognition
   D. metacognition

   Answer: B

15. Renee, a 6-year-old, is unable to answer the question, "How are a motorcycle and a bicycle alike?" Mohammed, a 17-year-old, answers the same question by saying, "They are both types of transportation." What statement about Renee and Wendy is most true?
A. Renee's inability to answer the question is very unusual for a child her age.
B. Mohammed has demonstrated the ability to think concretely.
C. Mohammed has demonstrated the ability to think abstractly.
D. According to Piaget's theory, Renee and Wendy are both developmentally delayed.

Answer: C

16. Heidi is going to a party after having braces put on her teeth. Heidi feels that everyone is staring at her and secretly thinking how funny she looks with braces. This is an example of _____.
A. impression formation
B. social cognition
C. a personal fable
D. the imaginary audience

Answer: D

17. Who coined the term adolescent egocentrism?
A. Piaget
B. Elkind
C. Binet
D. Sternberg

Answer: B

18. John is a junior in high school. Although he is sociable, he feels very self-conscious. He feels as if everyone is evaluating him. David Elkind refers to this loss of perspective in adolescence as _____.
A. self-reflection
B. personal fable
C. imaginary audience
D. impression formation

Answer: C

19. Chris and his parents had an argument because they did not want him to go to a New Year's Eve party across town. A few days after the argument, Chris' anger subsided because he realized his parents were worried about his safety. Which cognitive process did Chris use to reach this conclusion?
A. implicit personality theory
B. mutual role taking
C. automatization
D. social perspective taking

Answer: D

20. Research testing Elkind's theory of adolescent egocentrism have found that certain aspects _____.
    A. peaks at age 12 and then drastically declines
    B. may remain present throughout the adolescent and adult years
    C. is virtually a non-existent phenomenon in adolescence or adulthood
    D. less prevalent among college students

    Answer: B

21. Multidimensional thinking helps adolescents understand _____.
    A. sarcasm
    B. imaginary audiences
    C. formal operations
    D. concrete examples

    Answer: A

22. What thought process helps adolescents appreciate the sarcasm and satire of *Mad* magazine and *The Simpsons*?
    A. selective attention
    B. sensation-seeking
    C. mutual role taking
    D. multidimensional thinking

    Answer: D

23. _____ theorists believe that changes in cognitive abilities appearing during adolescence are qualitative, while _____ theorists believe they are quantitative.
    A. Cognitive-developmental; information-processing
    B. Cognitive-developmental; behavioral decision
    C. Information-processing; cognitive-developmental
    D. Information-processing; behavioral decision

    Answer: A

24. Dr. Martino argues that development proceeds in stages and that each stage is marked by fairly consistent behavior. Then, as the child's biological development progresses and new experiences are acquired, a shift occurs and development breaks through to the next level. Dr. Martino's view is most consistent with that expressed by the _____.
    A. triarchic theory of intelligence
    B. information-processing perspective
    C. psychometric theory
    D. Piagetian perspective

    Answer: D

25. Piaget believed that at the heart of formal operational thinking is an abstract system of
A. concrete operations
B. information-processing
C. propositional logic
D. social cognition

Answer: C

26. According to Piaget, the period of cognitive development which is based on theoretical, abstract principles of logic is called _____.
A. sensorimotor
B. preoperational
C. concrete operations
D. formal operations

Answer: D

27. Juan is 5 years old. His language skills are excellent, but his thinking skills demonstrate limitations such as egocentrism. What Piagetian stage of thought would you suspect he is in?
A. formal operational
B. sensorimotor
C. concrete operational
D. preoperational

Answer: D

28. Rose solves a chemistry problem by systematically testing several hypotheses. According to Piaget, which stage is Rose functioning at?
A. preoperational
B. concrete operations
C. formal operations
D. sensorimotor

Answer: C

29. LaToya has a secure relationship with her parents, whereas Karen has an insecure one. Based on research cited in the text, who is more likely to display formal operational thinking?
A. LaToya
B. Karen
C. both girls
D. unable to determine

Answer: A

30. Dr. Brown argues that adolescents can solve problems better than younger children because they can store more information in memory and because they have more effective strategies. Dr. Brown's view is most consistent with which of the following perspectives?
   A. triarchic theory of intelligence
   B. information-processing perspective
   C. psychometric theory
   D. Piagetian perspective

   Answer: B

31. Julia can use deductive reasoning to help resolve interpersonal problems among her friends, but she is unable to apply deductive reasoning successfully in her high school chemistry class. Julia's inconsistency in deductive reasoning illustrates _____.
   A. adolescent egocentrism
   B. the competence-performance distinction
   C. the propositional fallacy
   D. behavioral decision theory

   Answer: B

32. Unlike adolescents using formal-operational thinking, younger children who engage in concrete-operational thinking are more likely to: _____.
   A. systematically generate all possible solutions to a problem
   B. be aware of why they could not solve a problem
   C. have a hard time solving problems that require them to take different perspectives
   D. consider and anticipate all solutions to a problem

   Answer: C

33. The transition from concrete operational thought to formal operational thought occurs
   _____.
   A. very suddenly and evenly across all domains of functioning
   B. at the same age, regardless of the environment
   C. very gradually and unevenly across domains of functioning
   D. the change is barely noticeable

   Answer: C

34. Which of the following statements about the competence-performance distinction is false?
   A. competence to reason deductively does not become available until early adolescence
   B. older adolescents perform better than their younger peers when the tasks are personally relevant
   C. younger adolescents perform the same as older adolescents when the tasks are personally relevant
   D. performance is dependent on both competence and contextual factors

   Answer: C

35. For which of the following subjects will Andrew, a competent 12th grader, display the worst reasoning ability?
   A. adolescent dating
   B. misbehavior in school
   C. retirement planning
   D. driving a motor vehicle

   Answer: C

36. Which of the following criticisms has been leveled against Piaget's theory of cognitive development?
   A. There is little applicability in explaining cultural differences.
   B. It is too abstract to explain cognitive functioning during adolescence.
   C. It fails to explain how some young children can show advanced thinking.
   D. It fails to explain learning problems.

   Answer: C

37. Tommy notices that his father is sad. In response, he brings his father a red toy truck. Tommy assumes that the toy, which pleases him, will also please his father. Tommy's behavior illustrates the Piagetian concept of _____.
   A. reversibility
   B. object permanence
   C. conservatism
   D. egocentrism

   Answer: D

38. Jesse is in the 7th grade at a school that has open classrooms with multiple teachers instructing their classes in one large area. Which of the following cognitive processes will help Jesse focus on his teacher?
   A. working memory
   B. selective attention
   C. long-term memory
   D. divided attention

   Answer B

39. While studying for her biology exam, Jennifer watches her favorite show on TV. This is an example of _____.
   A. selective attention
   B. divided attention
   C. short-term memory
   D. long-term memory

   Answer: B

40. Charlie is able to tune out the television so that he can focus on his art project, which is due in class tomorrow. This is an example of _____.
    A. selective attention
    B. divided attention
    C. short-term memory
    D. long-term memory

    Answer: A

41. Which of the following statements about the changes in information-processing abilities during adolescence is *false*?
    A. There are advances in short-term but not long-term memory.
    B. The speed of processing information increases.
    C. Adolescents are more "planful" than children.
    D. There are advances in selective and divided attention.

    Answer: A

42. In Sternberg's problem-solving experiments, it was found that the ability to consider and compare alternatives in solving analogies was tied to the adolescent's _____.
    A. level of formal schooling
    B. IQ score
    C. contextual intelligence
    D. increased memory capacity

    Answer: D

43. The ability to complete activities with little effort or thought has been referred to as_____.
    A. divided attention
    B. propositional logic
    C. metacognition
    D. automatization

    Answer: D

44. Kevin has been driving for a year now, and appears to be more relaxed at the wheel. According to Robbie Case, this improvement is probably due to _____.
    A. Kevin's improved knowledge about cars
    B. the decline in the mental effort needed to engage in automatized activities
    C. Kevin's level of formal schooling
    D. his increase in memory functioning

    Answer: B

45. Who developed the first intelligence test?
    A. Wechsler
    B. Binet
    C. Elkind
    D. Piaget

    Answer: B

46. The first intelligence test was derived in France for the purpose of determining whether
_____.
A. a student should be graduated from high school
B. an individual was qualified to serve in the army
C. a student would profit from formal education
D. a student was qualified for a job

Answer: C

47. Steve gets all A's in his course work but has a hard time relating to the real world. According to
Sternberg, Steve is above average in _____ intelligence but below average in _____ intelligence.
A. componential; experiential
B. componential; contextual
C. experiential; componential
D. contextual; experiential

Answer: B

48. According to Alfred Binet's method, a child who was of average intelligence would have an IQ
score of _____.
A. 100
B. 200
C. 150
D. There is no "average" IQ.

Answer: A

49. Sternberg's "triarchic theory of intelligence" proposes that to assess an individual's intellectual
capabilities it is necessary to look at three distinct, but interrelated, types of "intelligence,"
_____.
A. verbal, mathematical, and spatial
B. componential, experiential, and contextual
C. componential, kinesthetic, and experiential
D. verbal, mathematical, and interpersonal

Answer: B

50. Sam took an IQ test in 4th grade and scored below average. Sam's middle school is administering
the test again. This time, Sam's score is likely to be _____.
A. below average
B. average
C. above average
D. there's no way to predict

Answer: A

51.   The finding that African-American and Hispanic American adolescents receive lower scores on
      IQ tests than European American adolescents is probably due to the _____.
      A. lack of schooling ethnic minorities receive
      B. genetic differences between these groups
      C. biased construction of these tests
      D. instability of intelligence during adolescence

      Answer: C

52.   According to Gardner's theory of multiple intelligences, sports figures Babe Ruth, Michael
      Jordan, Joe Montana, and Martina Navratalova are all considered above average in _____.
      A. spatial intelligence
      B. componential intelligence
      C. kinesthetic intelligence
      D. experiential intelligence

      Answer: C

53.   Although IQ tests are widely used, critics of these tests claim that they _____.
      A. are uncorrelated to future success in school
      B. are not stable over time
      C. lack internal consistency
      D. are culturally biased

      Answer: D

54.   During adolescence, individuals' IQ scores _____, while their mental abilities _____.
      A. remain stable; increase
      B. remain stable; decrease
      C. increase; remain stable
      D. decrease; remain stable

      Answer: A

55.   Adolescents who score higher than their peers on an IQ test will probably _____.
      A. score lower than their peers on their next IQ test
      B. continue to score higher than their peers on future IQ tests
      C. score the same as their peers on their next IQ test
      D. cannot make a prediction based on the instability of intelligence

      Answer: B

56.   It now appears that the only reliable sex difference in mental abilities is in the area of _____.
      A. spatial abilities
      B. verbal abilities
      C. math abilities
      D. creative abilities

      Answer: A

57. A(n) _____ test is used to measure a student's current level of achievement, while a(n) _____ test is used to predict a student's future performance.
   A. IQ; Wechsler
   B. IQ; Aptitude
   C. Aptitude; SAT
   D. Aptitude; IQ

   Answer: B

58. A(n) _____ test is used to predict a student's future performance, and the _____ is an example of such a test.
   A. IQ; Wechsler
   B. IQ; SAT
   C. Aptitude; Weschler
   D. Aptitude; SAT

   Answer: D

59. The SAT measures what Sternberg calls _____.
   A. componential intelligence
   B. experiential intelligence
   C. contextual intelligence
   D. kinesthetic intelligence

   Answer: A

60. Which of the following is the SAT designed to measure?
   A. practical intelligence
   B. creativity
   C. "street smarts"
   D. "school smarts"

   Answer: D

61. Research conducted on the predictive validity of the SAT found that _____.
   A. SAT verbal scores may be a more valid predictor for college English grades for females than for males
   B. SAT verbal scores may be a more valid predictor for college English grades for males than for females
   C. SAT math scores may be a more valid predictor for college math grades for males than for females
   D. SAT math scores may be a more valid predictor for college math grades for females than for males

   Answer: C

62.   A group of males and females are administered intelligence tests. Which of the following statements regarding the groups is most true?
A. The males will score slightly higher on measures of quantitative ability.
B. Females will score higher on tests that require one to mentally manipulate things.
C. Females will score higher in overall intelligence.
D. Males will score higher on measures requiring comprehension of written passages.

Answer: A

63.   Mary is having trouble understanding how to do a math problem. Her teacher asks her just the right question and Mary understands the problem. Vygotsky would refer to the social support provided by the teachers as _____.
A. ladder
B. enabler
C. pillar
D. scaffold

Answer: D

64.   According to Vygotsky, adolescents learn best when _____.
A. their lessons are within their zone of proximal development
B. a more experienced instructor is present
C. the instructor engages in scaffolding
D. all of the above

Answer: D

65.   The growth of _____ during adolescence is directly related to an improved ability to think abstractly.
A. long-term memory
B. social cognition
C. automatization
D. short-term memory

Answer: B

66.   Which of the following is _not_ one of the changes in social cognition during adolescence?
A. impression formation
B. social conventions
C. automatization
D. social perspective taking

Answer: C

67. An intuitive understanding of human behavior and motivation that results from gains in impression formation during early adolescence is called _____.
   A. implicit personality theory
   B. social perspective taking
   C. the imaginary audience
   D. a personal fable

   Answer: A

68. Billy is able to convince his parents to get him his own phone line by pointing out advantages for his parents as well as himself. According to Selman, Billy has reached which stage of social perspective taking _____.
   A. critical thinking
   B. selective attention
   C. mutual role taking
   D. concrete operations

   Answer: C

69. When the teacher asks a question in class, students raise their hands to answer. This example illustrates _____.
   A. social conventional behavior
   B. a specialized structural system
   C. metacognitive behavior
   D. dominance theory

   Answer: A

70. According to research on behavioral decision theory, adolescents often decide to engage in behavior that seems risky to adults because adolescents _____.
   A. cannot consider as many consequences for their actions as do adults
   B. have thinking processes that are still predominantly preoperational
   C. place a different value on the possible consequences than do adults
   D. wish to assert their independence from adults in every possible way

   Answer: C

71. Which theory helps researchers understand adolescent risk-taking?
   A. behavioral decision theory
   B. alternative choices theory
   C. desirability theory
   D. cognitive development theory

   Answer: A

72. Are adults, or adolescents, more likely to think of themselves as invulnerable?
    A. adults
    B. adolescents
    C. both are equally likely
    D. neither group thinks of themselves a invulnerable

Answer: C

73. What emotional characteristic makes an individual more likely to engage in risky behaviors?
    A. depression
    B. moodiness
    C. sensation-seeking
    D. anxiety

Answer: C

74. Which of the following statements about our current educational system is _false_?
    A. Most high schools reward rote memorization of facts.
    B. The system often does not stimulate critical thinking.
    C. Most high schools promote analytical and in-depth thinking.
    D. School curricula do not adapt to the cognitive changes that occur during adolescence.

Answer: C

75. Thinking that is characterized as in-depth, analytical, and discriminating has been referred to as
    _____.
    A. social conventional thinking
    B. critical thinking
    C. metacognitive thinking
    D. cohort specific thinking

Answer: B

Essay Questions

76.　In what five ways are the intellectual abilities of adolescents superior to those of children? Explain and give a concrete illustration of each developmental trend.

Sample Answer:
There are five chief ways in which the thinking of adolescents is more advanced, more efficient, and more effective than that of children. First, during adolescence individuals become better able to think about what is possible, instead of limiting their thought to what is real. Second, they become better able to think about abstract things, rather than being limited to the concrete. Third, during adolescence individuals begin thinking more often about the process of thinking itself. Fourth, adolescents' thinking tends to become multidimensional, rather than limited to a single issue. Finally, adolescents are more likely than children to see things as relative, rather than absolute. Several examples of each of these trends are given in the text.

Key Points
a) Think about what is possible
b) Think about abstract concepts
c) Think about thinking - metacognition
d) Thinking is multidimensional
e) See things as relative rather than absolute

77.　Dr. Herrmann is a firm believer in Piaget's theory of cognitive development. Although you respect Piaget's theory, you are aware of several criticisms. Provide Dr. Herrmann with two criticisms (and be sure to support these criticisms with research examples)

Sample Answer:
Piaget overestimated the language abilities of children and therefore underestimated their cognitive abilities. Studies have shown that children will do better on intelligence tests that do not depend on verbal language skills (e.g., when they are able to point to pictures). Also, Piaget's stages are not accurate age-wise. For instance, some children will do certain tasks earlier (they can be taught to perform tasks earlier). Lastly, environmental influences play a role. Some cultures do not exhibit formal operations at all and one study found that schooling in rural vs. urban areas effected the onset of formal operational thought (e.g., students in the urban areas acquired formal operations before those in the rural areas).

Key Points
a) Overestimated language abilities of children
b) Stages may not be accurately connected to appropriate ages.
c) Does not take into account cultural factors

78. Describe a class that Lev Vygotsky would teach. What components would be important in his classroom? What tactics would the teacher employ to facilitate learning?

> *Sample Answer:*
> *Vygotsky argued that children and adolescents learn best in their zone of proximal development, or in everyday situations when they encounter tasks that are neither too simple nor too advanced, but just slightly more challenging than their abilities permit them to solve on their own. The role of the teacher is to "scaffold," or to help structure the learning situation so that it is within reach of the student. Therefore, Vygotsky would use real-life examples, and have students practice what they learn. For example, a class on amphibians might take place at a local pond.*
>
> Key Points
> a) Zone of proximal development
> b) Role of the teacher is to scaffold
> c) Use real-life examples to have students practice what they learn

79. Steve gets all A's in his course work but has a hard time relating to the real world. Jessica has been failing her courses but is an exceptional artist. The guidance counselor, Miss Willingham, has stated that Steve is "smarter" than Jessica. Do you agree or disagree with Miss Willingham's conclusion? Support your answer.

> *Sample Answer:*
> *Disagree with Miss Willingham's conclusion. Sternberg's triarchic theory of intelligence shows that intelligence consists of three different components:*
>
> *1) componential - school smarts*
> *2) experiential - creativity & insight*
> *3) contextual - street smarts*
>
> *Steve excels in the componential aspects of intelligence but falls behind in the contextual aspects of intelligence. Jessica excels in the experiential aspect of intelligence but falls behind in the componential area. Each on is more skilled in a certain aspect of intelligence and less skilled in another. Because no single aspect of intelligence is more important than another, it is not a valid conclusion to state that Steve is smarter than Jessica or vice-versa.*
>
> Key Points
> a) Sternberg's Triarchic Theory of Intelligence would lead us to disagree.
> b) Steve exhibits componential aspects (school smarts).
> c) Jessica exhibits experiential aspects (creativity & insight).

80. Mr. Goldberg, a high school teacher, approaches you (a brilliant adolescent psychologist) regarding two of his students. He is concerned about their behavior and hopes that you can explain what is going on. One of his students, Sharon, occasionally engages in unprotected sex. The other student, Michael, constantly wears pants to hide what he believes are skinny legs. Using David Elkind's research results, how would you characterize Sharon's behavior? How would you characterize Michael's behavior? Be sure to justify your answer.

Sample Answer:
These two phenomenon result from Elkind's theory of adolescent egocentrism. Sharon's behavior is a classic example of what Elkind refers to as the personal fable. She believes that what she does and what happens to her is unique. Her belief is that nothing will happen to her if she occasionally engages in unprotected sex. Michael's behavior is related to what Elkind refers to the imaginary audience. He believes that everyone's thoughts are about him -- that they are constantly looking at him (as if he were on stage).

Key Points
a) David Elkind's theory of adolescent egocentrism
b) Sharon's behavior may be characterized by the personal fable.
c) Michael exhibits portions of the imaginary audience phenomenon

CHAPTER 3
TEST ITEMS

◆

Social Transitions

Multiple Choice Items

1. Which of the following is *not* one of the areas of fundamental change in adolescence?
    A. biological
    B. social
    C. conceptual
    D. cognitive

    Answer: C

2. Kaji, a 16-year-old male, has gone through the rite of passage and is now considered a warrior by his tribesmen. This change in Kaji's role and status may be referred to as _____.
    A. extrusion
    B. scarification
    C. social redefinition
    D. the marginal man

    Answer: C

3. The universal process through which an individual's position or status is changed by society is called _____.
    A. extrusion
    B. social redefinition
    C. social specification
    D. self-image stability

    Answer: B

4. Today, people go through _____ earlier than 100 years ago, but tend to stay in _____ longer.
    A. puberty; school
    B. marriage; school
    C. school; puberty
    D. school; marriage

    Answer: A

5. What process is less vivid and ceremonial in contemporary America than it is among an African tribal society?
   A. social redefinition
   B. giving birth
   C. communication
   D. going to school

   Answer: A

6. Compared to 100 years ago, the adolescent period has been _____ and the transition into adulthood _____.
   A. shortened; abbreviated
   B. lengthened; prolonged
   C. shortened; more continuous
   D. lengthened; abbreviated

   Answer: B

7. Camille is entering adolescence. She is likely to experience change in all of the following domains except _____.
   A. identity
   B. sexuality
   C. autonomy
   D. physiology

   Answer: D

8. The designated age at which an individual is recognized as an adult member of the community in contemporary society is called _____.
   A. the age of majority
   B. juvenile attainment
   C. quinceañera
   D. the marginal age

   Answer: A

9. For American adolescents, the age of majority is _____.
   A. 13
   B. 15
   C. 18
   D. 21

   Answer: D

10. Jacob is looking forward to the upcoming presidential election because he is now able to cast his vote. Based on your knowledge of the social redefinition of adolescence, what has Jacob attained?
   A. the marginal age
   B. juvenile attainment
   C. quinceañera
   D. the age of majority

   Answer: D

11. Dr. Jones argues that adolescence is primarily a social invention rather than a biological or cognitive phenomenon. Her view that the broader environment influences our conception of adolescence is most in line with the _____.
   A. Piagetian perspective
   B. psychometric perspective
   C. inventionist perspective
   D. contextual perspective

   Answer: C

12. Which of the following statements about the inventionist perspective is true?
   A. Adolescence is a separate period that has been largely determined by the broader social environment.
   B. Adolescence is driven by the physiological changes of puberty.
   C. The cognitive advances of adolescence are what make this period distinct from all others.
   D. Adolescence is not a distinct period in the life cycle and should not be regarded as such.

   Answer: A

13. Among those who study adolescence, an inventionist is one who _____.
   A. develops new products aimed predominantly at the adolescent population
   B. argues that adolescence is a period in the life cycle is mainly a social invention
   C. believes that many of the problems in adolescence are merely invented by the popular press
   D. believes that adolescents need to be kept away from the labor force for their own safety

   Answer: B

14. Prior to the industrial revolution, the term "child" referred to
   A. ages 3 - 12
   B. ages 5 - 10
   C. anyone under age 18
   D. ages 3 - 21

   Answer: C

15. Adolescence was not considered a distinct transitional period until _____.
    A. the publication of Seventeen magazine
    B. the creation of Child Labor Laws
    C. the industrial revolution
    D. it has always been recognized as a distinct part of development

    Answer: C

16. In the 19th century, what distinguished children from adults?
    A. what job they performed
    B. whether they owned property
    C. marital status
    D. religious confirmation

    Answer: B

17. The term "adolescent" became widely used at what time?
    A. since the 15th century
    B. since the 18th century
    C. since the 19th century
    D. during the 20th century

    Answer: C

18. Which of the following was *not* an outcome of the industrial revolution?
    A. a shortage of job opportunities
    B. the lengthening of schooling for adolescents
    C. an increase in crime
    D. increased opportunities for adolescents in the work place

    Answer: D

19. The status of adolescents as full-time students arose as a result of _____.
    A. the industrial revolution
    B. increases in scientific knowledge
    C. political changes due to the Civil War
    D. the advent of technical careers

    Answer: A

20. Prior to industrialization, the term "youth" referred to
    A. all children
    B. ages 12 - 24
    C. ages 10 - 18
    D. ages 3 - 12

    Answer: B

21. Which of the following contributed to the invention of the "teenager"?
    A. industrialization
    B. economic freedom
    C. higher education
    D. student activism

    Answer: B

22. Today, adolescence has been redefined as a time of _____ , rather than _____ .
    A. participation; preparation
    B. preparation; participation
    C. working; schooling
    D. apprenticeship; autonomy

    Answer: B

23. The Boy Scouts is an example of an organization that grew out of the _____ school of thought.
    A. extrusionist
    B. Piagetian
    C. child protectionist
    D. inventionist

    Answer: C

24. During the industrial revolution, child protectionists argued that _____ .
    A. a separate justice system must exist for juveniles
    B. adolescents needed parental permission to marry
    C. young people needed to be kept away from the labor force for their own good
    D. adolescent music was too controversial and needed to be censored

    Answer: C

25. Contemporary adolescents spend _____ time working with their parents and _____ with their peers preparing for the future.
    A. less, more
    B. less; less
    C. more; less
    D. more; more

    Answer: A

26. Popularized about 50 years ago, this expression refers to young people in a more frivolous and lighthearted manner than the term adolescent.
    A. marginal man
    B. youth
    C. teenager
    D. punk

    Answer: C

27. The agenda for adolescents in the 1800s was more _____ oriented, whereas the agenda for adolescents in the 1990s is more _____ oriented.
    A. production; family
    B. production; consumer
    C. consumer; production
    D. consumer; family

Answer: B

28. Which of the following was _not_ a result of industrialization?
    A. new patterns of work
    B. less time in school
    C. increased school preparation
    D. less time working with family members

Answer: B

29. Which of the following did _not_ contribute to the redefinition of the term "youth"?
    A. increased materialism among college students
    B. a growing college population
    C. a rise in student activism
    D. changes in attitudes and values among college students

Answer: A

30. Which of the following terms is often used to describe individuals who are in many ways more mature than adolescents, but not as mature as adults?
    A. teenager
    B. youth
    C. twenty-something
    D. emancipated minor

Answer: B

31. An example of a change in interpersonal status would include _____.
    A. getting a driver's license
    B. moving from the "children's" table to the adult table at Thanksgiving
    C. turning 8
    D. being able to see an "R" rated movie

Answer: B

32. A double shift in social status takes place during adolescence with an increase in both _____ and _____.
    A. privileges; expectations
    B. school work; discipline
    C. discipline; restrictions
    D. restrictions; expectations

Answer: A

33. A fourteen-year-old robs a supermarket. This behavior would be referred to as a _____, and would be punished in _____.
    A. majority offense; criminal justice system
    B. minority offense; juvenile justice system
    C. status offense; juvenile justice system
    D. majority offense; juvenile justice system

    Answer: B

34. Jennifer, who is 16, ran away with her friend Tonya who is 18. The police, however, only arrested Jennifer for running away because for a minor, running away is considered _____.
    A. the age of majority
    B. extrusion
    C. status offense
    D. juvenile truancy

    Answer: C

35. Jurors are most likely to recommend the death penalty for an adolescent convicted of first degree murder if the adolescent _____.
    A. has a history of violent crime
    B. is 16 or older
    C. has been previously convicted for a similar crime
    D. shows no remorse for the crime

    Answer: B

36. Legal decisions have tended to support adolescent autonomy when the behavior at issue is _____.
    A. viewed as potentially dangerous
    B. supported by the adolescents' parents
    C. also legal for adults
    D. viewed as having potential benefit

    Answer: D

37. Which of the following would _not_ be considered an initiation ceremony?
    A. graduating from high school
    B. a quinceañera
    C. a Bas Mitzvah
    D. obtaining a driver's license

    Answer: D

38. The phenomenon of extrusion is the practice in which children are _____.
    A. punished for failing to obey their elders
    B. prematurely forced into adult roles
    C. separated from members of the opposite sex
    D. expected to sleep in other households

    Answer: D

39.   In contemporary society, many young people are sent off to summer camps, boarding schools, or colleges. An analogous practice in traditional societies is known as _____.
         A. extrusion
         B. initiation
         C. avoidance
         D. socialization

         Answer: A

40.   The timetable for the process of social definition among adolescents occurs earlier among _____ than among _____.
         A. East Germans; West Germans
         B. European Americans; Asian Americans
         C. Asian Americans; European Americans
         D. rural youth; urban youth

         Answer: B

41.   Which of the following themes is generally not a universal element in the process of social redefinition?
         A. the accentuation of physical and social differences between males and females
         B. the real or symbolic separation of the adolescent from his or her parents
         C. the separation of adolescents experiencing menarche from elder members of the community
         D. the passing on of cultural, historical, and practical information

         Answer: C

42.   The separation of males and females during the social redefinition process has been referred to as _____.
         A. quinceañera
         B. extrusion
         C. brother-sister avoidance
         D. cohorts

         Answer: C

43.   Brother-sister avoidance refers to a practice in which _____.
         A. siblings are separated at birth and not permitted to see one another until adolescence
         B. brothers and sisters are forbidden to be seen with each other in public during religious holidays
         C. adolescent brothers and sisters may not interact with each other until one or both are married
         D. brothers may not see their sisters until they have reached menarche

         Answer: C

44. The Bas Mitzvah, the confirmation, and the quinceañera are all examples of _____.
A. extrusion
B. inventionism
C. initiation ceremonies
D. universal rights of passage

Answer: C

45. Which of the following is *not* an example of the contemporary version of scarification?
A. brushing teeth
B. using make-up
C. shaving face or legs
D. ear piercing

Answer: A

46. The Bar Mitzvah and Bas Mitzvah are contemporary examples of traditional society's practice of _____.
A. extrusion
B. brother-sister avoidance
C. cohorts
D. counterculture

Answer: B

47. In contemporary society, siblings of the opposite sex often seek more privacy from one another after one or both have matured physically. A practice resembling this in less industrialized societies is called _____.
A. familial reorganization
B. sibling resocialization
C. brother-sister avoidance
D. matrilocal age grading

Answer: C

48. For Sally's 13th birthday, her mother has agreed to let her get her ears pierced. In traditional societies, this type of body ritual may be equated to _____.
A. epiphysis
B. extrusion
C. voodoo
D. scarification

Answer: D

49. The adolescent who is caught in the transitional space between childhood and adulthood has been referred to by Lewin as _____.
A. the marginal man
B. the peripheral person
C. a teenager
D. a member of the youth culture

Answer: A

50. The messages that society sends adolescents are
A. full of sexual innuendos
B. unclear and inconsistent
C. outdated
D. inappropriate for young people

Answer: B

51. One who is caught in a transitional space between childhood and adulthood could be called a(n) _____.
A. inter-phase
B. juvenile delinquent
C. marginal man
D. status offender

Answer: C

52. Charles feels older than most of the other kids in his grade. He is more likely to engage in all of the following activities *except* _____.
A. spending more time with peers
B. greater achievement in school
C. feel more autonomous
D. engage in problem behavior

Answer: B

53. Initiation ceremonies for young women in traditional societies most often coincide with _____.
A. marriage
B. menarche
C. extrusion
D. brother-sister avoidance

Answer: B

54. Adolescents in the late 19th entered the labor force _____ today's adolescents.
   A. earlier than
   B. later than
   C. at the same time as
   D. unable to determine

   Answer: A

55. Which of the following statements about adolescents' passage into adulthood is _false_?
   A. The transition into adulthood was more prolonged 100 years ago than it is today.
   B. The transition into adulthood was characterized by a relatively long period of semi-autonomy 100 years ago.
   C. Adolescents married much earlier 100 years ago than they do today.
   D. Adolescents entered the labor force earlier 100 years ago than they do today.

   Answer: C

56. Compared with contemporary youth, adolescents living in the late 19th century left home _____ and left school _____.
   A. earlier; later
   B. earlier; earlier
   C. later; earlier
   D. later; later

   Answer: C

57. Dr. Ramirez believes that the passage into adulthood is a gradual process in which the adolescent assumes the roles and status of adulthood bit by bit. This view is most closely associated with

   _____.
   A. the continuous transition
   B. the discontinuous transition
   C. the longitudinal perspective
   D. the abstemious approach

   Answer: A

58. Dr. Goodrich believes that the passage into adulthood is a sudden change in which adult roles and statuses are abruptly assumed. This view is most closely associated with _____.
   A. the continuous transition
   B. the discontinuous transition
   C. the longitudinal perspective
   D. the abstemious approach

   Answer: B

59. Since Mark was 5 years old, he has been helping his father maintain the family farm. Now, 30 years later, Mark owns the farm and is teaching his own son how to manage it. Based on your knowledge about the continuity of adolescence, how would you describe Mark's transition?
A. attenuated
B. longitudinal
C. discontinuous
D. continuous

Answer: D

60. In contemporary society, the transition into adult work roles is fairly _____.
A. discontinuous
B. continuous
C. smooth
D. none of the above

Answer: A

61. The current school-to-work transition in America is considered a _____.
A. functional transition
B. discontinuous transition
C. continuous transition
D. consonant transition

Answer: B

62. Critics of the American educational system have proposed to reduce the discontinuity in the school-to-work transition by establishing _____.
A. youth apprenticeships
B. private schools for gifted students
C. in-home tutors
D. family support systems

Answer: A

63. Besides going to college, what can aid the transition from high school to adult work?
A. youth apprenticeships
B. discontinuous jobs
C. youth hostels
D. extrusion

Answer: A

64. Sociologist Margaret Marini has discovered that _____ were more likely to combine their school with work and family commitments than _____ .
A. lower class individuals; upper class individuals
B. upper class individual; lower class individuals
C. women; men
D. men; women

Answer: D

65. The transition into adulthood 100 years ago was characterized by _____ prior preparation for family roles and _____ prior preparation for work roles.
A. more; less
B. more; more
C. less; more
D. less; less

Answer: B

66. In 1934, anthropologist Ruth Benedict suggested that the turmoil experienced during adolescence was due to _____.
A. discontinuous transitions
B. the hormonal changes associated with puberty
C. the overwhelming of adolescents with adult responsibilities
D. the practice of youth apprenticeships

Answer: A

67. Compared to 100 years ago, contemporary adolescents take on full-time employment _____ and live under adult supervision _____ than adolescents in earlier times.
A. later; more
B. later; less
C. earlier; more
D. earlier; less

Answer: B

68. Elder's study of the Great Depression revealed that adolescents who experienced hardship during those years were more likely to _____.
A. complete their schooling
B. postpone marriage and childbearing
C. be involved in adult-like tasks at an earlier age
D. suffer from unemployment as adults

Answer: C

69. The National Research Council suggests that high rates of youth unemployment, juvenile delinquency, and teenage alcoholism may all stem from _____.
   A. the educational system's emphasis on rote memorization tasks
   B. the continuous nature of the adolescent transition into adulthood
   C. the surge in hormones during the pubertal transition
   D. the lack of clarity and continuity in the transition from adolescence to adulthood

   Answer: D

70. Which of the following students will have the most difficulty negotiating the transition into adolescence?
   A. Brian, an Asian American
   B. Ken, a European American
   C. Charlie, a Hispanic American
   D. Mara, a European American

   Answer: C

71. By the year 2020, minority children will account for what percentage of all U.S. children?
   A. 25 percentage
   B. 33 percentage
   C. 50 percentage
   D. 75 percentage

   Answer: C

72. The transition into adulthood is more likely to be impeded among minority teenagers because they _____.
   A. are more likely to grow up poor
   B. experience more prejudice and discrimination
   C. are more economically dependent on their parents than their white peers
   D. are more likely to be involved in gangs

   Answer: A

73. Which of the following is *not* associated with transition difficulties in adolescence?
   A. spending a lot of time with peers
   B. being a member of a minority group
   C. living in poverty
   D. the absence of affluent neighbors

   Answer: A

74. How does poverty adversely affect the behavior and development of adolescents?
   A. Social problems are contagious and can spread from one adolescent to another.
   B. Poverty in neighborhoods breeds social isolation.
   C. Adolescents growing up in poverty are more likely to be exposed to violence.
   D. All of the above are true.

   Answer: D

75.   Tamika and Theresa both live in single-parent households and survive on welfare. Tamika, however, lives in a better neighborhood than Theresa. According to community researchers, who is more likely to drop out of school or become pregnant?
       A. Tamika
       B. Theresa
       C. both Tamika and Theresa have an equal chance
       D. unable to determine

       Answer: B

Essay Questions

76.   "The social redefinition of the adolescent typically involves a two-sided change in status." Discuss the meaning of this statement and provide several illustrations of a two-sided change in status found in contemporary society.

       Sample Answer:
       This statement refers to the notion that the social redefinition of the adolescent brings with it changes in rights and privileges, on the one hand, as well as changes in responsibilities and obligations, on the other. A good answer would indicate a thorough understanding of the concept of social redefinition as involving one or more status changes. The dual-sided shift in status characteristics of social redefinition can be illustrated with a variety of interpersonal, economic, political, or legal examples, many of which are given in the text.

77.   You have been appointed to design a program for youth who are not college bound. How would you help these adolescents make the transition from high school to work? What components would be important to include in this program?

       Sample Answer:
       A program to help adolescents who are not bound for college would include a number of components. First, adolescents should spend time in voluntary, nonmilitary service activities so they can learn responsibility and adult roles. Second, it is important to bring adolescents into contact with adult mentors. Third, it is also important to focus on strengthening families and communities along with the adolescent. Finally, one must remember that this program should address the educational, employment, interpersonal, and health needs of adolescents from all walks of life.

       Key Points
       a) Have adolescents spend time in voluntary, nonmilitary service activities so they can learn responsibility and adult roles.
       b) Bring adolescents into contact with adult mentors.
       c) Help to strengthen families and communities.
       d) Try to address both the educational, employment, interpersonal, and health needs of adolescents from all walks of life.

78.   Since Mark was 5 years old, he has been helping his father maintain the family farm. Now, 30
       years later, Mark owns the farm and is teaching his own son to manage it. Mark's brother,
       Jeffrey, attended high school and then spent several years working at various jobs. Who had the
       easier transition into adolescence? How do you know this? (HINT: Whose theory would best
       explain this transitional experience?)

       Sample Answer:
       Mark's transition was easier than Jeffrey's. This is according to Benedict's theory of
       clarity and continuity. Since Mark was raised to do his father's job, this is considered a
       continuous process. Jeffrey's cycle was discontinuous (his job and school were
       unrelated) and therefore it would have been a rougher transition. A discontinuous
       transition is one in which the individual receives little prior preparation and is thrust
       rather suddenly into adult roles and responsibilities. This is generally the case in
       contemporary America, where young people receive little prior preparation in work,
       family, or citizenship roles before becoming adults.

       Key Points
       a) Benedict's theory of clarity and continuity.
       b) Mark had a continuous transition (easier).
       c) Jeffrey had a discontinuous transition (more difficult) which is more typical of today's
          adolescent.

79.   Applying what you have learned about initiation ceremonies, design an initiation ceremony for
       American adolescents in the 19th century. Describe at what age this would take place. What
       general themes would be present within your ceremony?

       Sample Answer:
       An initiation ceremony for American adolescents would include three themes. First, it
       would include extrusions, or the symbolic separation of the young person from his or her
       parents. Second, an accentuation of the physical and social differences between males
       and females would take place (i.e. brother-sister avoidance). Finally, this ceremony
       would include the passing of cultural, historical and practical information. This would
       take place at puberty, when the adolescent is biologically an adult.

       Key Points
       a) Extrusion - symbolic separation of the young person from his or her parents
       b) Accentuation of physical and social differences between males and females (brother
          -sister avoidance)
       c) Passing on of cultural, historical and practical information

80.   Amanda, a 13-year-old Hispanic girl, lives below the poverty line with her mother in an impoverished neighborhood. Based on what you know about the affects of poverty on the transition to adulthood, what would you predict for Amanda? Be sure to include the role of race and geography in your answer.

Sample Answer:
Poverty indirectly affects adolescents in their transition from childhood to adulthood. Poverty is associated with many factors that contribute to transition difficulties, such as failure in school, unemployment, and out-of-wedlock pregnancy. Minority children, urban and rural children, and children from single-parent households are more likely to be poor and therefore more likely to experience difficult transitions into adulthood than suburban, white children from intact households. These factors disrupt the transition into adulthood by limiting individuals' economic and occupational success. Adolescents from neighborhoods of concentrated poverty have even more difficulty transitioning to adulthood because of the social isolation they experience in their poor neighborhoods as well as the increased community violence, exposure to stress, and the increased likelihood of developing behavioral and emotional problems.

Key Points
a) Transition is more difficult (school failure, unemployment, teenage pregnancy).
b) Minority children and children from single parent families are the more likely to be poor than white children and children from intact families.
c) Those in poor neighborhoods are the most vulnerable to future problems (social isolation, violence, stress).

CHAPTER 4
TEST ITEMS

◈

Families

<u>Multiple Choice Items</u>

1.   The tensions that are often assumed to be inherent in the relations between adolescents and adults are referred to as the _____.
   A. parent-child rift
   B. generation gap
   C. empty nest syndrome
   D. midlife crisis

   Answer: B

2.   As Alex enters adolescence, he and his parents are experiencing severe relationship problems. These difficulties are most likely the result of _____.
   A. the "storm and stress" of the adolescent period
   B. the generation gap between parents and their adolescents
   C. earlier childhood problems that have not been resolved
   D. introduction into the high school system

   Answer: C

3.   Peers usually have more influence than parents on matters of _____.
   A. work
   B. education
   C. personal traits
   D. values

   Answer: C

4.   The popular notion of a generation gap has only been supported in differences between parent-child _____.
   A. values and attitudes
   B. personal taste
   C. mother-daughter relationships
   D. father-son relationships

   Answer: B

5.   Jim and Stacey are the parents of two pre-teen girls. Throughout the girls' childhood, the family has enjoyed fairly harmonious relationships. The likelihood that they will experience serious problems as the girls go through adolescence is _____.
A. highly likely
B. average
C. not likely
D. cannot predict

Answer: C

6.   When it comes to matters like religion, adolescents are more likely to be influenced by _____ over _____.
A. friends; parents
B. media; friends
C. media; parents
D. parents; friends

Answer: D

7.   Adolescents are most likely to conform more to their parents than their peers on which of the following questions?
A. Is Madonna a great singer?
B. Do I look better in large or medium T-shirts?
C. Would I make a good nurse?
D. Should I get my nose pierced?

Answer: C

8.   Mark is a teenager who generally respects his parents. On which of the following issues, however, is Mark most likely to side with his friends and against his parents?
A. on how to wear his hair
B. on the issue of capital punishment
C. on the choice of religious preference
D. on the value of a college education

Answer: A

9.   According to Smetana, adolescents often judge keeping one's room clean and style of dress as _____, while parents tend to judge these issues as _____.
A. personal; conventional
B. personal; moral
C. conventional; personal
D. moral; personal

Answer: A

10.   Luis and Carla Hernandez are getting a divorce. _____ predict that the family will to through a period of disequilibrium before it can adjust to this challenge.
        A. Family systems theorists
        B. Ethnographers
        C. Marital counselors
        D. Sociologists

        Answer: A

11.   One reason that the adolescent years may constitute a difficult period of adjustment is that parents _____.
        A. are frequently becoming more involved in building their own careers
        B. seem to be pushing children toward financial independence at increasingly earlier ages
        C. are often home too often and don't give their children adequate freedom
        D. may also be experiencing identity crises of their own

        Answer: D

12.   All of the following are generally considered components of a midlife crisis except _____.
        A. changes in physical appearance and health
        B. changes in sexual functioning
        C. changes in cognitive functioning
        D. questioning the meaning of one's career

        Answer: C

13.   Concerns of adolescents and their parents are often complementary. All of the following issues concern both adolescents and their parents except _____.
        A. the future
        B. sexual appeal
        C. money
        D. their bodies

        Answer: C

14.   Adults tend to be _____ when their children are adolescents than the past generation.
        A. younger
        B. less busy
        C. more conservative
        D. older

        Answer: D

15.   Victoria has four children. Which child's transition into adolescence is likely to affect her the most adversely?
        A. Jim, her first born son
        B. Caitlin, her second born daughter
        C. Carter, her third born son
        D. Joseph, her fourth born son

        Answer: A

16. One reason for imbalance or disequilibrium in the family during the adolescent years is that parents _____.
    A. are too involved in their own careers to notice their children
    B. may be experiencing their own type of "identity crisis"
    C. may be pushing their child toward financial independence too early
    D. are too restrictive of their adolescents' finances

    Answer: B

17. The identity crisis of adolescence may interact with the _____ in increasing family conflict.
    A. hormonal surges of puberty
    B. stage theorists' description of cognitive development
    C. intergenerational conflict with parents
    D. midlife crisis of adults

    Answer: D

18. What parent-child relationship is most distant during adolescence?
    A. mother-daughter
    B. father daughter
    C. mother-son
    D. father-son

    Answer: B

19. Which group of parents reports the most dissatisfaction with their marriage?
    A. parents of infants
    B. parents of children
    C. parents of adolescents
    D. parents of young adults

    Answer: C

20. Felicia is very warm and accepting to both of her two children, but she also sets firm rules that the children must follow with very few exceptions. According to Baumrind, the characteristics that best describe her are _____.
    A. responsive and demanding
    B. demanding and submissive
    C. lenient and indulgent
    D. submissive and responsive

    Answer: A

21. Max tells his friends that his mother is a "real marshmallow" who does whatever he wants and who never enforces the rules she tries to set. If Max's statement is true, his mother is best characterized as _____.
A. authoritarian
B. nonresponsive
C. nondemanding
D. demanding

Answer: C

22. Joshua's parents set rules for him, but he feels that when a rule seems unfair, he can discuss it with his parents and, even if they don't agree to change the rule, they at least listen to his opinions. Joshua's parents fit best into which of the following parenting styles?
A. authoritative
B. authoritarian
C. indulgent
D. indifferent

Answer: A

23. Tammy's father has absolute standards and expects Tammy to conform to them without exception. If she disobeys he generally punishes her, and sees no reason why he should explain his rules to Tammy. Instead, his response is, "I'm the father and I love you. I know what's best for you." Her father is best described as having what kind of parenting style?
A. authoritative
B. authoritarian
C. indulgent
D. indifferent

Answer: B

24. Judy's parents express love toward her and they let her, for the most part, establish her own schedule. She eats when she's hungry, has full run of the house, and sleeps when she's tired. This parenting style fits best with which of the following?
A. authoritative
B. authoritarian
C. indulgent
D. indifferent

Answer: C

25. Don's teacher is concerned about him because he is moody, fearful, withdrawn, and indifferent to new experiences. He also shows signs of developing low self-esteem. Based on Baumrind's classification of parenting styles, the best guess is that Don's parents are _____.
A. authoritative
B. authoritarian
C. indulgent
D. indifferent

Answer: B

26. Research on the nature of parent-adolescent relationships reveals that _____.
   A. Most adolescents experience considerable storm and stress in relationships with parents.
   B. Most adolescents resent their parents and rebel against their restrictions.
   C. Most adolescents appear to maintain positive, supportive and mutually-respective relationships
      with parents.
   D. Most adolescents become even closer to parents, and report almost no disruptions in their
      relationships with them.

   Answer: C

27. Jessica was physically and psychologically abused by her mother throughout childhood. Jessica is
   likely to develop which of the following problems?
   A. depression
   B. behavior problems
   C. later involvement in domestic violence
   D. all of the above

   Answer: D

28. Marcus feels like his parents don't care about him since they allow him to set his own rules and
   they seldom provide much support. He even wishes they would punish him because that would at
   least indicate they are paying attention to him. Marcus' parents would be described best as fitting
   into which of Baumrind's parenting styles?
   A. authoritative
   B. authoritarian
   C. indulgent
   D. indifferent

   Answer: D

29. Optimal development during adolescence appears to be facilitated by the _____ style of
   parenting.
   A. authoritative
   B. authoritarian
   C. indulgent
   D. neglectful

   Answer: A

30. Which statement about parenting is true?
   A. All parenting styles remain constant as adolescents age.
   B. Parenting styles are very consistent among ethnic minority groups.
   C. Parenting styles vary greatly depending on the gender of the adolescent.
   D. Parenting styles are related to academic achievement in school.

   Answer: D

31. Which of the following adolescents is likely to be aggressive?
    A. Sam, whose parents are indulgent
    B. Maya, whose parents are responsive
    C. Katie, whose parents employ physical punishment
    D. Bill, whose parents are authoritative

    Answer: C

32. According to Baumrind, children of indulgent parents tend to be _____.
    A. more involved in delinquent behavior
    B. less able to assume positions of leadership
    C. more impulsive
    D. less socially adept

    Answer: B

33. Michelle is in late adolescence. She excels in school, holds an after-school job, and participates in community service projects on the weekends. Michelle also has lots of friends at school. Her parents are most likely _____.
    A. indulgent
    B. authoritative
    C. indifferent
    D. authoritarian

    Answer: B

34. Which of the following is the most powerful predictor of healthy psychosocial growth during adolescence?
    A. positive and warm family relationships
    B. family composition
    C. the presence of siblings
    D. father's employment

    Answer: A

35. Which of the following parenting styles is most closely associated with overall psychological competence?
    A. authoritative
    B. authoritarian
    C. indulgent
    D. indifferent

    Answer: A

36. The three main components of authoritative parenting include all of the following, *except*
_____.
   A. warmth
   B. control
   C. structure
   D. autonomy support

Answer: B

37. Who is likely to be least affected by having non-demanding parents?
   A. Gwen, an Asian girl
   B. Carlos, a Hispanic boy
   C. Noah, an African American boy
   D. Jack, a white boy

Answer: A

38. Which type of parenting is the most prevalent among ethnic minorities?
   A. authoritative
   B. authoritarian
   C. indulgent
   D. indifferent

Answer: B

39. Research on ethnic differences in family relationships during adolescence shows all of the
following except _____.
   A. parent-adolescent conflict appears to be more common among Asian families than European
American families
   B. strict control among Korean parents is viewed as a sign of warmth and concern
   C. there is just as much variation within cultures as there is between cultures
   D. immigrant families have a difficult time adapting old-culture parenting styles to new-culture
expectations

Answer: A

40. Hauser has referred to verbal interactions that are judgmental or devaluing of a family member's
opinion as _____.
   A. coercive interactions
   B. enabling interactions
   C. indifferent interactions
   D. constraining interactions

Answer: D

41. According to the research, one of the most effective ways for helping adolescents to assume greater autonomy involves _____.
    A. engaging in discussions with adolescents and respecting their opinions
    B. giving adolescents free reign
    C. helping adolescents better enforce rules for their younger siblings
    D. restricting their activities so they avoid any mistakes

    Answer: A

42. Over the course of adolescence, relationships among siblings become more egalitarian but _____distant and _____emotionally intense.
    A. more; less
    B. less; more
    C. more; more
    D. less; less

    Answer: A

43. All of the following statements accurately reflect research on adolescent-sibling relationships *except* _____.
    A. companionship, warmth, and closeness are regular features of adolescent-sibling relationships
    B. adolescent-sibling relationships involve more conflict than adolescent-friend relationships
    C. adolescent-sibling relationships are characterized by a large increase in sibling rivalry
    D. all of these statements accurately reflect research on adolescent-sibling relations

    Answer: C

44. Throughout adolescence, the highest levels of conflicts that adolescents report take place with their _____.
    A. parents
    B. friends
    C. teachers
    D. siblings

    Answer: D

45. According to research by Plomin and Daniels, siblings are actually quite different from each other. Which of the following has *not* been used to explain this difference?
    A. Siblings only share a portion of their genes.
    B. Siblings may experience their family environment very differently.
    C. Siblings go through the pubertal transition at different times.
    D. Siblings may have very different experiences outside the family.

    Answer: C

46.   Which of the following has _not_ contributed to the transformation of family life in the past forty
        years?
        A. divorce
        B. fathers' employment
        C. mothers' employment
        D. poverty

        Answer: B

47.   What percentage of American children born in the 1980s will spend a portion of their life living
        in a single-parent household?
        A. 10 percent
        B. 25 percent
        C. 50 percent
        D. 75 percent

        Answer: C

48.   Which of the following adolescents is most likely to experience their parents' divorce?
        A. Janet; a white adolescent
        B. John; a white adolescent
        C. Jeff; a black adolescent
        D. Bruce; a Hispanic adolescent

        Answer: C

49.   Social scientists who study large-scale changes in the composition of the population are called
        _____.
        A. stenographers
        B. census tract scientists
        C. ethnographers
        D. demographers

        Answer: D

50.   African American adolescents are _____ likely to experience their parents divorce and _____
        likely to experience their remarriage.
        A. more; less
        B. more; more
        C. less; more
        D. less; less

        Answer: A

51. The _____ may act as a buffer for children growing up in single-parent households and plays an important role in the socialization of African American youth.
   A. extended family
   B. school guidance counselor
   C. involvement in religious activities
   D. peer group

   Answer: A

52. Matthew and Ryan both live in single-parent households. Matthew interacts with his grandparents every day, while Ryan has no contact with his extended family members. Who will be more likely to engage in adolescent misbehavior?
   A. Matthew
   B. Ryan
   C. both will be equally delinquent
   D. it depends on whether Matthew has brothers and sisters

   Answer: B

53. Which of the following statements regarding divorce in America is true?
   A. The divorce rate has been steadily rising since 1980.
   B. African-American youth are more likely to experience their parents' remarriage than other adolescents.
   C. The rate of divorce is lower for second marriages than for first marriages.
   D. Social support from relatives has been found to buffer the effects of living in a single-parent household.

   Answer: D

54. Adolescents from divorced families frequently display all of the following negative effects except _____.
   A. social rejection due to stigma
   B. lower academic achievement
   C. engage in alcohol/drug use
   D. engage in sexual intercourse earlier

   Answer: A

55. Research on the effects of divorce on children and adolescents has revealed that _____.
   A. the disruptive effects of divorce are greater for girls than they are for boys
   B. adolescent boys tend to become more depressed about the divorce than do adolescent girls
   C. social and emotional turmoil is usually greatest for adolescents about 2-3 years before separation
   D. adolescents who align themselves with one parent or the other during a divorce had difficulty achieving independence

   Answer: D

56.   Karen's parents are planning on getting a divorce. Based on the research cited in the text, who
       will Karen be most likely to live with following the divorce?
       A. paternal relatives
       B. maternal relatives
       C. her father
       D. her mother

       Answer: D

57.   Who is most likely to have difficulty adjusting to his or her parents divorce?
       A. Alice; a 16-year-old who lives with her father
       B. Paul; a 16-year-old who lives with his father
       C. Martha; a 10-year-old who lives with her mother
       D. Hans; a 10-year-old who lives with his mother

       Answer: D

58.   Although young children may seem unaffected by a divorce at the time, problems may emerge
       when they are adolescents. This delayed effect is called _____.
       A. a sleeper effect
       B. a deferred effect
       C. sluggish adjustment
       D. a generational tendency

       Answer: A

59.   Although Sarah's parents divorced seven years ago, the counselor at school attributes Sarah's poor
       school performance and delinquent behavior to the divorce. This counselor is probably referring
       to the _____.
       A. deferred effect of divorce
       B. sleeper effect of divorce
       C. generation gap between adolescents and parents
       D. sluggish adjustment of adolescence

       Answer: B

60.   The factor that seems <u>most</u> important in influencing how well children adjust to divorce over time
       is _____.
       A. the educational level of the parent
       B. the degree of conflict between parents
       C. the age of the parents
       D. the sex of the custodial parent

       Answer: B

61. Which group of adolescents is likely to exhibit the most problems?
    A. a 10-year-old female in a two-parent home
    B. a 12-year-old male living with his mother and grandmother
    C. a 13 year-old female growing up in a stepfamily
    D. a 17-year-old deciding between work and college

    Answer: C

62. Current research on the effects of remarriage indicate that _____.
    A. younger children have more problems than older children
    B. boys and girls show equal distress
    C. boys have more problems than girls
    D. girls have more problems than boys

    Answer: D

63. Which of the following statements about stepfamilies is _false_?
    A. Adolescents have an easier time adjusting to a stepfather if they have a good relationship with their biological father.
    B. Younger adolescents have a harder time adjusting to stepfamilies than older adolescents.
    C. Adolescents growing up in stepfamilies have more problems than adolescents growing up in single-parent families.
    D. Girls show more difficulty in step-families than boys.

    Answer: B

64. According to Hetherington, stepparents should _____.
    A. enforce discipline early on in order to establish firm boundaries for the child
    B. develop close relationships with their step-children quickly
    C. defer matters of discipline to the child's biological parent early on
    D. forbid step-children to form close relationships with their noncustodial biological parent

    Answer: C

65. Girls, compared to boys, are _____ adversely affected by their parents' remarriage, and _____ adversely affected by their mothers' employment.
    A. more; less
    B. less; more
    C. less; less
    D. more; more

    Answer: A

66. Full-time maternal employment during the high school years is associated with lowered school performance among _____.
    A. girls from upper-middle class homes
    B. boys from upper-middle class home
    C. girls from lower class homes
    D. boys from lower class homes

    Answer: B

67. When comparing girls with working mothers to girls of mothers who stay at home, which of the following statements is true?
    A. Girls with working mothers tend to perform more poorly in school.
    B. Girls with working mothers usually hold more sex-stereotyped attitudes than daughters of mothers who stay at home.
    C. Girls with working mothers tend to be less positively adjusted.
    D. Girls with working mothers have higher career aspirations than do girls whose mother do not work.

    Answer: D

68. Jason's performance in school has dropped since his mother went back to work. It is most likely that _____.
    A. Jason's mother works part-time instead of full-time
    B. Jason lives in a lower-class neighborhood
    C. Jason lives in an upper-middle-class neighborhood
    D. Jason has a poor relationship with his sister

    Answer: C

69. All of the following have been used to explain why boys are more adversely affected by maternal employment than girls *except* _____.
    A. mothers' work stress affects boys more negatively
    B. boys require more parental monitoring than girls
    C. there are increased household demands placed on children whose mothers work
    D. boys argue with working mothers more often than with non-working mothers

    Answer: A

70. The impact of a mother's employment on adolescent development seems to vary with _____.
    A. the type of job the mother has
    B. the father's employment status
    C. the age of the mother
    D. the family's level of appreciation

    Answer: D

71. Denise's parents have both been laid off from work and are unable to pay the bills. Denise's parents are likely to do all of the following *except* _____.
A. become less nurturing toward Denise
B. begin using harsher and more inconsistent discipline than they had in the past
C. engage in drug and alcohol abuse
D. feel more depressed

Answer: C

72. Lydia's parents are both unemployed. As a result, Lydia is _less_ likely to _____.
A. engage in delinquent behavior
B. become irritable or depressed
C. be career-oriented
D. have responsibilities around the house

Answer: C

73. Disruptions in family finances lead to more _____.
A. frequent conflict among fathers and sons
B. drug and alcohol abuse among parents
C. consistent discipline
D. frequent conflict among mothers and daughters

Answer: A

74. Poor children, compared to their middle-class peers, are more likely to _____.
A. be victims of violence
B. feel alienated from school
C. neither (a) nor (b)
D. both (a) and (b)

Answer: D

75. Kim lives in a poor neighborhood. As a result, Kim's mother drives her to school each morning and refuses to let her go out after dark. According to the text, Kim's mother is _____.
A. suffering from the empty nest syndrome
B. using the promotive strategy
C. using the prohibitive strategy
D. using the restrictive strategy

Answer: D

Essay Questions

76.   Tammy's father has absolute standards and expects Tammy to conform to them without exception. If she disobeys, he generally punishes her, and he sees no reason why he should explain his rules to Tammy. Instead, his response is, "I'm the father and I love you. I know what's best for you." Kathy's father set rules for her, but she feels that when a rule seems unfair, she can discuss it with him, even if he doesn't agree to change the rule, he at least listens to her opinions. What type of parenting style does Tammy's father employ? Kathy's father? Based on what you know about the effects of parenting on adolescence, what will Tammy be like? Kathy? (HINT: Be sure to define each style and discuss the outcomes.)

> *Sample Answer:*
> *Tammy's father is authoritarian. Authoritarian parenting involves high demandingness and low responsiveness. The standards and boundaries are set and the child is expected to adhere to them. Children who experience authoritarian parenting are less curious, less socially adept, passive, and less self-assured. They aren't allowed to make decisions for themselves.*
>
> *Kathy's father is authoritative in style. In authoritative parenting, there is a lot of demandingness and a lot of responsiveness. Things are discussed - there is give-and-take dialogue leads to intellectual development and psychosocial competence. Children who experience authoritative parenting are adept, curious, creative, socially competent, scholastically competent, and self-assured. They can problem solve and empathize.*

Key Points
a) Tammy comes from an authoritarian home (high demandingness/low responsiveness).
b) Kathy comes from an authoritative home (high demandingness/high responsiveness).
c) Kathy will be more well adjusted than Tammy.

77.   Jack and Jill's parents have recently divorced. As a school psychologist, what can you predict about their behavior now, and in the future? (HINT: Who will probably have custody of them? How will a remarriage affect them)

> *Sample Answer:*
> *Jack and Jill will both probably show signs of anger, blaming, depression, and decreased school performance. Within two years their behavior will most likely return to normal because they will have adapted (parental monitoring resumes, financially more stable). Jack will probably be affected worse by the divorce than Jill. However, Jack will adjust better to a remarriage than Jill because Jack has more to gain from a remarriage (male role model). The mother will most likely have custody and some research suggests (Dornbusch) that children do better in mother custody or joint custody arrangements. Other studies (Lee), however, suggest Jack would probably do better with his father and Jill would do better with her mother (living with the same sex-parent).*

Key Points
a) Jack and Jill's behavior will deteriorate.
b) Mother will most likely have custody.
c) Jill will have a more difficult time with her mother's remarriage than Jack.

78. Researchers have found that siblings' scores on standard measures of personality traits are virtually uncorrelated. Discuss how parental treatment of their children can serve as a nonshared environmental influence.

> *Sample Answer:*
> *Because siblings share common genetic and environmental influences (shared environmental influences), they are expected to develop similar personalities. However, adolescents vary widely in personalities. Research suggests that nonshared environmental influences are stronger than shared environmental influences during adolescence. One important nonshared environmental influence during adolescence is differential treatment by parents. Parents may treat their children differently because of their own conscious and unconscious preferences, difference in their children's temperaments, and changes in their child-rearing philosophies over time.*

> Key Points
> a) Nonshared environmental influences are stronger than shared environmental influences during adolescence.
> b) Parental treatment of their children can be a nonshared environmental influence (parents treat one child differently from the other).
> c) Three factors contribute to parental treatment as nonshared environmental influences:
>   1) conscious and unconscious preferences
>   2) difference in the child's preferences
>   3) changes in child-rearing philosophies over time.

79. Wendy and her mother are arguing over her messy room. Wendy feels that this is her space, and that she can do what she wants with it. Wendy's mom argues that it is her house and that Wendy's room is a reflection of their family lifestyle. Outline reasons for their disagreement using the recent research on intergenerational differences in values and attitudes.

> *Sample Answer:*
> *According to Judith Smetana, a major contributor to adolescent-parent bickering is the fact that teenagers and their parents define the issues of contention very differently. Parents are likely to see these as issues of right and wrong - not in a moral sense, but as matters of custom or convention. Adolescents, in contrast, are likely to define these same issues as matters of personal choice. Therefore, they are clashing over the definition of the issue than over the specific details. The struggle, then, is over who has the authority and whose jurisdiction the issue falls into.*

> Key Points
> a) Adolescents and parents clash more over the definition of an issue then over the specific details.
> b) Wendy's mom sees this issues as a matter of right and wrong while Wendy sees it as a matter of personal choice.

80. Michael's father, who is close to 40 years old, feels uncomfortable playing football with his adolescent son like they always used to do when Michael was younger. Outline three developmental concerns of Michael's dad that might account for this change.

Sample Answer:
A growing body of evidence suggests that the period surrounding age 40 can be a potentially difficult time for many adults. Some theorists describe this time as a midlife crisis. Many of the developmental concerns of parents and adolescents are complementary. Just as adolescents' bodies are changing, parents also feel increased concern about their physical attractiveness and sexual appeal. Secondly, while adolescents are thinking about their future, their parents are beginning to feel that the possibilities for change are limited. Parents' ideas are becoming more limited and they measure time in terms of how much longer they have to live. Finally, there is the issues of power, statues and entrance into the roles of adulthood. Parents have reached their occupational plateau and come to terms with their achievements, while their children are just embarking on these events. One possible solution would be to find alternative activities to enjoy together. Many adolescents also rely more on their peer groups to fulfill these roles.

Key Points
a) midlife crisis
b) biological changes – Parents feel increased concern about own bodies, about physical attractiveness and sexual appeal.
c) perceptions of time and the future – Parents are beginning to feel that the possibilities for change are limited.
d) issue of power, status and entrance into the roles of adulthood – Parents have reached occupational plateau and must deal with any gaps that exist between early aspirations and actual achievement.
e) solutions – finding new activities to share and turning to friends more

CHAPTER 5
TEST ITEMS

❖

Peer Groups

Multiple Choice Items

1. Judy and Jessica hang around people their same age. These people are most accurately described as _____.
    A. friends
    B. buddies
    C. peers
    D. chums

    Answer: C

2. The process of grouping individuals within social institutions on the basis of chronological age is called _____.
    A. mainstreaming
    B. tracking
    C. age grading
    D. reference grouping

    Answer: C

3. All of the following contributed to the rise of age segregation in contemporary society *except* _____.
    A. tougher child labor laws
    B. rise of secondary education
    C. decrease in family values
    D. increase of extra-curricular activities

    Answer: C

4. Following the end of World War II, many parents wanted to have children as soon as possible, creating what has come to be called the post-war _____.
    A. baby boom
    B. depression
    C. infantile fixation
    D. cohort effect

    Answer: A

5.   During the 1990s, the size of the adolescent population is expected to _____.
      A. decrease
      B. increase
      C. remain constant
      D. unable to predict

      Answer: B

6.   In *The Adolescent Society*, Coleman expressed concern over the finding that adolescents
      _____.
      A. showed high rates of drug and alcohol abuse
      B. reported frequent periods of loneliness
      C. placed less emphasis on academic success than their parents
      D. spent more time with their parents than with their peers

      Answer: C

7.   Which of the following did *not* contribute to the rise in adolescent peer groups?
      A. the spread of compulsory education and age-grading
      B. the increase in poverty among minority youth
      C. changes in the workplace
      D. the rapid population growth following World War II

      Answer: B

8.   Which of the following writers has been the most vocal proponent of the idea that there is a
      separate and troublesome "youth culture?"
      A. Margaret Mead
      B. Eleanor Maccoby
      C. Brad Brown
      D. James Coleman

      Answer: D

9.   According to some commentators, teenagers have become separate from adult society to such an
      extent that they have established their own society, which undermines parents' authority and
      emphasizes peer deviance. This society is called _____.
      A. the Woodstock generation
      B. the dead poet's society
      C. the lost boys
      D. the youth culture

      Answer: D

10.   A separate youth culture is said to promote all of the following *except* _____.
      A. academics
      B. sports
      C. dating
      D. partying

      Answer: A

11. Particularistic norms are most often found among people living in _____.
    A. extended families
    B. cliques
    C. postfigurative cultures
    D. cofigurative cultures

    Answer: C

12. A 1986 study showed that peers are most likely to pressure others to _____.
    A. use marijuana
    B. engage in sexual activity
    C. drink alcohol
    D. use cocaine

    Answer: C

13. In a particular tribe, relatives of the chief are allowed to choose their own mates, while others must abide by arranged marriages. This is an example of a _____.
    A. particularistic norm
    B. universalistic norm
    C. cofigurative culture
    D. prefigurative culture

    Answer: A

14. In contrast to the popular impression that adults have about peers during adolescence, _____.
    A. male peers exert less negative influence on adolescents than do female peers
    B. female peers exert less negative influence on adolescents than do male peers
    C. peers contribute positively to development during adolescence
    D. adolescents have a larger negative influence than most adults do.

    Answer: C

15. Adolescents who do not have close relationships with their peers may be ____ than other teens who are overly influenced by their peers.
    A. significantly better off
    B. more developmentally delayed
    C. at as great, or greater, risk for problems
    D. more developmentally advanced

    Answer: C

16. Universalistic norms are more often found in _____.
    A. extended families
    B. cliques
    C. postfigurative cultures
    D. cofigurative cultures

    Answer: D

17.   In the United States, all citizens over the age of 18 are allowed to vote. This is an example of
       _____.
       A. particularistic norm
       B. universalistic norm
       C. cofigurative culture
       D. prefigurative culture

       Answer: B

18.   Age segregation in schools is the most efficient way to educate children in societies that are
       _____.
       A. particularlistic
       B. universalistic
       C. postfigurative
       D. prefigurative

       Answer: B

19.   As a Bushman, Iko can rely on his grandfather to teach him everything he needs to know to
       function in his culture. This is an example of a _____.
       A. nonfigurative culture
       B. prefigurative culture
       C. cofigurative culture
       D. postfigurative culture

       Answer: D

20.   Molly teaches her grandmother how to use her new digital answering machine. According to
       Mead, this is an example of a _____.
       A. nonfigurative culture
       B. prefigurative culture
       C. cofigurative culture
       D. postfigurative culture

       Answer: B

21.   A teenager turning to a peer for advice would be more likely in which sort of culture?
       A. nonfigurative
       B. refigurative
       C. cofigurative
       D. postfigurative

       Answer: C

22. According to Margaret Mead, America today is most like a _____.
   A. cofigurative culture
   B. postfigurative culture
   C. universalistic culture
   D. monolithic culture

   Answer: A

23. Adolescents who find themselves teaching adults are likely to be living in which sort of culture?
   A. nonfigurative
   B. prefigurative
   C. cofigurative
   D. postfigurative

   Answer: B

24. Changes in patterns of work and family life have resulted in a large number of young people who are not supervised by their parents after school. These self-care adolescents are called _____ and are most likely to be from _____ neighborhoods.
   A. latchkey children; suburban
   B. latchkey children; urban
   C. baby boomers; suburban
   D. baby boomers; urban

   Answer: A

25. Which of the following adolescents is most likely to be a "latchkey" child?
   A. Lisa; an African American adolescent from an urban neighborhood
   B. Adam; an Asian American from a rural neighborhood
   C. Loryn; a white adolescent from a suburban neighborhood
   D. Maria; an Hispanic-American from a poor neighborhood

   Answer: C

26. Based on research cited in the text, latchkey children who _____ are no more susceptible to problem behavior than are children whose parents are home with them.
   A. go to a friend's house after school
   B. check in with their parents via telephone
   C. hang out at the mall
   D. none of the above, all latchkey children exhibit more problem behavior

   Answer: B

27. Stephanie is an adolescent who feels socially isolated, depressed and is involved in problem behavior. She is likely to have an after school environment consisting of _____.
   A. parental check-ins
   B. direct adult supervision
   C. self-care
   D. extracurricular activities

   Answer: C

28. Which adolescent is most likely to replace time spent with parents with time spent alone?
   A. Maya, a white female
   B. Rosalia, a Hispanic female
   C. Hillary, an African American female
   D. Mike, an Asian male

   Answer: D

29. Jordan is a pre-adolescent. Her friendship circle is largely comprised of other young girls. What has Jordan's social life been influenced by?
   A. age grading
   B. sex cleavage
   C. cliques
   D. the baby boom

   Answer: B

30. Marilyn, a typical high school freshman, has been asked to list the people in her life who are most important to her. Nearly half the list consists of _____.
   A. teachers
   B. relatives
   C. mixed-age peers
   D. same-age peers

   Answer: D

31. Eric, a 4th grader, spends a lot of time with his peers and is more likely to engage in which of the following activities _____.
   A. Little League Baseball
   B. going to the mall with his friends
   C. hanging out at his friend's house unsupervised
   D. girl-watching

   Answer: A

32.   Which of the following is most characteristic of childhood peer groups?
        A. mixed-sex groups
        B. less adult supervision
        C. sex cleavage
        D. the emergence of peer "crowds"

        Answer: C

33.   During childhood, boys typically associate with boys, while girls primarily associate with other
        girls. This separation of boys and girls has been referred to as _____.
        A. brother-sister avoidance
        B. sex cleavage
        C. youth culture
        D. sex grading

        Answer: B

34.   Steve eats lunch with Jeff, Hans, and Mike every day. After school they play computer games
        and talk about girls. This group of boys is called _____.
        A. a crowd
        B. a clique
        C. a reference group
        D. a youth culture

        Answer: B

35.   "Druggies," "jocks," and "nerds" are examples of _____.
        A. crowds
        B. cliques
        C. youth cultures
        D. gangs

        Answer: A

36.   _____ are settings for intimate interactions and friendships, while _____ are based on reputation,
        rather than on actual social interaction.
        A. Cliques; crowds
        B. Crowds; reference groups
        C. Reference groups; cliques
        D. Crowds; cliques

        Answer: A

37.   Exclusive social circles of friends are called _____.
        A. crowds
        B. cliques
        C. populars
        D. peers

        Answer: B

38. Mitch organizes a party for about 20 of his classmates who are all interested in theater, and they all watch a tape of the musical *The Phantom of the Opera*. This group of teenagers, who don't always hang out together, but share common interests, would most appropriately be labeled
_____.
   A. a gang
   B. a reference group
   C. a crowd
   D. a clique

Answer: C

39. A research technique in which the researcher "infiltrates" a group of individuals in order to study their behavior and relationships is called _____.
   A. naturalistic observation
   B. a longitudinal approach
   C. a demographic approach
   D. participant observation

Answer: D

40. Dr. Whitney wants to study the structure of adolescents' peer groups. She pretended to be a newcomer to the community and attended the local high school. She met a group of students and eventually joined their group. This type of observation is called _____.
   A. naturalistic observation
   B. an ethnographic approach
   C. a demographic approach
   D. participant observation

Answer: D

41. According to the research, conformity to peer pressure _____.
   A. peaks in adolescence and remains high into adulthood
   B. peaks in adolescence relative to childhood and adulthood
   C. shows a linear increase from childhood into adulthood
   D. shows a linear decrease from childhood into adulthood

Answer: B

42. In early adolescence, _____ friendships are most common, and in late adolescence, _____ friendships are common.
   A. same sex; opposite sex
   B. same sex; same sex
   C. opposite sex; same sex
   D. opposite sex; opposite sex

Answer: A

43. Dunphy suggests that peer groups change during the early adolescent years. Which of the following sequences provides an accurate description of the progression of peer group structure?
A. unisexual cliques; unisexual crowds; heterosexual dating
B. heterosexual crowds; unisexual cliques; heterosexual dating
C. unisexual cliques; heterosexual dating; heterosexual cliques
D. unisexual cliques, heterosexual cliques; heterosexual dating

Answer: D

44. Jacqueline, Kristine, Ruby, and Veronica all belong to the same clique. Jacqueline, who is considered the leader of the clique, plays on the volleyball team with Kristine. Ruby is a cheerleader and Veronica is the star of the school play. Which girl is most likely to start dating first?
A. Veronica
B. Ruby
C. Jacqueline
D. Kristine

Answer: C

45. Mixed-sex cliques start becoming more prevalent during _____.
A. childhood
B. pre-adolescence
C. middle adolescence
D. late adolescence

Answer: C

46. According to Kinney's research, youngsters who were "dweebs" in middle school _____.
A. were automatically labeled "dweebs" in high school
B. were the "popular" group in high school
C. could never become part of another crowd
D. had opportunities to shift status in high school

Answer: D

47. Adolescents are likely to be susceptible to peer influence when _____.
A. they possess social status near the middle of the peer group
B. they lack confidence in their abilities
C. they have low self esteem
D. all of the above

Answer: D

48.   In middle school, Carlos was involved in many school plays and musicals. Being part of the drama crowd was important for Carlos in what way?
        A. identity development
        B. dating opportunities
        C. occupied his free time
        D. improved relationships with parents

        Answer: A

49.   Adolescent peer groups fall along two dimensions _____.
        A. intelligence level; sociability
        B. adult orientation; peer orientation
        C. maturity; identity
        D. demandingness; responsiveness

        Answer: B

50.   A group against which an individual compares him or herself is called _____.
        A. a clique
        B. a reference group
        C. a crowd
        D. a youth culture

        Answer: B

51.   Greg is the star quarterback of the football team and hangs out with Larry who is the star pitcher of the baseball team. Ben also hangs out with Larry and Greg. When classmates refer to Ben, they call him a member of the "jocks." The crowd with which Ben associates serves as _____.
        A. a reference group
        B. a clique
        C. a youth culture
        D. a fraternity

        Answer: A

52.   Tommy values education and works hard in school but also enjoys hanging out with his friends on the weekend. Which peer crowd is Tommy most likely to belong to?
        A. "nerds"
        B. "populars"
        C. "partyers"
        D. "toughs"

        Answer: B

53. Ken cuts class with his friends and is disrespectful to his teachers. Which peer crowd is Ken most likely to belong to?
A. "populars"
B. "partyers"
C. "brains"
D. "jocks"

Answer: B

54. Self-esteem is _____ among students who are identified with peer groups that have relatively high status in their school.
A. lower
B. the same
C. higher
D. self esteem varies from person to person

Answer: C

55. Chuck is part of the "jock" crowd at his school. Greg is part of the "toughs". Which adolescent probably has high self-esteem?
A. Chuck
B. Greg
C. both, because they belong to a cohesive group
D. it depends upon their position within the groups

Answer: A

56. Adolescents from which of the following crowds experience more peer pressure to engage in delinquent behavior?
A. "jocks"
B. "populars"
C. "druggies"
D. "normals"

Answer: C

57. Which of the following adolescents is likely to have the lowest self-esteem?
A. Nadia, who is a star athlete
B. Suzanne, who is a popular girl
C. Joyce, who is considered "normal" by her peers
D. Janet, who is a "druggie"

Answer: D

58. According to Hollingshead, adolescents associate with peers based chiefly on _____.
   A. common interests
   B. gender
   C. religion
   D. social class

   Answer: D

59. By middle to late adolescence, cliques are often segregated by race. All of the following are possible explanations for this phenomenon *except* _____.
   A. differential abilities in athletics
   B. socioeconomic influences
   C. differential levels of academic achievement
   D. attitudes toward other races

   Answer: A

60. Adolescents who join antisocial peer groups are likely to have _____.
   A. been coerced by their peers to join
   B. had problematic parent-child relationships in childhood
   C. been involved in drugs and alcohol
   D. reported high levels of sensation-seeking behavior

   Answer: B

61. The term for Mexican American female gang members is _____.
   A. homies
   B. amigos
   C. cholas
   D. machimos

   Answer: C

62. Felicia has a problematic relationship with her parents. All of the following negative effects are likely to occur for Felicia *except* _____.
   A. development of an anti-social disposition
   B. active school involvement
   C. school failure
   D. rejection by classmates

   Answer: B

63. Gang affiliation during adolescence is thought by many experts to result from all of the following causes *except* _____.
   A. frustration over barriers to economic and social progress
   B. the lack of support and close relationships
   C. the tremendous incidence of absent fathers in families of gang members
   D. fewer satisfactory relationships in school and community

   Answer: C

64.   Dawn has always enjoyed school and excelled in her classes. In middle school, she has connected
       with a group of friends who also enjoy school. They often spend time studying together. This is
       an example of _____.
       A. selection
       B. socialization
       C. both a and b
       D. none of the above

       Answer: C

65.   Which of the following statements about cliques is *false*?
       A. Cliques are typically more emotionally salient for adolescents involved in antisocial behavior.
       B. Cliques are typically composed of adolescents from the same socioeconomic background.
       C. Cliques are typically composed of friends with similar interests and attitudes.
       D. Cliques rarely have members who differ in age.

       Answer: A

66.   Which of the following traits is not likely to lead to rejection in the adolescent peer group?
       A. aggression
       B. conceit
       C. intelligence
       D. tactlessness

       Answer: C

67.   All of the following are classifications for unpopular or disliked adolescents *except* _____.
       A. aggressive
       B. withdrawn
       C. aggressive-withdrawn
       D. offensive-reclusive

       Answer: D

68.   Who is at the greatest risk of developing psychological problems as a result of peer rejection?
       A. an aggressive child
       B. a withdrawn child
       C. an aggressive-withdrawn child
       D. a reclusive child

       Answer: C

69.   Esther has been rejected by her peers because she is withdrawn and reclusive. Esther is most
       likely to be at risk for _____.
       A. conduct problems
       B. diminished social competence
       C. aggressive behavior in adulthood
       D. drug and alcohol abuse

       Answer: B

70. In Graham's study of African American adolescents, high levels of aggressive behavior were associated with _____.
     A. a deficit in social information processing
     B. excessive involvement in antisocial peer groups
     C. low self-esteem during middle childhood
     D. authoritative parenting

     Answer: A

71. Karen, a 9th grader, was mad at Cheryl for spilling juice on Karen's shirt. Karen spread a rumor that Cheryl had gossiped about her friends. Karen is using _____ to express her aggression toward Cheryl.
     A. relational aggression
     B. hostile attributional bias
     C. aggressive-withdrawal
     D. bullying

     Answer: A

72. Dan planned a party and invited his whole English class by passing out personal invitations. Dan accidentally forgot to make an invitation for Sam. Sam assumed he wasn't invited and became irate at Dan for excluding him. This is an example of _____.
     A. relational aggression
     B. hostile attributional bias
     C. aggressive-withdrawal
     D. bullying

     Answer: B

73. Hostile attributional bias _____.
     A. plays a central role in the aggressive behavior of rejected adolescents
     B. plays a small role in the aggressive behavior of rejected adolescents
     C. helps rejected adolescents gain acceptance
     D. is the only factor in determining the behavior of rejected adolescents

     Answer: A

74. Which group is more likely to use relational aggression?
     A. young girls
     B. young boys
     C. adolescent girls
     D. adolescent boys

     Answer: C

75. Arthur, an unpopular 10th grader, has two older brothers who were very popular in high school. Arthur is more likely than his brothers to _____.
A. drop out of high school
B. express autonomy
C. develop a mature relationship with his parents
D. value school

Answer: A

Essay Questions

76. Discuss the significance of the book *The Adolescent Society* in shaping our ideas about peer relations during adolescence.

> *Sample Answer:*
> *The Adolescent Society (1961), written by James Coleman, was based on a study of ten Midwestern high schools. Coleman examined the prevailing value systems in each of the schools and concluded that a separate "youth culture" prevailed among high school students. This culture, claimed Coleman, did not value the same things as did adult society. Specifically, Coleman argued that adolescents placed little value on academic achievement; rather, they placed a premium on athletic success (for boys) and social success (for girls) as routes to status and popularity. The study popularized the concept of the youth culture and helped fuel arguments that the adolescent peer group represents a force that may be antithetical to the influence of adults on adolescents. It prompted many social scientists to suggest that steps should be taken to integrate young people into adult society more effectively.*

> Key Points
> a) Adolescents do not value the same things as adult society.
> b) Adolescents place little value on academic achievement.
> c) Peer groups are a negative influence and contribute to the "youth culture".

77.	Marji, a 10-year-old preadolescent, is going to enter junior high next year. Based on your knowledge of adolescent development, what can you predict about Marji's peer relations? (HINT: How do childhood peer relations differ from adolescent peer groups?)

Sample Answer:
During the teenage years, peer groups change in significance and structure along four main developments. First, there is a sharp increase in the sheer amount of time individuals spend with their peers during adolescence. Time during and after school and on the weekend evening is largely spent with age mates. Second, during adolescence, peer groups function much more often without adult supervision than they do during childhood. As children grow into adolescents, adults allow more time without adult supervision. Third, during adolescence, more and more contact with peers is with opposite-sex friends. Sex segregation of peer groups is less common later in adolescence. Fourth, adolescence marks the emergence of larger collectives of peers, or "crowds." Children's peer relationships are mainly limited to pairs of friends and relatively small groups.

Key Points
a) Sharp increase in time spent with peers
b) Less adult supervision of adolescents
c) Increased contact with opposite-sex friends
d) Larger collectives of peers emerge (crowds).

78.	Why is there a racial separation in adolescents' peer groups? Discuss ways in which society can break this cycle of separation.

Sample Answer:
There are three major explanations for racial separation in adolescents' peer groups. First, because adolescents' cliques are often segregated along socioeconomic lines, peer groups that appear to be segregated because of race actually may be separated on the basis of class, since higher numbers of minority youngsters come from economically poorer families. Second, there is a difference in the levels of academic achievement of white and African American adolescents. As we have learned about peer groups, adolescents who are friends usually have similar attitudes toward school and achievement levels. Finally, there is an attitude difference between these groups. In one study, white adolescents perceived their African American peers as aggressive and hostile while the black students felt that the white students were conceited and prejudiced. These perceptions make the formation of interracial peer groups unlikely. One way to break out of this cycle of misunderstanding is to bring white and black youngsters together at an early age, before they have time to build up stereotypes.

Key Points
a) Cliques are often segregated along socioeconomic lines.
b) There are differing levels of academic achievement among white and African American adolescents.
c) Attitudinal (African Americans are perceived as aggressive whereas whites are perceived as conceited and prejudiced).
d) A way out of this cycle is to bring white and black youngsters together from an early age.

79. Discuss the factors that have contributed to the rise of adolescent peer groups in modern society.

> *Sample Answer:*
> *Age segregation in contemporary society has largely been responsible for the prominence of adolescent peer groups. This separation of adults from adolescents has been due mostly to three major changes in contemporary lifestyles: changes in schools, changes in the workplace, and changes in the family. As a result, adolescent peer groups have gained prominence. The rise of free secondary education during the first quarter of this century has been the major school contribution that has made age segregation the norm. Additionally, youth organizations have contributed to age segregation. Concurrent with the rise in free secondary education was the implementation of stricter child labor laws, which forced previously employed adolescents out of their jobs and into secondary schools. Finally, today's family is much smaller than it was in previous times. Therefore, children in one family are usually close in age, diminishing the possibility of children interacting with siblings of differing ages.*

> Key Points
> a) Age segregation.
> b) Rise in free secondary education.
> c) Implementation of strict child labor laws.
> d) Family composition is smaller.

80. Using the example of *cholas*, explain how adolescent gangs look much like other types of adolescent cliques. Then outline two reasons why individuals would want to find membership in a gang.

> *Sample Answer:*
> *A recent study of Mexican American female gang members, or cholas, illustrated that adolescent gangs look much like other types of adolescent cliques. They are both groups of adolescents who are similar in background and orientation, share common interests and activities, and use the group to derive a sense of identity. Research shows that problematic parent-child relationships that are hostile lead to the development of an antisocial disposition in the child, and this disposition contributes, in elementary school, to academic failure and rejection by classmates. Therefore, this lack of support in the home and at school could push one to find support outside of these elements, in a gang.*

> Key Points
> a) Come from similar backgrounds, orientations.
> b) Share common interests and activities.
> c) Use the group to derive a sense of identity.
> d) Problematic parent-child relationships may push adolescents to find support outside home.
> e) School failure and rejection by classmates results in the same thing.

CHAPTER 6
TEST ITEMS

◆

Schools

Multiple Choice Items

1. In America, what percentage of individuals between the ages of 14 and 17 are in school?
   A. 25 percent
   B. 50 percent
   C. 75 percent
   D. 95 percent

   Answer: D

2. Today, the typical student attends nearly _____ of their classes throughout the year.
   A. 50 percent
   B. 75 percent
   C. 90 percent
   D. 100 percent

   Answer: C

3. The proportion of the adolescent population enrolled in school increased dramatically between _____.
   A. 1910 and 1940
   B. 1940 and 1960
   C. 1950 and 1970
   D. 1970 and 1990

   Answer: A

4. The average American school year is _____ days long.
   A. 100
   B. 150
   C. 180
   D. 220

   Answer: C

5.   Compared with their counterparts fifty years ago, today's American adolescents _____.
       A. spend more days per year in school
       B. spend fewer days per year in school
       C. are absent from school more often
       D. are less likely to continue their schooling beyond the twelfth grade

       Answer: A

6.   Changes in the structure of secondary schools have been linked to broader societal revolutions.
       All of the following factors have contributed to these changes *except* _____.
       A. industrialization
       B. agriculture decline
       C. immigration
       D. changing teaching methods

       Answer: D

7.   Which of the following did not contribute to the rise in compulsory education?
       A. immigration
       B. desegregation
       C. industrialization
       D. urbanization

       Answer: B

8.   During the 1920s, the _____ was designed to meet the needs of a diverse population of young
       people.
       A. comprehensive high school
       B. middle school
       C. vocational school
       D. parochial school

       Answer: A

9.   The perceived threat of the Soviets Union's space program in the early 1950s sparked which of
       the following changes in American high schools?
       A. Increased attention was paid to religious and moral education.
       B. Requirements for classes in European history were intensified.
       C. Students were obligated to take more foreign language courses.
       D. Increased emphasis was placed on math and science education.

       Answer: D

10.   Before schools became compulsory, what were high schools designed for?
       A. keeping delinquent children out of trouble
       B. finishing school for elite youngsters
       C. vocational instruction
       D. general education

       Answer: B

11. Which of the following is not an example of higher order thinking?
    A. rote memorization
    B. interpretation
    C. analysis
    D. evaluation

    Answer: A

12. During this course, you have been asked to interpret and analyze adolescent behavior. This type of thinking is referred to as _____.
    A. inductive reasoning
    B. deductive reasoning
    C. higher-order reasoning
    D. intuitive processing

    Answer: C

13. Cross-cultural comparisons during the 1980s revealed that American adolescents were scoring significantly lower on achievement tests than those in many industrialized countries. As a result, during the late 1980s, education reformers called for _____.
    A. more emphasis in the classroom on higher-order thinking
    B. schools to be desegregated
    C. work-study programs and classes in career education
    D. more courses in math and science

    Answer: A

14. The National Commission on Excellence in Education recommends that schools adopt which of the following policies for dealing with disruptive students?
    A. Ignore the behavior so as not to reinforce it.
    B. Discipline the disruptive student in front of their peers.
    C. Remove the disruptive student from the classroom.
    D. Praise the behavior in order to minimize its impact.

    Answer: C

15. In preparing for this exam, Marc memorized the names and theories of researchers mentioned in the textbook, while Suzanne compared each theory to the others. Who is using higher-order thinking?
    A. Marc
    B. Suzanne
    C. both Marc and Suzanne
    D. neither Marc nor Suzanne

    Answer: B

16. Ms. Willingham sets high standards for her students but is very responsive to their needs. What type of teaching style is this characteristic of?
    A. autocratic
    B. authoritarian
    C. authoritative
    D. permissive

    Answer: C

17. Which of the following statements about classroom environment is true?
    A. Moderate, rather than strict, control in the classroom promotes positive student behavior.
    B. Classroom climate has little effect on achievement.
    C. Teachers who focus on discipline promote the most positive climate.
    D. Classrooms that are very task-oriented tend to make students feel more comfortable and secure.

    Answer: A

18. What kind of family environment most closely resembles the optimal classroom environment?
    A. authoritarian
    B. authoritative
    C. indifferent
    D. autocratic

    Answer: B

19. Stephen comes from an economically disadvantaged family. He also has trouble keeping up with his classmates in school. Which of the following can Stephen expect to experience at his school?
    A. more attention from his teachers
    B. a leadership position in a club
    C. low self-esteem
    D. challenging and engaging classes

    Answer: C

20. According to a national survey, how many students in American public schools have been victims of violence?
    A. 1 out of 4
    B. 2 out of 4
    C. 1 out of 40
    D. 2 out of 40

    Answer: A

21. Generalizing from the text, what might be a way to improve students' experience at school?
    A. shorten the school day
    B. group students according to ability
    C. reduce the class size
    D. encourage teachers to assign work that is relevant to the real world

    Answer: D

22. Principal Goldman wants to increase his students' academic achievement. He should consider doing all of the following *except* _____.
   A. monitoring students progress and providing feedback
   B. encouraging teachers to have high expectations
   C. involving parents in all activities
   D. increasing his school size

Answer: D

23. Which of the following statements is true?
   A. As class size increases; academic achievement decreases.
   B. As class size increases; academic achievement increases.
   C. As school size increases; academic achievement increases.
   D. As school size increases; academic achievement decreases.

Answer: A

24. Which has a greater effects on students' scholastic achievement: school size or class size?
   A. school size
   B. class size
   C. both school size and class size are extremely important
   D. neither school size nor class size have an impact on students' achievement

Answer: A

25. Comparisons of large and small schools reveal that _____.
   A. small schools actually offer more varied curricula
   B. students in large schools are more likely to participate in school activities
   C. small schools have more material resources
   D. students in small schools are more likely to participate in school activities

Answer: D

26. During school, Nancy is taught to take pride in her work and respect her teachers. When she gets home, Nancy cleans her room, finishes her homework, and eats supper with her parents. According to Coleman, this similarity between school and home is considered _____.
   A. an anomic community
   B. a functional community
   C. a utilitarian community
   D. a transmittal community

Answer: B

27. According to evidence cited in the text, the ideal size of a school for adolescents is between _____.
    A. 100 - 500 students
    B. 200 - 600 students
    C. 500 - 1000 students
    D. 2000 - 4000 students

    Answer: C

28. Jean attends a high school with over 3,000 students. Gil's high school has 900 students. Who is more likely to achieve more and behave better?
    A. Jean
    B. Gil
    C. Both have equal chances for high achievement.
    D. Cannot determine, need more information.

    Answer: B

29. Which of the following is *not* a benefit that small schools offer?
    A. More participation in extra-curriculars by all students.
    B. More students can take leadership positions and responsibility.
    C. More varied instruction.
    D. Students feel more connected.

    Answer: C

30. Jillian's family is moving to another town. Her parents are concerned that Jillian will have a difficult time adjusting to the new school. Which of the following difficulties should they anticipate for Jillian?
    A. decline in grades
    B. feelings of anonymity
    C. lowered self-esteem
    D. all of the above

    Answer: D

31. Marnia attends a school with seventh and eighth graders as well as adolescents who are one or two years younger. This type of educational institution is called a _____.
    A. junior high school
    B. parochial school
    C. comprehensive high school
    D. middle school

    Answer: D

32. Which manner of dividing grades has the best outcomes for students' psychosocial well-being?
    A. K-4, 5-7, 8-12
    B. K-6, 7-8, 9-12
    C. K-8, 9-12
    D. K-12

    Answer: C

33. Of the following, who is least likely to suffer from the adverse consequences of changing schools?
    A. Barbara, an African-American adolescent
    B. Bruce, a Mexican-American adolescent
    C. Nora, a suburban adolescent
    D. Marsha, an urban adolescent

    Answer: C

34. Shelli and Suzanne are in two different school systems. Shelli's system is an 8-4 arrangement whereas Suzanne's is a 6-3-3 system. Research suggests that _____.
    A. Shelli will have higher self-esteem than Suzanne
    B. Shelli will have lower self-esteem than Suzanne
    C. Shelli and Suzanne will both have high self-esteem
    D. Shelli and Suzanne will both have low self-esteem

    Answer: A

35. Contrary to Simmons and Blyth, Eccles argues that the difficulty adolescents experience in the transition to junior high school is due to the _____.
    A. increased pressure from parents to succeed
    B. teachers' beliefs about junior high students
    C. change in curriculum and choice of extracurricular activities
    D. increased class size

    Answer: B

36. Simmons and Blyth suggest that the transition into junior high is stressful because _____.
    A. the freedom to choose courses is too overwhelming
    B. students are not able to use higher-order thinking until the middle of eighth grade
    C. there are a variety of other physical, psychological, and social changes taking place at this time
    D. most junior high schools are located outside of familiar neighborhoods

    Answer: C

37. The process of separating students into different levels of classes within the same school is called
_____.
A. mainstreaming
B. desegregation
C. acceleration
D. tracking

Answer: D

38. Which of the following statements about tracking is *false*?
A. Teaching quality is more or less the same in different tracks.
B. Students who are tracked tend to socialize mainly with peers from the same academic group.
C. Tracking can cause hostility between students in different tracks.
D. Tracking procedures often discriminate against minority and poor students.

Answer: A

39. Even though Scott has some difficulty in English, his school places him in the highest track. Scott's school follows which type of tracking system?
A. exclusive
B. comprehensive
C. meritocratic
D. inclusive

Answer: D

40. Placing students in tracks that match their abilities is called _____.
A. exclusive
B. comprehensive
C. meritocratic
D. inclusive

Answer: C

41. Kelly is at a high school with tracked classes. She has been placed in the average track. What type of effects is this placement likely to have on her?
A. positive
B. negative
C. negligible
D. cannot predict

Answer: C

42. Which statement about tracking is true?
A. Students assigned to lower tracks are more likely to graduate from college.
B. Minority students are more frequently assigned to college tracks.
C. Assignment to a lower track contributes to a sense of alienation and failure.
D. Tracking encourages students to work harder.

Answer: C

43. Amy is in a classroom where she feels alienated from other students and unmotivated. Amy is considering dropping out. Which statement about her situation is most likely true?
   A. Amy's school is not using a tracking system.
   B. Amy was assigned to a college preparatory track and is feeling less encouraged.
   C. Amy was assigned to an appropriate track.
   D. Amy was assigned to a lower track.

   Answer: D

44. All of the following are alternatives to academic tracking *except* _____.
   A. the involvement of parents in the educational process
   B. increasing school size
   C. cooperative learning
   D. assignment of actual work experience for academic credit

   Answer: B

45. The criterion most commonly used to identify gifted children eligible for special programs is _____.
   A. early language development
   B. higher-order thinking
   C. IQ scores
   D. class performance

   Answer: C

46. Michelle has been placed in a school program for gifted children. She was probably selected because she _____.
   A. has a high IQ
   B. is a creative thinker
   C. developed language skills early
   D. earns good grades

   Answer: A

47. Susannah's school psychologist has recently determined that Susannah has a learning disorder. Her parents are concerned about the affects this will have. Which of the following is an effect the psychologist might warn her parents about?
   A. Susannah may have trouble making friends.
   B. She is more likely to drop out of school.
   C. She will have more trouble coping with school.
   D. All of the above.

   Answer: D

48. A learning disability _____.
    A. is related to emotional problems such as divorce
    B. may be due to a neurological problem
    C. is usually related to hearing impairments
    D. can be corrected with special tutoring

    Answer: B

49. According to the text, _____ do better in math during elementary school and _____ do better in high school.
    A. boys; girls
    B. girls; boys
    C. boys; boys
    D. girls; girls

    Answer: B

50. Although Chris is mentally retarded, he goes to a regular grade school, takes classes in social studies, music, and physical education with the non-handicapped students, and goes to special classes to learn about reading and arithmetic. This situation is an example of _____.
    A. mainstreaming
    B. functional education
    C. higher-order learning
    D. education compensation

    Answer: A

51. Under current federal law, children with learning disabilities must be _____.
    A. mainstreamed as much as possible
    B. educated by tutors at home
    C. enrolled in special schools
    D. placed in after-school "catch up" programs

    Answer: A

52. Martin, an African-American adolescent, is attending a predominantly white school, whereas Vicki, a European-American, attends a predominantly black school. Studies suggest that _____.
    A. Martin will have higher self-esteem than Vicki
    B. Martin will have lower self-esteem than Vicki
    C. both Martin and Vicki will have high self-esteem
    D. both Martin and Vicki will have low self-esteem

    Answer: D

53. By the 1960s, after Brown v. Board of Education of Topeka, schools were called upon to
_____.
   A. offer more courses in math and science
   B. implement desegregation programs
   C. provide opportunities for work-study programs
   D. become more academically demanding

   Answer: B

54. Gary, an African American, attends a desegregated high school. Based on research cited in the
text, Gary is therefore _____.
   A. more likely to graduate from high school
   B. more likely to have higher self-esteem
   C. less likely to continue his education after high school
   D. less likely to work in an integrated environment

   Answer: A

55. Which of the following features may contribute to segregation within a desegregated school?
   A. tracking
   B. seating assignments
   C. ability grouping
   D. all of the above

   Answer: B

56. As a parent, you have the opportunity to send your child to either a public or a private school.
Based on research cited in the text, where is your child more likely to succeed scholastically?
   A. in a private school
   B. in a public school
   C. in a private school for the first few years and then a public school for the remaining years
   D. there are no differences between public and private schools

   Answer: A

57. Which students are most likely to reveal the differences in achievement between public and
private high schools?
   A. freshman and sophomores
   B. juniors and seniors
   C. all grade levels reveal differences
   D. there are no differences in achievement

   Answer: B

58. Which school-related factor is the most important in influencing psychosocial development during adolescence?
    A. class size
    B. course offerings
    C. extra-curricular opportunities
    D. immediate school/class environment

Answer: D

59. Which of the following school factors is most important in influencing adolescents' learning and psychosocial development?
    A. school climate
    B. size of the school
    C. amount of money spent on extracurricular activities
    D. racial composition of the school

Answer: A

60. What is one of the most important influences on the adolescent's experience in school?
    A. extracurricular activities
    B. teacher training
    C. length of school day
    D. school climate

Answer: D

61. Which of the following has the least effect on learning and achievement?
    A. teacher-student interaction
    B. use of class time
    C. teacher expectations for students
    D. racial composition of the school

Answer: A

62. The extent to which students are psychologically committed to learning and mastering the material rather than simply completing the assigned work is called _____.
    A. self-fulfilling prophecy
    B. student engagement
    C. tracking
    D. desegregation

Answer: B

63. Research has shown that teachers tend to favor high-achieving students by providing extra cues for answers and more positive nonverbal behaviors than for lower-achieving students. Such evidence provides support for the notion that teachers' expectations may contribute to _____.
   A. superior performance of lower-achieving students
   B. better performance of all students
   C. lower performance of all students
   D. the self-fulfilling prophecy

   Answer: D

64. In elementary school Trinh was considered an above-average student whereas his classmate, Kendra was considered a below-average student. When Trinh and Kendra graduate from high school, where are they likely to be standing academically?
   A. Trinh will be have improved and Kendra will have deteriorated.
   B. Trinh and Kendra both will have improved.
   C. Trinh and Kendra both will have similar academic standing as in elementary school.
   D. Trinh will have deteriorated and Kendra will have improved.

   Answer: A

65. Kerry and Kristie's teacher accidentally got their test scores mixed up and mistakenly thought Kerry was the more intelligent of the two girls. At the end of the year, her records demonstrated that, indeed, Kerry had gained more and performed at a higher level than Kristie. This is best thought of as an example of _____.
   A. goodness-of-fit
   B. the self-fulfilling prophecy
   C. mainstreaming
   D. higher-order thinking

   Answer: B

66. Mitch attends a high school where 95 percent of the students are involved in extracurricular activities. This will probably also mean that at Mitch's school _____.
   A. teachers track their students
   B. academic standards are low
   C. student enrollment is low
   D. there is more variation in instruction

   Answer: C

67. Teachers are most likely to attribute a girl's poor performance in math to her lack of _____ and a boy's poor performance to his lack of _____ .
   A. effort; effort
   B. ability; ability
   C. effort; ability
   D. ability; effort

   Answer: D

68. Today, approximately _____ of all young people continue their education beyond high school.
A. one-fourth
B. one-third
C. one-half
D. three-fourths

Answer: C

69. What two dominant characteristics distinguish the development of postsecondary education in contemporary America from that in other parts of the world?
A. diversity and accommodation
B. diversity and accessibility
C. diplomacy and accessibility
D. democracy and accommodation

Answer: B

70. Which of the following is an accurate description of European countries' school systems?
A. European schools are more accessible to the general population.
B. European schools are more diverse than American schools.
C. European countries have shorter school years than American schools.
D. European countries separate students into college and noncollege-bound tracks early in adolescence.

Answer: D

71. Of the students who enter college, what percent graduate from the same college four years later?
A. 20 percent
B. 40 percent
C. 75 percent
D. 95 percent

Answer: B

72. The "forgotten half" is a term that refers to adolescents who _____.
A. are placed in special education programs in high school
B. do not go on to college after high school
C. attend high schools in rural areas
D. are identified by their peers as loners

Answer: B

73. During the school year, the rate of academic progress was equal between African-American and European-American students. During the summer months _____.
A. European-American students' scores declined
B. African-American students' scores declined
C. Both European-American and African-American students' scores declined.
D. Both European-American and African-American students' scores remained the same

Answer: B

74. Generalizing from the text, who would benefit most from summer school?
   A. Ron; an African-American
   B. Bill; a European-American
   C. both Ron and Bill
   D. neither Ron nor Bill

   Answer: A

75. According to adolescents, what is the best thing about school?
   A. learning new information
   B. being with friends
   C. interacting with the teachers
   D. participating in extracurricular activities

   Answer: B

Essay Questions

76. Tracking is an important issue in today's classrooms. Define this issue and illustrate three reasons why this can be problematic.

   Sample Answer:
   Tracking is the process of separating students into different levels of classes within the same school. Students placed in the lower tracks or in low-ability groups within classrooms receive a markedly inferior education than do those in the higher tracks or groups. Once a student is placed in a lower track, it is very difficult for the student to move up. Tracking also may contribute to the polarization of the student body into different subcultures that feel hostile toward each other.

   Key Points
   a) Tracking is the process of separating students into different levels of classes within the same school.
   b) The problem exists most in the low-tracks or low-ability groups who receive inferior education.
   c) It is very difficult for students to move up tracks.
   d) Tracking can contribute to polarization of the students.

77. You and your spouse are about to purchase a new house. The yellow house is located in a town with a 6-3-3 type school system. The blue house is located in a town with an 8-4 school system. Let's assume that both homes are equally desirable. On that note, based on the two school systems, which house would you buy? Why? Support your answer with evidence.

Sample Answer
The blue house would probably be the "better buy". Based on research conducted by Simmons & Blyth's, it was found that an 8-4 school system may be better for an adolescent. During the school transition, many children are experiencing puberty at the same time - fewer changes during this time would be beneficial. The theory of developmental readiness is also a part of the reasoning for buying the blue house. It has been shown that it is more difficult for an adolescent to experience multiple changes such as school and puberty at the same time. Only one change (8-4) would be experienced and the child will probably do better, especially if you have a girl. Studies show that a 6-3-3 system causes more problems for girls (low self-esteem) than boys.

Key Points
a) The blue house – 8-4 school system
b) Simmons and Blyth found that less change is beneficial.
c) Developmental Readiness hypothesis
d) 6-3-3 was found to effect girls self esteem more negatively.

78. When it comes to school size, is bigger better?

Sample Answer:
According to studies by Roger Barker and his colleagues, students may benefit from attending smaller schools. Although large schools are able to offer a more diverse curriculum and a more varied menu of extracurricular activities, the far greater number of students in large schools makes participation in school activities more difficult. In his terms, large schools are more likely to be "over-manned," that is, they have high ratios of students per activity. As a result, students in small schools are more likely to feel needed, more likely to be placed in positions of leadership, and more likely to have had experiences that they feel have helped them to develop their skills and abilities. For academically marginal students, especially, large schools can be quite alienating.

Key Points
a) Smaller schools are better.
b) Easier to participate
c) Lower ratios of students per activity
d) Students feel needed, have positions of leadership.

79.   The principal of your high school has come to you for advice on how to make the school a better place. According to your reading, outline four of the five necessary characteristics needed for a good school.

Sample Answer:
First, good schools should emphasize intellectual activities. This ensures that students will learn and graduate. Second, good schools have teachers who are committed to their students and who are give a good deal of freedom and autonomy by the school administration in the way that this commitment is expressed in the classroom. Third, good schools constantly monitor themselves and their students to become even better. Fourth, good schools are well integrated into the communities they serve. Finally, good schools must have active students who participate in the process of education.

Key Points
a) Emphasize intellectual activities
b) Committed teachers
c) Monitor their own progress
d) Will integrated into community
e) Students who participate in their education

80.   What is "the forgotten half," and how have America's schools contributed to its problems?

Sample Answer
The term "forgotten half" refers to the nearly 50 percent of the adolescent population that does not go on to college after high school. As manufacturing jobs began to be replaced by minimum-wage service jobs, the chances of making a decent living without college experience worsened appreciably. As a result of this and the worsening economic climate of the eighties and nineties, today's high school graduates without college experience must survive on about one-third the income that their counterparts earned in the early 1970s. American high schools have contributed to this problem by failing to provide equal opportunities for learning and higher-order thinking in the general and vocational tracks, by failing to provide adolescents in these classes with adequate preparation for the world of work, and by providing counseling geared mainly toward helping college-bound students to continue their educations.

Key Points
a) "Forgotten half" refers to adolescents who don't go to college after high school.
b) Harder to make a living without a college education) High schools fail to provide equal opportunities for learning.
d) High schools fail to provide adequate preparation and counseling.

CHAPTER 7
TEST ITEMS

◆

Work and Leisure

Multiple Choice Items

1. Today's teenagers spend the most hours _____.
    A. in school
    B. with members of their families
    C. on leisure activities
    D. working

    Answer: C

2. Adolescents spend the least amount of time on _____ activities and the most amount of time on _____ activities.
    A. productive; maintenance
    B. productive; leisure
    C. maintenance; productive
    D. maintenance; leisure

    Answer: B

3. The power of the adolescent as a consumer has increased due to _____.
    A. growth of single-parent households
    B. growth of dual-worker households
    C. adolescents doing some of the family's shopping
    D. all of the above

    Answer: D

4. Younger adolescents spend most of their leisure time _____ whereas older adolescents spend more time _____.
    A. playing; watching television
    B. outdoors; playing sports
    C. socializing; listening to music
    D. watching television; socializing

    Answer: D

5.   What percentage of high school juniors and seniors have worked during the school year?
     A. 25 percent
     B. 50 percent
     C. 80 percent
     D. 95 percent

     Answer: C

6.   According to your text, adolescents spend _____ the number of hours each week on part-time
     jobs as on _____.
     A. 2 times; homework
     B. 3 times; homework
     C. 4 times; extracurricular activities
     D. 5 times; extracurricular activities

     Answer: C

7.   American high school students spend fewer than _____ hours per week on homework, while
     Japanese high school students average closer to _____.
     A. 10; 20 hours per week
     B. 20; 20 hours per week
     C. 5; 5 hours per day
     D. 5; 5 hours per week

     Answer: C

8.   What percentage of today's high school student have *not* worked before graduating?
     A. 20 percent
     B. 80 percent
     C. 25 percent
     D. 70 percent

     Answer: A

9.   From 1900-1940, the employment of American teenagers in the formal labor force _____.
     A. declined
     B. increased
     C. remained unchanged
     D. fluctuated

     Answer: A

10. All of the following contributed to the rise of the adolescent workplace *except* _____.
     A. industrialization
     B. the expansion of the service sector
     C. the expansion of the retail sector
     D. an increase in the cost of living for the typical teenager

     Answer: A

11. In the United States today, working during high school is most common among _____ adolescents.
    A. poor
    B. middle-class
    C. African American
    D. Hispanic American

    Answer: B

12. Which of the following characteristics of the retail and restaurant industries contributed to the rise in adolescent employment?
    A. need for part-time workers
    B. abundance of low wage positions
    C. short shift schedules
    D. all of the above

    Answer: D

13. Which of the following adolescents will be most likely to get a part-time job during high school?
    A. Kelly, an urban girl
    B. Mary Jo, a suburban girl
    C. Darius, an African American boy
    D. Teddy, an inner-city boy

    Answer: B

14. Which of the following groups of teenagers has the greatest difficulty obtaining employment?
    A. females
    B. males
    C. suburban teens
    D. minority youth

    Answer: D

15. Who is more likely to hold a part-time job during high school?
    A. Gino; a Canadian adolescent
    B. Cheri; a Swedish adolescent
    C. Hope; a Japanese adolescent
    D. Selena; an American adolescent

    Answer: D

16. An adolescent who works in a government-sponsored apprenticeship and spends more time outside of school doing homework is most likely from _____.
    A. America
    B. Europe
    C. Africa
    D. Any of the above places

    Answer: B

17. Who is more likely to be employed during the school year?
    A. Daryl
    B. Theresa
    C. both Daryl and Theresa are equally likely to be employed
    D. Theresa during early adolescence and Daryl during late adolescence

    Answer: C

18. Parker is looking for a job. What type of job is he *least* likely to take?
    A. gardener
    B. newspaper carrier
    C. janitor
    D. nurses' aide

    Answer: D

19. Kathy and Ira are working during the school year so that during the spring break they can go to Mexico. Based on research cited in the text, who will probably make more money?
    A. Kathy
    B. Ira
    C. Kathy and Ira will make the same amount.
    D. Differences in salary will not be apparent until Kathy and Ira enter the adult work force.

    Answer: B

20. Which of the following jobs would be *least* likely to be held by an adolescent girl?
    A. fast-food worker
    B. baby-sitter
    C. housecleaner
    D. newspaper carrier

    Answer: D

21. Hillary is a high school senior. Which of the following jobs is she most likely to have?
    A. food server at a restaurant
    B. baby-sitter
    C. gardener
    D. housekeeper

    Answer: A

22. Ryan did a survey at his middle school of the most common after school jobs for the eighth grade class. What are his results likely to say?
    A. movie theater usher and nurses' aide
    B. baby-sitting and lawn work
    C. fast-food worker and clothing store cashier
    D. receptionist and paper carrier

    Answer: B

23. Overall, the greatest number of working high school students are employed in _____.
A. construction and manual labor
B. restaurants and retail establishments
C. offices and other clerical settings
D. factories and manufacturing plants

Answer: B

24. Stan's parents both work long hours. They are concerned that he doesn't have enough interaction with adults. If they want him to be exposed to more adult interaction, which of the following activities should they _not_ encourage him to do?
A. join the wrestling team
B. run for student council
C. get a job at the local music store
D. try out for the school play

Answer: C

25. Which of the following is true of most adolescents' jobs?
A. They encourage adolescents to behave independently.
B. They require challenging decision-making.
C. Adolescents are rarely required to use skills taught in school.
D. Adolescents receive strict instruction from supervisors

Answer: D

26. One of the major differences between the "old" and "new" adolescent workplace is that the former _____.
A. only pertained to the most affluent families
B. paid significantly better
C. involved greater contact with adults
D. was not related to future career paths

Answer: C

27. Robert, a 15-year-old, works for a fast-food restaurant. How old is Robert's supervisor most likely to be?
A. the same age as Robert
B. not much older than Robert
C. in his early 30's
D. middle-aged

Answer: B

28. Jamie works at McDonald's. She had a bad day at work. Who is she *least* likely to talk to about her bad day?
   A. other adolescents at work
   B. her friends at school
   C. her adult supervisor at work
   D. her parents

   Answer: C

29. Elder's study of boys who took part-time jobs during the Great Depression showed that they

   _____.
   A. had higher rates of depression than adults
   B. were more cynical about the workplace
   C. became more "adult-like"
   D. were more likely to engage in delinquent behavior

   Answer: C

30. Ruben works over twenty hours a week during the school year and Marianne does not work at all. Ruben, compared to Marianne, is more likely to _____.
   A. become more socially responsible
   B. know how to manage his money better
   C. endorse unethical business practices
   D. not engage in drug and alcohol use

   Answer: C

31. Which of the following is *not* an effect of premature affluence?
   A. increased cynicism about the value of hard work
   B. increased social belongingness
   C. increased drug and alcohol use
   D. increased materialistic attitudes

   Answer: B

32. Lisa earns approximately $300 a month from her part-time job. She is most likely to spend the money on _____.
   A. family necessities
   B. personal luxuries
   C. household expenses
   D. college expenses

   Answer: B

33. Which of the following is an adolescent the *least* likely to spend their job earnings on?
   A. drugs and alcohol
   B. designer clothing
   C. higher education
   D. stereo equipment

   Answer: C

34. Having more income than one can manage during early adolescence has been called _____.
   A. precocious income
   B. displacement abundance
   C. occupational disparity
   D. premature affluence

Answer: D

35. All of the following are effects of premature affluence *except* _____.
   A. increased cynicism about the value of hard work
   B. increased interest in buying drugs and alcohol
   C. tendency to develop more materialistic attitudes
   D. a greater desire to save for college

Answer: D

36. The average working high school student earns _____ per month in wages.
   A. $50
   B. $150
   C. $200
   D. $300

Answer: D

37. Alison is more likely to spend her money on _____, and Jack is more likely to spend his money on _____.
   A. clothes; food
   B. clothes; clothes
   C. food; clothes
   D. food; food

Answer: A

38. Jahmal is the manager of a Taco Bell restaurant. His employees have worked there between 9 months and 18 months. How many of the employees have probably committed a delinquent act at work?
   A. 5 percent
   B. 10 percent
   C. 25 percent
   D. 60 percent

Answer: D

39. The commission of acts at work that are illegal or unethical is called _____.
   A. occupational deviance
   B. displacement
   C. premature affluence
   D. vocational transgression

Answer: A

40. Adolescents who work more than twenty hours weekly are more likely than their peers to
_____.
A. be absent from school
B. graduate from high school
C. spend more time on their homework
D. be less cynical about the work place

Answer: A

41. Which of the following statements about adolescent drug and alcohol use is true?
A. Adolescents who use drugs and alcohol are more likely to choose to work long hours.
B. Adolescents who work are less likely to use drugs and alcohol.
C. Adolescents who work under high stress are less likely to use drugs and alcohol.
D. Adolescents who work long hours are more likely to get involved with drugs and alcohol.

Answer: D

42. Pam uses marijuana every weekend. It is most likely that _____.
A. Pam is unemployed
B. Pam works long hours
C. Pam is spending too much time with her supervisor
D. Pam's job is not very stressful

Answer: B

43. Experts believe that working more than _____ a week may jeopardize adolescents' schooling.
A. 5 hours a week
B. 10 hours a week
C. 15 hours a week
D. 20 hours a week

Answer: D

44. Which of the following is _not_ associated with adolescents who work?
A. greater absences from school
B. greater enjoyment of school
C. less time spent on homework
D. earn lower grades

Answer: B

45. Lourdes' parents are disappointed with her grades. She is involved in many work and leisure activities. Which activity is most likely contributing to her poor school performance?
A. basketball team
B. shopping at the mall with friends
C. working part-time at a restaurant
D. watching TV

Answer: C

46. Which of the following was *not* reported by Steinberg as a characteristic of adolescents who worked more than twenty hours per week?
   A. lowered school achievement
   B. more deviant conduct in school
   C. more involvement in extracurricular activities
   D. taking less demanding classes

   Answer: C

47. What percentage of teens are out of school, unemployed, and looking for full-time work?
   A. 5 percent
   B. 15 percent
   C. 25 percent
   D. 40 percent

   Answer: A

48. Which of the following statements about unemployed youth is *false*?
   A. The majority of unemployed youth are high school dropouts.
   B. Minority youth are more likely to be unemployed than white youth.
   C. The majority of unemployed youth are unmotivated to find work.
   D. The majority of adolescents who are unemployed stay unemployed only for short periods of time.

   Answer: C

49. An unemployed youth would most likely be _____.
   A. a minority and from a low-income family
   B. a white male
   C. an American Indian
   D. a minority and from a high-income family

   Answer: A

50. Who is more likely to experience unemployment?
   A. Jamie; a college graduate
   B. Florence; a high school graduate
   C. neither Jamie nor Florence because both have degrees
   D. both are extremely likely to be unemployed

   Answer: B

51. Adults worry that leisure activities may be interfering with the more "important" tasks of adolescence, such as school. This has been referred to as _____.
   A. occupational deviance
   B. the displacement hypothesis
   C. premature affluence
   D. social loafing

   Answer: B

52.   Aside from athletics, which type of extracurricular activity is most popular among adolescents?
      A. music-related
      B. academic-related
      C. occupational-related
      D. church-related

      Answer: A

53.   Kent has been involved in minor delinquent behavior. In order to curb this type of behavior,
      Kent's parents should _____.
      A. encourage Kent to get a full-time job
      B. encourage Kent to get a part-time job
      C. enroll Kent in a larger school
      D. enroll Kent in an after-school activity

      Answer: D

54.   Jeb has the choice of several after school activities. Statistically, which will he be the most likely
      to join?
      A. the chorus
      B. the science club
      C. the baseball team
      D. the debate team

      Answer: C

55.   The most popular type of extracurricular activities are_____.
      A. athletics
      B. music
      C. academic clubs
      D. occupational clubs

      Answer: A

56.   All of the following statements about extracurricular activities are true *except* _____.
      A. African American students are more likely to participate than white students.
      B. extracurricular activities provide greater opportunities for cross-racial friendships
      C. students from larger schools are more likely to participate than students from smaller schools
      D. athletics are the most popular type of extracurricular activity

      Answer: C

57.   Participation in non-athletic extracurricular activities is higher among _____ than among _____.
      A. boys; girls
      B. rural students; suburban students
      C. white students; African American students
      D. students from large schools; students from small schools

      Answer: B

58. To evaluate the cause and effect of extracurricular activities, what type of study has been used?
    A. cross-sectional
    B. prospective
    C. longitudinal
    D. all of the above

    Answer: C

59. According to your text, what is one serious caution regarding participation in athletics for adolescents?
    A. steroid use
    B. injury
    C. amenhorrea
    D. lower self-image

    Answer: B

60. Which of the following students is more likely to engage in more cross-racial friendships?
    A. Sal, who earns straight As
    B. Melanie, who works part-time
    C. Danielle, who participates in extracurricular activities after school
    D. Ian, who attends a private school

    Answer: C

61. The chief route to popularity for boys is _____ and the primary route for girls is _____.
    A. athletics; athletics
    B. athletics; cheerleading
    C. not to participate in extracurricular activities; cheerleading
    D. athletics; not to participate in extracurricular activities

    Answer: B

62. Virginia is the most popular girl in school. She is probably _____.
    A. a cheerleader
    B. an athlete
    C. very aggressive
    D. not very intelligent

    Answer: A

63. The primary socialization factor of leisure activities for adolescent girls is _____.
    A. ethics
    B. achievement
    C. competitiveness
    D. physical attractiveness

    Answer: D

64. Typically, a female who participated in _____ would be less popular than a female who participated in _____.
   A. sports; cheerleading
   B. cheerleading; sports
   C. orchestra; sports
   D. cheerleading; orchestra

Answer: A

65. For adolescents, although time spent with the mass media has increased, time spent with the _____ has decreased.
   A. radio
   B. part-time jobs
   C. television
   D. magazines

Answer: C

66. Keeshon's mom enters the room to see 15-year-old Keeshon and his dad working on a puzzle while listening to music. Who is most likely to identify "listening to music" as the primary activity?
   A. Keeshon
   B. his dad
   C. his mom
   D. all three are equally likely

Answer: A

67. Joel used to watch a lot more TV as a young adolescent. Now, he watches less because he spends more time. _____.
   A. listening to music
   B. at his part-time job
   C. hanging out with his friends
   D. alone in his room

Answer: A

68. Who is most likely to watch the most TV?
   A. Selma; a junior high student
   B. Stephanie; a high school sophomore
   C. Dick; a high school senior
   D. Gertie; a college freshman

Answer: A

69. _____ adolescents are more likely to watch TV , and _____ adolescents are more likely to listen to music.
   A. Older; older
   B. Younger; younger
   C. Older; younger
   D. Younger; older

Answer: D

70. The Experience Sampling Method involves _____.
   A. observing individuals in their natural setting
   B. witnessing change in the makeup of the population
   C. adolescents carrying beepers and reporting their moods when paged
   D. researchers becoming participants during their observations

Answer: C

71. The Experience Sampling Method was created by _____.
   A. Greenberger
   B. Larson
   C. Steinberg
   D. Bachman

Answer: B

72. Emma is dancing to her favorite song on the radio when her electronic pager goes off. Emma proceeds to pull out a notebook and record her current emotional state. This type of data collection is called _____.
   A. ethnography
   B. participant observation
   C. Experience Sampling Method
   D. demography

Answer: C

73. When are adolescents usually in the "worst" mood?
   A. when they are with friends
   B. when they are working
   C. when they are with their family
   D. when they are alone

Answer: D

74. Between grades 5 and 9, adolescents' moods while with their families follow a(n) _____ pattern.
   A. increasingly positive
   B. increasingly negative
   C. neutral
   D. curvilinear

Answer: D

75.   Research on the sexual or aggressive images in rock music lyrics and on MTV suggests that
_____.

A. they may cause adolescents to become more aggressive
B. they may cause adolescents to become sexually active
C. both (a) and (b)
D. neither (a) nor (b)

Answer: D

Essay Questions

76.   Propose three suggestions that may help noncollege-bound high school students prepare for the
world of work and avoid unemployment. Discuss how they might work.

Sample Answer:
Most high schools today cater to the needs of their college-bound students. Noncollege-
bound students are often forgotten and do not receive the training they need to prepare
them for the work force. Three suggestions have been proposed to help combat this
problem: community service, youth services, and apprenticeship programs. Community
service opportunities for noncollege-bound students will help integrate them into the
community while enhancing feelings of confidence and responsibility and exposing them
to adult role models. Improving youth services and youth organizations will help non-
college-bound students by offering job placement services and counseling for summer
and volunteer work. Apprenticeship programs like those in Europe help noncollege-
bound students because they provide on-the-job training that is relevant to the adult work
force.

Key Points
a) Most high schools today cater to the needs of college-bound students.
b) Three suggestions have been made to combat the problem:
    1. Community service: integrate adolescents into the community, enhance feelings of
       confidence and responsibility, expose them to adult role models.
    2. Improve youth services and strengthen youth organizations: employment services
       like job placement will help combat unemployment.
    3. Implement apprenticeship programs: provide on-the-job training, relevant to post
       -school careers.

77. How are American adolescents different from their European counterparts in terms of the types of jobs they hold? Name four reasons for these differences.

Sample Answer:
American adolescents are more likely to hold paying part-time jobs during the school year, and less likely to work in school-sponsored or government-sponsored apprenticeships. One reason for this difference could be that part-time employment opportunities are not as readily available elsewhere as they are in America. Second, the scheduling of part-time jobs in other countries is not well suited to the daily routines of students. Third, in other industrialized countries, the employment of youth is associated with being poor. Fourth, schools in other countries demand much more out-of-school time.

Key Points
a) Americans are more likely to hold paying part-time jobs during the school year.
b) Europeans are more likely to work in school-sponsored or government-sponsored apprenticeships.
c) Scheduling of part-time jobs in other countries is not well suited to their daily routines.
d) Employment of children in other industrialized countries is associated with being poor.
e) Schools in other countries demand much more out-of-school time.

78. How would you characterize the work settings of the typical American teenager? How are adolescents affected by working long hours during the school year?

Sample Answer:
Most young people – at least those old enough to work in the formal labor force – are employed in retail or service jobs, many in the food-service industry. The average worker works about fifteen to twenty hours weekly. With occasional exceptions, most teenagers' jobs are repetitive, monotonous, and unlikely to be intellectually stimulating. Some are even highly stressful, requiring that youngsters work under intense time pressure without much letup. Young people spend as much time on the job interacting with other adolescents as with their elders, and are unlikely to form close relationships with adults at work. Working more than twenty hours a week may jeopardize adolescents' schooling, as is indicated by reports of increased absences, lower participation in extracurricular activities, less time spent on homework, and lower grades among teenagers who work long hours. Such adolescents may even be at increased risk of dropping out of school. Working long hours is also associated with increased drug and alcohol use. Young people who spend more time at work report growing more distant from their parents and friends, perhaps because they miss out on family and weekend activities.

Key Points
a) Most adolescent jobs are in the retail or service industry and are not very stimulating.
b) Most adolescents do not form close relationships with their adult employers.
c) Adolescents who work more than twenty hours per week tend to engage in more delinquent activity and do worse in their schooling.

79.   Discuss the role that extracurricular activity participation plays in sex-role socialization.

> *Sample Answer:*
> *Many leisure activities for adolescents are structured to socialize them into traditional sex roles. For boys, the road to popularity is determined by participation in athletics, which emphasizes traditional adult male values: achievement, toughness, dominance, and competition. For girls, popularity is the result of participation in cheerleading. Cheerleading emphasizes appearance, neatness, and a bubbly personality. These characteristics are common stereotypical attributes of adult females. Adolescent boys and girls are more likely to be admired when they participate in "sex-appropriate" activities.*

> Key Points
> a) Many leisure activities are structured to socialize adolescents into traditional sex roles.
> b) Athletics leads to popularity for boys.
> c) Athletics emphasizes achievement, toughness, dominance and competition: traditional values for adult males.
> d) Cheerleading leads to popularity for girls.
> e) Cheerleading emphasizes appearance, neatness, personality: traditional values for adult females.
> f) Boys and girls are more likely to be admired when they participate in "sex-appropriate" activities.

80.   Outline the recent findings regarding the effects of athletics on the lives of adolescents and then illustrate one important reason why it is difficult to draw conclusions from this research. What type of study could best determine this effect?

> *Sample Answer:*
> *It is difficult to draw firm conclusions regarding the effect of extracurricular activities on adolescents because few studies separate cause and effect. However, there have been few longitudinal studies that have tried to evaluate cause and effect.. Results from studies suggest that participation in extracurricular activities - especially in athletics of fine arts - seems to improve students' performance in school, to reduce the likelihood of dropping out, to deter delinquency and drug use, and to enhance students' psychological well-being and social status.*

> Key Points
> a) Participation in athletics seems to improve students performance in school, reduce the likelihood of dropping out of school, and deter delinquency and drug use.
> b) It also enhances students' psychological well-being and social status.
> c) It is difficult to separate cause and effect - longitudinal studies can help do this.

CHAPTER 8
TEST ITEMS

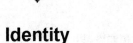

Identity

Multiple Choice Items

1. Analogy: Adulthood is to adolescence as midlife crisis is to _____.
    A. false-self behavior
    B. code switching
    C. psychosocial moratorium
    D. identity foreclosure

    Answer: C

2. Researchers have identified all of the following factors as critical components of the development of identity during adolescence, *except* _____.
    A. self-esteem
    B. sense of identity
    C. self-conception
    D. self-regulation

    Answer: D

3. Maria sees herself as an only child, as a person who likes art and music, who is shy, and who likes to read. Maria's description fits best with the idea of _____.
    A. self-conception
    B. self-esteem
    C. self-attribution
    D. self-control

    Answer: A

4. Gwen has recently been preoccupied with trying to understand what kind of person she is. As an exercise, she writes out a list of twenty traits that she thinks best describe her. According to the text, Gwen is focusing on her _____.
    A. identity
    B. self-conception
    C. self-esteem
    D. socialization

    Answer: B

5.   As adolescents develop, their self-conceptions become more _____.
      A. negative
      B. optimistic
      C. disorganized
      D. differentiated

      Answer: D

6.   Which of the following statements about self-conception is most likely to be made by a child
      rather than by an adolescent?
      A. "I am not a classifiable person."
      B. "Most people think I'm very secure, but really I'm pretty shy."
      C. "I am a girl; I have two brothers; I like to read."
      D. "I am honest; I am helpful; I am friendly."

      Answer: C

7.   When asked to describe himself, Aaron stated, "Most of my friends think I don't care about
      school, but I really study a lot at night because school is important to me." This is an example of
      how adolescent self-conceptions become more _____.
      A. detailed
      B. logical
      C. differentiated
      D. intensified

      Answer: C

8.   According to Harter, which of the following is one of the characteristics that distinguish between
      the adolescent's and the child's self-concept?
      A. Adolescents tend to view the self as involving more dimensions than do children.
      B. Adolescents distinguish among actual, ideal and feared selves.
      C. The adolescent's self varies over time and across situations.
      D. All of the above

      Answer: D

9.   Adolescents who have more complex self-conceptions are less likely _____.
      A. to be depressed
      B. to achieve more in school
      C. to have lots of friends
      D. to be foreclosed

      Answer: A

10. Which of the following adolescents is _least_ likely to engage in false-self behavior?
   A. Kassim, who has low self-esteem
   B. Emily, who has high support from her parents
   C. Joy, who has problems with depression
   D. Eddie, who has a sense hopelessness

   Answer: B

11. Adolescents are most likely to exhibit false-self behavior with their _____.
   A. friends
   B. parents
   C. dates
   D. siblings

   Answer: C

12. Kikko hates country music but told Keith, who is a big Garth Brooks fan and her latest love interest, that she adored country music and would love to go with him to see Garth in concert. This type of behavior is called _____.
   A. the negative identity
   B. code switching
   C. identity confusion
   D. the false-self

   Answer: D

13. Amy, a 16-year-old girl, is shy around boys though she would really like to be more outgoing. This reflects _____.
   A. the drive toward positive self-esteem
   B. the discrepancy between her ideal and actual selves
   C. a false sense of self-concept
   D. all of the above

   Answer: B

14. Adolescents are most likely to behave _____ in romantic situations and with a classmate, and they are least likely to engage in _____ with parents.
   A. falsely; inauthentic behavior
   B. authentically; inauthentic behavior
   C. inauthentically; false-self behavior
   D. authentically; true-self behavior

   Answer: C

15. Someone who engages in false-self behavior most likely _____.
     A. reports less emotional support from parents and peers
     B. has low self-esteem
     C. is depressed
     D. all of the above

     Answer: D

16. Which dimension of the Five-Factor Model measures how organized someone is?
     A. Extroversion
     B. Agreeableness
     C. Neuroticism
     D. Conscientiousness

     Answer: D

17. Who is most likely to score high in the Extroversion dimension of the Five-Factor model?
     A. Maya, a white girl
     B. Andrea, a delinquent girl
     C. Saul, an inner-city boy
     D. Carl, an African American boy

     Answer: B

18. How much do people's personalities differ before and after adolescence?
     A. They are much different.
     B. There are a few major changes.
     C. They remain about the same
     D. It's different for everyone.

     Answer: C

19. Which of the following is not one of the personality dimensions of the Five-Factor Model?
     A. Neuroticism
     B. Openness to Experience
     C. Agreeableness
     D. Gender Intensification

     Answer: D

20. What does the Five-Factor Model describe?
     A. research methodology
     B. personality dimensions
     C. false-self behavior
     D. self-esteem dimensions

     Answer: B

21.   Temperament and personality tend to become _____ as we _____.
        A. stable; take more classes
        B. unstable; get older
        C. stable; get older
        D. unstable; take more classes

        Answer: C

22.   How one feels emotionally about one's own traits and abilities defines the concept of _____.
        A. self-regulation
        B. self-esteem
        C. self-attribution
        D. self-control

        Answer: B

23.   Larry feels inferior to most of his friends, but he does feel he is well-liked by younger children.
        Larry's sentiments are best thought of as an example of his _____.
        A. self-regulation
        B. self-esteem
        C. self-attribution
        D. self-conception

        Answer: B

24.   Moment-to-moment shifts in self-assessment are referred to as _____.
        A. crystallized self-esteem
        B. fluid self-esteem
        C. barometric self-esteem
        D. baseline self-esteem

        Answer: C

25.   During childhood, Cathy had high self-esteem. As she enters adolescence, Cathy's self-esteem is
        most likely to _____.
        A. increase
        B. remain the same or increase
        C. remain the same or decrease
        D. decrease

        Answer: B

26.   Based on the research findings of Simmons and her colleagues, which of the following statements
        about young adolescents' self-esteem, self-consciousness, and self-image is _false_?
        A. Early adolescents' self-esteem remains stable.
        B. Early adolescents have lower self-esteem.
        C. Early adolescents are more self-conscious.
        D. Early adolescents have a more unstable self-image.

        Answer: A

27. How does Rosenberg define "barometric self-esteem"?
    A. the relationship between self-concept and weather
    B. how situational factors cause fluctuations in our feelings about ourselves.
    C. how an adolescent interacts with family, peers and teachers on a daily basis
    D. none of the above

    Answer: B

28. Contrary to previous research, Simmons found that early adolescents' self-esteem declined. According to Rosenberg, this decline is due to _____.
    A. the base-line self-esteem
    B. the storm and stress of adolescence
    C. the development of negative identity
    D. barometric self-esteem

    Answer: D

29. Jason is normally a very outgoing, confident young man, but this morning he is embarrassed and quiet because his mother yelled at him in front of his friends as she dropped him off at school. His present mood is reflective of a change in his _____.
    A. crystallized self-esteem
    B. fluid self-esteem
    C. barometric self-esteem
    D. baseline self-esteem

    Answer: C

30. One's stable, general feelings about one's self are called _____.
    A. baseline self-esteem
    B. fluid self-esteem
    C. barometric self-esteem
    D. crystallized self-esteem

    Answer: A

31. Although Samantha experiences normal fluctuations in her feelings about herself, generally speaking, she is confident that she is a good, kind, honest, hard-working young woman. These traits are thus reflective of her _____.
    A. baseline self-esteem
    B. fluid self-esteem
    C. barometric self-esteem
    D. crystallized self-esteem

    Answer: A

32. The negative self-assessment that is sometimes seen in young adolescents is most likely a function of _____.
   A. crystallized self-esteem
   B. fluid self-esteem
   C. barometric self-esteem
   D. baseline self-esteem

Answer: C

33. Tawatha's parents are worried that as she enters adolescence, her self-image will greatly decrease. During what time should Tawatha's parents expect the most fluctuations in her self-image?
   A. When she is 8-11 years old.
   B. When she is 12-14 years old.
   C. When she is 15-18 years old.
   D. When she is 19-21 years old.

Answer: B

34. Which adolescent would be _least_ adversely affected by a bad grade in math class?
   A. one with low baseline self-esteem
   B. one with low barometric self-esteem
   C. one with high barometric self-esteem
   D. one with high baseline self-esteem

Answer: D

35. Which of the following factors is the most important predictor of overall self-esteem?
   A. athletic ability
   B. academic ability
   C. physical self-esteem
   D. moral conduct

Answer: C

36. According to Harter, which of the following aspects of self-esteem is most likely to influence adolescents' overall self-esteem?
   A. academic self-esteem
   B. athletic self-esteem
   C. physical self-esteem
   D. moral self-esteem

Answer: C

37. Which of the following groups of adolescents feel least positive about themselves?
   A. White females
   B. White males
   C. Black females
   D. Black males

Answer: A

38. What is the most important predictor of overall self-esteem in adolescents?
A. athletic ability
B. academic ability
C. family relationships
D. appearance

Answer: D

39. Susan, a white adolescent, is more likely to be vulnerable to disturbances in _____ than any other group of youngsters.
A. self-concept
B. self-image
C. false-self behavior
D. family relationships

Answer: B

40. Tony, a Black adolescent, and Vicki, a White adolescent, both attend a predominantly Black school. Studies predict that _____.
A. Tony will have higher self-esteem than Vicki
B. Tony will have lower self-esteem than Vicki
C. both Tony and Vicki will have high self-esteem
D. both Tony and Vicki will have low self-esteem

Answer: A

41. How does the self-esteem of Jamal, an African-American adolescent, compare to that of Steven, his Caucasian counterpart?
A. It is much lower.
B. It is much higher.
C. It is comparable to, or greater.
D. No comparison can be made.

Answer: C

42. Among the following adolescents, who is most likely to have high self-esteem?
A. Kim; a lower-class African-American
B. Rose; a middle-class White
C. Frank; a lower-class White
D. Scott; a middle-class African-American

Answer: D

43. Which of the following adolescent's self-esteem is most likely affected by their academic success?
    A. Stacey, a White adolescent
    B. Bill, an Asian-American adolescent
    C. Henry, a Mexican-American adolescent
    D. Cathy, an African-American adolescent

    Answer: B

44. Involvement in delinquent activity may lead to _____ in self-esteem.
    A. an increase
    B. a decrease
    C. stability
    D. no relationship

    Answer: A

45. Which of the following statements about self-esteem in children is true?
    A. Having high self-esteem boosts achievement.
    B. High achievement boosts self-esteem.
    C. High achievement and high self-esteem each boost the other characteristic.
    D. For the most part, self-esteem and achievement are unrelated characteristics.

    Answer: B

46. In an experiment, a researcher sprays half of his sample of adolescent males with a cologne containing pheromones, while the other half is sprayed with the same cologne minus the pheromones (a "placebo" cologne). The researcher then measures the amount of time that adolescent females spend talking with each male participant. The presence/absence of the pheromones is the _____ in this experiment and the amount of time adolescent females spend talking with the male participants is the _____.
    A. dependent variable; independent variable
    B. dependent variable; control variable
    C. independent variable; dependent variable
    D. independent variable; control variable

    Answer: C

47. In a research study, the _____ is the variable that is manipulated and the _____ is the outcome of interest.
    A. independent variable; dependent variable
    B. independent variable; control variable
    C. dependent variable; independent variable
    D. dependent variable; control variable

    Answer: A

48. According to Erikson, at what age does a coherent sense of identity typically emerge?
A. 15
B. 18
C. 24
D. 30

Answer: B

49. Erik Erikson's theory of psychosocial development differed from Freud's psychosexual theory in that _____.
A. Erikson emphasized the positive contributions that adolescence can make to behavior and development across the lifespan.
B. Freud viewed adolescence as a period involving the distinctive developmental challenge of the identity crisis.
C. Erikson emphasized pathological aspects of human development.
D. All of the above

Answer: A

50. The key to resolving the crisis of identity versus identity diffusion, according to Erikson, is _____.
A. identity achievement
B. family relationships
C. interactions with others
D. peer relationships

Answer: C

51. According to Erikson, the major crisis of adolescence is called _____.
A. basic trust versus mistrust
B. autonomy versus shame and doubt
C. industry versus inferiority
D. identity versus identity diffusion

Answer: D

52. Kurt is 15 and spends most of his energy wondering who he is and what kind of person he will become. Erikson would describe him as facing the crisis called _____.
A. basic trust versus mistrust
B. autonomy versus shame and doubt
C. industry versus inferiority
D. identity versus identity diffusion

Answer: D

53. According to Erikson, a necessary "time out" for adolescents is called _____.
    A. psychosocial moratorium
    B. a period of crystallization
    C. deindividuation
    D. a period of separation

    Answer: A

54. Who is the most likely to experience a state of moratorium?
    A. an adolescent who is extremely close to his or her parents
    B. a college freshman
    C. males
    D. females

    Answer: B

55. Dr. Smith argues that adolescence is such a demanding time that adolescents need several years with as few responsibilities as possible so they can sort out their identities. His argument focuses on the idea of _____.
    A. individuation
    B. separation
    C. crystallization
    D. psychosocial moratorium

    Answer: D

56. Since Jerry became an adolescent, he has experimented with different roles and personalities. Jerry's parents are telling all their friends that this is just as "phase" he's going through. According to Erikson, this "phase" is called _____.
    A. identity foreclosure
    B. psychosocial moratorium
    C. identity confusion
    D. negative identity

    Answer: B

57. Identity that is incoherent, disjointed, and characterized by an incomplete sense of self is called _____.
    A. false-self behavior
    B. moratorium
    C. identity diffusion
    D. marginal identity

    Answer: C

58.   Alex has been classified as lacking commitment and exploration. What identity status would
       Alex fall under?
       A. achieved
       B. foreclosed
       C. diffusion
       D. moratorium

Answer: C

59.   James has flunked out of high school, has severed all of his ties with family and friends, and has
       no sense of where he is headed. According to Erikson, James is experiencing _____.
       A. identity diffusion
       B. negative identity
       C. identity foreclosure
       D. psychosocial moratorium

Answer: A

60.   Jane, the adolescent daughter of the local police chief, has recently been hanging out with a
       rowdy group of youth who have vandalized a number of public buildings. Jane has most likely
       adopted a _____.
       A. false-self behavior
       B. negative peer culture
       C. negative identity
       D. all of the above

Answer: C

61.   What largely determines whether an adolescent's search for self-definition will take the form of a
       full-blown crisis or a more manageable challenge?
       A. ethnic identity
       B. family relations
       C. school environment
       D. social context

Answer: D

62.   Sixteen-year-old Mercedes believes that the death penalty is wrong because her parents, friends,
       and church say so. She has never really thought about the issue, but has accepted this view as her
       own. What is her identity status?
       A. achievement
       B. foreclosure
       C. diffusion
       D. moratorium

Answer: B

63. Identities that are undesirable to parents and community members are referred to by Erikson as
_____.
    A. negative identities
    B. marginal identities
    C. false identities
    D. offensive identities

Answer: A

64. Whose research supports Erikson's theory on identity development?
    A. Phinney
    B. Harter
    C. Marcia
    D. Gilligan

Answer: C

65. According to Marcia's research, which identity status is associated with healthy development?
    A. achievement
    B. foreclosure
    C. moratorium
    D. diffusion

Answer: A

66. Generalizing from Marcia's research on identity, who is most likely to become an authoritarian parent?
    A. Sanjay; identity achieved
    B. Ann; identity diffusion
    C. Michele; psychosocial moratorium
    D. Tara; identity foreclosed

Answer: D

67. Ethnic identity may be sped up if parents teach their children _____.
    A. to ignore society's conflicting messages about race
    B. to respect their elders
    C. to attend church regularly
    D. about racism

Answer: D

68. Vedica is attending her high school graduation and her mother, a devout Hindu, wants Vedica to wear a sari. Vedica refuses because she wants to "be like all the other kids." This type of ethnic identity is called _____.
    A. marginality
    B. assimilation
    C. separation
    D. biculturalism

    Answer: B

69. Anu has been accused by peers of her ethnic group of "acting white." Which type of ethnic behavior is Anu probably demonstrating?
    A. marginality
    B. assimilation
    C. separation
    D. biculturalism

    Answer: B

70. Minority adolescents who switch between two different cultural groups' norms for behavior, depending on the situation, are engaging in _____.
    A. marginality
    B. separation
    C. assimilation
    D. code switching

    Answer: D

71. Possessing both highly masculine and highly feminine traits is called _____.
    A. marginality
    B. virile
    C. androgyny
    D. code switching

    Answer: C

72. Increased pressure to behave in sex-appropriate ways is called _____.
    A. gender intensification
    B. self-image stability
    C. sex-role stereotyping
    D. androgyny

    Answer: A

73. According to Gilligan, women define their identity in terms of _____.
   A. achievement
   B. competition
   C. independence
   D. interpersonal relationships

   Answer: D

74. Being androgynous may have _____ effects for girls and _____ effects for boys.
   A. positive; positive
   B. positive; negative
   C. negative; positive
   D. negative; negative

   Answer: B

75. Who has the highest self esteem?
   A. Paul; who is extremely masculine
   B. David; who is extremely feminine
   C. Roger; who is androgynous
   D. Donald; who is both masculine and feminine

   Answer: A

Essay Questions

76. How do self-conceptions change in childhood and adolescence? Discuss two major patterns of change that occur and give illustrations of each.

   Sample Answer:
   "Self-conceptions" refers to the ways in which individuals think about themselves or the attributes and characteristics they cite in describing themselves. Between childhood and adolescence, self-conceptions become more abstract, more differentiated, and better organized. An example of growing abstraction would be the increased use of psychological characteristics. An example of growing differentiation would be the use of self-descriptions that distinguish between behavior in different situations. An example of increased organization would be the more coherent integration found in adolescents' self-descriptions than in those of children.

   Key Points
   a) Self-conceptions are the ways individuals think about themselves.
   b) Self-conceptions become more abstract, more differentiated and better organized as one gets older.

77. Discuss the distinction between baseline and barometric self-esteem, and why the difference between the two is important in adolescent research.

> *Sample Answer:*
> *Different research projects investigating whether self-esteem fluctuates in adolescence have yielded conflicting results. While some investigators have shown that there is no apparent loss of self-esteem during adolescence, others suggest that, especially during early adolescence, fluctuations in self-image may arise. According to sociologist Morris Rosenberg, it is important to differentiate between two aspects of self-perceptions in looking at studies of fluctuations in self-esteem. The barometric aspect of our self-esteem refers to the extent to which our feelings about ourselves shift and fluctuate rapidly, moment to moment. Baseline self-esteem, in contrast, is less transitory and less likely to fluctuate moment to moment. Instead, it is relatively stable over time and unlikely to be easily shifted by immediate experiences. Studies that report high stability in self-esteem over adolescence are likely tapping baseline self-esteem, while studies that show fluctuation and volatility in self-image during early adolescence are probably focusing on barometric self-image.*

> Key Points
> a) Baseline self-esteem is relatively stable over time.
> b) Barometric self-esteem refers to how our feelings about ourselves shift from moment to moment.
> c) High stability over time in baseline self-esteem.

78. Has research on Erikson's theory of adolescent identity development supported his view? How have researchers gone about testing Erikson's model, and what have they found?

> *Sample Answer:*
> *Generally speaking, research on Erikson's theory has been supportive of the notion that identity development proceeds through stages of experimentation and consolidation, although there appears to be a good deal more back-and-forth shifting between various points in the identity development process than one might have predicted. Using an approach developed by James Marcia, researchers have rated individuals on two dimensions: the degree to which they have made commitments and the degree to which they engaged in a sustained search in the process. Results have indicated (a) that individuals can be reliably classified into different identity statuses, (b) that personality differences among individuals who have been classified into different statuses are reasonable and support the validity of the classification scheme, and (c) that late adolescence, especially the college years, appears to be an important time for the consolidation of a coherent sense of identity.*

> Key Points
> a) Research has been supportive of the notion that identity development proceeds through stages.
> b) Marcia rates individuals on two dimensions: degree to which they have made commitments, and degree to which they engaged in sustained search in the process.
> c) Results show that individuals can be classified into different identity statuses.

79.   Discuss some ways in which identity development among ethnic minorities is similar to and
       different from that among white adolescents.

       Sample Answer:
       Although research on identity development among ethnic minorities is just beginning,
       evidence does suggest that the process through which identity development occurs is
       similar in many American ethnic groups. One important difference, however, is that
       having a strong ethnic identity is associated with higher self-esteem among minority
       youngsters, especially among black and Hispanic youth, although this is not the case
       among white youth. Some research does suggest that developing a coherent sense of
       identity is much more complicated for minority adolescents than for their majority
       counterparts, probably because of the context in which they live (including racial
       stereotypes, a limited number of role models, and mixed messages about the costs and
       benefits of identifying too closely with the majority culture). Perhaps tied to this is the
       fact that a number of studies have suggested that the prevalence of identity foreclosure is
       higher among minority youth.

       Key Points
       a) Ethnic development among minorities and whites is similar.
       b) One difference is that having a strong ethnic identity is associated with higher self
          -esteem among minority adolescents than for whites.

80.   Using the terms gender intensification hypothesis and androgyny, explain how the relation
       between gender-role stereotypes and adolescent identity can be confusing for females.

       Sample Answer:
       The gender intensification hypothesis states that sex differences result from an
       acceleration in males and females socialization to act in stereotypically masculine and
       feminine ways. During adolescence, as gender differences increase, females feel caught
       between what they have been told is correct for their gender (nurturance and caring) and
       what they can see is valued by society (assertiveness and independence). Therefore,
       females who exhibit androgynous qualities (both high in masculine and feminine traits)
       are likely to have a better self-image due to these confusing societal messages.

       Key Points
       a) Gender intensification hypothesis: Sex differences result from an acceleration in their
          socialization to act in stereotypically masculine and feminine ways.
       b) Androgyny: Individuals who are both highly masculine and highly feminine.
       c) Confusion for females: During adolescence, when gender differences increase, females
          feel caught between what they have been told is correct for their gender (nurturance
          and caring) and what they can see is valued by society (assertiveness and
          independence).
       d) Benefits of androgyny to adolescents' self-image is greater for girls than boys.

CHAPTER 9
TEST ITEMS

◆

Autonomy

Multiple Choice Items

1. The psychosocial domain concerning the development and expression of independence is called
    _____.
    A. autocracy
    B. autonomy
    C. detachment
    D. morality

    Answer: B

2. Cara hates that her mother always asks her where she is going and who she is hanging out with.
    Cara's attempts to keep secrets is her attempt to establish _____.
    A. autonomy
    B. independence
    C. maturity
    D. both a and b

    Answer: A

3. While _____ refers to individuals' capacity to behave on their own, _____ has
    emotional and cognitive as well as behavioral components.
    A. independence; self-sufficiency
    B. autonomy; independence
    C. independence; autonomy
    D. autonomy; self-sufficiency

    Answer: C

4. Erik Erikson believed that _____ is the central issues of toddlerhood, just as _____ is
    the central issue of adolescence.
    A. identity; autonomy
    B. autonomy; identity
    C. identity; rebellion
    D. autonomy; academics

    Answer: B

5.   Jane has decided not to go along with her friends and drink after school. She realizes that this is wrong, and decides not to give in to the peer pressure. What type of autonomy is Jane exhibiting?
        A. behavioral
        B. emotional
        C. value
        D. none of the above

        Answer: C

6.   Peter is noticing changes in the expression of affection and distribution of power in his relationships with his parents. He is less likely to rush to them with a problem, and is spending more time with his friends. What type of autonomy is developing with Peter?
        A. behavioral
        B. emotional
        C. value
        D. none of the above

        Answer: B

7.   Which of the following aspects of autonomy involves the capacity to make independent decisions and follow through with them?
        A. behavioral autonomy
        B. psychosocial autonomy
        C. emotional autonomy
        D. value autonomy

        Answer: A

8.   As Barbara moves into adolescence, her relationship with her mother and father changes. She is becoming less dependent on them and more dependent on herself. She also realizes that her parents are not always right. Which type of autonomy is Barbara expressing?
        A. behavioral autonomy
        B. psychosocial autonomy
        C. emotional autonomy
        D. value autonomy

        Answer: C

9.   Which of the following types of autonomy refers to that aspect of independence related to changes in an individual's close relationships?
        A. behavioral autonomy
        B. psychosocial autonomy
        C. emotional autonomy
        D. value autonomy

        Answer: C

10. Karen's parents have noticed that throughout Karen's adolescent years, their relationship has transformed. What type of autonomy is Karen expressing?
    A. emotional
    B. cognitive
    C. behavioral
    D. all of the above

    Answer: A

11. Which of the following behaviors is characteristic of increased emotional autonomy among adolescents?
    A. Adolescents are eager to get their parents help and advice with problems.
    B. Adolescents feel their parents are all-knowing and all-powerful.
    C. Adolescents are able to see their parents as people.
    D. Adolescents have difficulty sympathizing with their parents' problems.

    Answer: C

12. In classical psychoanalytic theories, the process of separation that occurs during early adolescence is referred to as _____.
    A. detachment
    B. separation anxiety
    C. distinction
    D. individuation

    Answer: A

13. Which of the following statements about autonomy is *false*?
    A. Adolescents are less emotionally dependent on their parents than they were as children.
    B. Children are closer to their parents than adolescents.
    C. An absence of conflict between an adolescent and his or her parents indicates a delay in autonomy development.
    D. In general, adolescents get along very well with their parents.

    Answer: C

14. Who would agree that the physical changes of puberty cause substantial disruption and conflict inside the family system?
    A. Anna Freud
    B. Erik Erikson
    C. Peter Blos
    D. Heinz

    Answer: A

15. What statement regarding Anna Freud's theory of family relationships is *false*?
   A. Recent studies have not supported her ideas.
   B. Detachment in adolescence is a result of tensions between family members.
   C. Emotional autonomy during adolescence involves a transformation of family relationships.
   D. Intrapsychic conflicts that have been repressed since early childhood are reawakened at early adolescence by the resurgence of sexual impulses

Answer: C

16. Recent research indicates that _____ has negative effects on adolescents' mental health, while _____ has positive ones.
   A. detachment; nondependency
   B. detachment; individuation
   C. individuation; nondependency
   D. individuation; detachment

Answer: B

17. According to Peter Blos, a late adolescent who is gradually and progressively sharpening his/her sense of self as autonomous, competent, and separate from one's parents is developing a sense of
   _____.
   A. autonomy
   B. individuation
   C. self-evaluation
   D. morality

Answer: B

18. Tyler's parents comment that his first year in college has been very good for him because he has learned to accept responsibility for his actions. Tyler's parents are describing _____.
   A. individuation
   B. crystallization
   C. specification
   D. psychosocial moratorium

Answer: A

19. According to research by Steinberg and Silverberg, which of the following aspects of emotional autonomy would you expect an adolescent to develop last?
   A. individuation
   B. de-idealization of parents
   C. seeing parents as people
   D. nondependence

Answer: C

20.	According to the text, who is more likely to begin the process of individuation first: Jeanne, whose parents have been divorced for five years, or Paul, whose parents are married?
	A. Jeanne
	B. Paul
	C. both Jeanne and Paul will begin the process at the same time
	D. unable to determine

	Answer: A

21.	Rosalia is realizing that her parents sometimes make mistakes. What type of emotional autonomy is she exhibiting?
	A. nondependent
	B. individuated
	C. de-idealized
	D. none of the above

	Answer: C

22.	Which stage is the earliest step toward emotional autonomy?
	A. de-idealization
	B. individuation
	C. detachment
	D. justice orientation

	Answer: A

23.	Darnell and his father argue all the time about what occupational field Darnell should eventually pursue. What level of autonomy is Darnell likely to be at?
	A. He lacks autonomy.
	B. He has a low level of autonomy.
	C. He has an average level of autonomy.
	D. He has a high level of autonomy.

	Answer: A

24.	Jeremy's father has made great attempts to offer Jeremy enabling support throughout adolescence. In what way is this likely to affect Jeremy's development?
	A. more individuation
	B. higher ego development
	C. higher psychosocial competence
	D. all of the above

	Answer: B

25. Mrs. Smith is unable to accept her son's long hair and loud music. She responds to his individuality by devaluing and judging rather than questioning and probing. What type of behavior is Mrs. Smith demonstrating?
A. enabling
B. autonomous
C. constraining
D. distracting

Answer: C

26. Seth and his father are discussing politics. Seth says that the government is a corrupt institution and should be overthrown. His father responds, "That's the dumbest thing I've ever heard! What are you, some kind of moron?" This type of interaction has been characterized by Hauser as

_____.
A. coercive behavior
B. constraining behavior
C. repressive behavior
D. judgmental behavior

Answer: B

27. According to Hauser and Allen, parents who exhibit _____ behavior facilitate more healthy autonomous development, while parents who exhibit _____ behavior facilitate less healthy autonomous development.
A. constraining; enabling
B. constraining; repressive
C. enabling; constraining
D. repressive; enabling

Answer: C

28. Healthy individuation and positive mental health are fostered by _____ family relationships.
A. constraining
B. authoritarian
C. close
D. distant

Answer: C

29. Which of the following types of parenting promotes healthy emotional autonomy in adolescents?
A. authoritarian
B. autocratic
C. authoritative
D. permissive

Answer: C

30. Michelle's parents believe in a relaxed rules and guidelines. They believe that rules and regulations will inhibit Michelle's discovery of herself as a person. In what way is this parental philosophy *not* likely to affect Michelle?
   A. Michelle will be emotionally detached from her parents.
   B. Michelle will be genuinely autonomous.
   C. Michelle will be psychosocially dependent upon her friends.
   D. Michelle's social life will be important to her.

   Answer: B

31. Kristie believes that her parents are too strict and has decided not to abide by their rules. She refuses to do her chores around the house and breaks curfew every night. Kristie is probably from _____.
   A. a permissive home
   B. an authoritarian home
   C. an authoritative home
   D. an autocratic home

   Answer: B

32. When Lenny gets frustrated or upset, he turns to his peers rather than his parents for support. As a matter of fact, Lenny relies on his peers more than his parents for most things. Lenny is probably from _____.
   A. a permissive home
   B. an authoritarian home
   C. an authoritative home
   D. an autocratic home

   Answer: A

33. Behavioral autonomy is characterized by which of the following activities?
   A. able to turn to others for advice when appropriate
   B. can weigh alternative courses of action
   C. can reach an independent conclusion about how to behave
   D. all of the above

   Answer: D

34. Which of the following types of households create adolescents who do not develop healthy autonomy, have difficulty complying with rules, and are usually dependent on their friends?
   A. authoritarian
   B. autocratic
   C. authoritative
   D. permissive

   Answer: D

35. Before Shirley fills out her course registration for fall semester, she asks her parents which courses they think she should take. Shirley also consults the guidance counselor at school as well as some of her close friends. Which type of autonomy is Shirley expressing?
   A. value autonomy
   B. behavioral autonomy
   C. emotional autonomy
   D. psychosocial autonomy

   Answer: B

36. According to research conducted by Lewis, the decision-making abilities of teenagers _____.
   A. increase throughout adolescence
   B. decrease throughout adolescence
   C. increase during early adolescence and then remain constant
   D. remain constant throughout adolescence

   Answer: A

37. Mark is a teenager who generally respects his parents. On which of the following issues, however, is Mark most likely to side with his friends and against his parents?
   A. on how to wear his hair
   B. on the issue of capital punishment
   C. on the choice of religious preference
   D. on the value of a college education

   Answer: A

38. Peers usually have more influence than parents on matters of _____.
   A. work
   B. education
   C. personal taste
   D. admired personal qualities

   Answer: C

39. Carrie's parents have repeatedly told her not to pierce her belly button despite her argument that all of her friends are getting their belly buttons pierced. Carrie's urge to pierce her navel probably stems from _____.
   A. her desire to rebel against her parents
   B. her need to express her true identity
   C. her desire to be a true individual
   D. her desire to conform to her peers

   Answer: D

40. Albert always follows the clothing trends his friends start at school. Carl ignores the trends at school and strictly adheres to his parents' guidelines for dressing. Which adolescent is genuinely autonomous?
A. Albert
B. Carl
C. Neither Albert nor Carl
D. Both Albert and Carl

Answer: C

41. If an adolescent is making a decision regarding long-term occupational plans, he or she is likely to go to _____ for advice.
A. his or her parents
B. a friend
C. an acquaintance
D. no one

Answer: A

42. For which of the following questions is an adolescent most likely to turn to outside experts for advice?
A. What steps do I need to take to get admitted to college?
B. Does this outfit look nice?
C. Are my friends really nerds?
D. Is the University of Michigan a fun place to go to college?

Answer: A

43. In early and middle adolescence, adolescents become more _____ with respect to parents, and more _____ with respect to peers.
A. autonomous; conformist
B. conformist; autonomous
C. autonomous; autonomous
D. conformist; conformist

Answer: A

44. Which statement about conformity to peers is most true?
A. Conformity is higher during later adolescence.
B. Conformity is low when the behavior in question is antisocial.
C. Conformity is higher during early and middle adolescence than later adolescence, especially when the behavior in question is antisocial.
D. Conformity to peers is low during early and middle adolescence.

Answer: C

45. During late adolescence, the conformity to peer pressure _____ and the strength of peer pressure _____.
   A. increases; increases
   B. increases; decreases
   C. decreases; decreases
   D. decreases; increases

   Answer: D

46. At which of the following ages would you expect susceptibility to peer pressure to be the greatest?
   A. 8 years
   B. 11 years
   C. 14 years
   D. 19 years

   Answer: C

47. Craig is always the first to go along with the deviant activities his friends suggest. With which style of parenting was Craig probably raised?
   A. authoritarian
   B. permissive
   C. authoritative
   D. autocratic

   Answer: B

48. Which of the following statements about peer pressure is false?
   A. During adolescence, susceptibility to peer pressure increases and then falls.
   B. During adolescence, susceptibility to parental pressure increases and then falls.
   C. Susceptibility to parental pressure decreases throughout adolescence.
   D. The strength of peer pressure increases throughout adolescence.

   Answer: C

49. Autonomy from parents and peers increases in which of the following stages?
   A. early adolescence
   B. middle adolescence
   C. early and middle adolescence
   D. middle childhood

   Answer: B

50. According to Bronfenbrenner, the perspective on development that emphasizes the broad context in which development occurs is called _____.
   A. social psychology
   B. ecology of human development
   C. the exo-system orientation
   D. neighborhood research

   Answer: B

51. Dr. Eccles is interested in whether the ways in which adolescents are treated by their parents affect the ways in which they behave with their friends. Based on the ecological perspective of human development, which of the four levels is this question addressing?
A. micro-systems
B. meso-systems
C. exo-systems
D. macro-systems

Answer: B

52. Dr. Davies conducts research on family relations during adolescence. Based on the ecological perspective of human development, Dr. Davies can best be described as focusing on the _____ level.
A. micro-systems
B. meso-systems
C. exo-systems
D. macro-systems

Answer: A

53. According to the ecological perspective on human development, research that examines the linkages among different contexts of adolescence is called _____.
A. micro-systems
B. meso-systems
C. exo-systems
D. macro-systems

Answer: B

54. According to the ecological perspective on human development, research that examines the broader context of culture and historical time is called _____.
A. micro-systems
B. meso-systems
C. exo-systems
D. macro-systems

Answer: D

55. Feldman and her colleagues have found evidence for variations in autonomy expectations as a function of _____.
A. gender
B. birth order
C. ethnicity
D. all of the above

Answer: C

56. Which adolescent is _least_ likely to seek autonomy from her parents?
    A. Kerry, an Asian adolescent
    B. Mikayla, an Anglo adolescent
    C. Felicia, a Hispanic adolescent
    D. Fatima, an African American adolescent

    Answer: A

57. Which of the following is an example of value autonomy?
    A. establishing more adult-like relationships with family members
    B. relying less on your parents for emotional support
    C. refusing to cheat on an exam even when the teacher is not in the room
    D. seeking the advice of others when faced with a serious question

    Answer: C

58. The most prominent theory of moral development was espoused by _____ and stems from the work of _____.
    A. Piaget; Gilligan
    B. Gilligan; Kohlberg
    C. Kohlberg; Gilligan
    D. Kohlberg; Piaget

    Answer: D

59. As a child, Joe doesn't understand that he simply cannot take the things he wants. As he gets older, he comes to understand about the concept of ownership. This change is an example of _____.
    A. moral development
    B. peer pressure
    C. self-reliance
    D. detachment

    Answer: A

60. According to Kohlberg, reasoning that is based on rewards and punishments is called _____.
    A. principled
    B. conventional
    C. postconventional
    D. preconventional

    Answer: D

61. Postconventional reasoning has also been referred to as _____.
    A. emotional reasoning
    B. principled moral reasoning
    C. self-reliant reasoning
    D. autonomous reasoning

    Answer: B

62.	According to Kohlberg, moral development is linked to _____ development.
	A. cognitive
	B. physical
	C. emotional
	D. psychosocial

	Answer: A

63.	A person who obeys the rules because of a sense of social obligation is functioning at which level of moral development?
	A. principled
	B. conventional
	C. postconventional
	D. preconventional

	Answer: B

64.	Sally is asked who is naughtier, Bobby who accidentally broke three of his mother's cups or Brian who got angry and smashed one of the cups on the floor. She says, "Bobby, because he broke more cups." Sally's level of moral development fits best with which of the following stages?
	A. principled stage
	B. conventional stage
	C. postconventional stage
	D. preconventional stage

	Answer: D

65.	According to Kohlberg, the majority of adolescents probably function at which of the following moral reasoning levels?
	A. principled
	B. conventional
	C. postconventional
	D. preconventional

	Answer: B

66.	Advanced levels of moral reasoning are indicative of which parenting style?
	A. authoritarian
	B. permissive
	C. neglectful
	D. authoritative

	Answer: D

67. Mark complains to his mother that there is nothing wrong with drinking a little beer because, "Everyone my age does it once in a while." Mark's level of moral development would be described as _____.
   A. preconventional stage
   B. conventional stage
   C. postconventional stage
   D. anticonventional stage

   Answer: B

68. According to Gilligan, the moral perspective typically used by women is oriented toward _____.
   A. justice
   B. equality
   C. care
   D. reciprocity

   Answer: C

69. The content area of moral reasoning, according to Kohlberg, is oriented toward _____.
   A. justice
   B. equality
   C. care
   D. reciprocity
   Answer: A

70. Which of the following statements about political thinking in adolescence is true?
   A. Adolescents are more likely to be Republicans than Democrats.
   B. Adolescents believe in autocratic rule and take an acquiescent stance toward government.
   C. Adolescence are not politically influenced by the their living environment.
   D. Adolescents are more likely to challenge authority and argue that laws should be reexamined.

   Answer: D

71. At which of the following ages would we expect an adolescent's political views to be most rigid?
   A. 12 years
   B. 15 years
   C. 18 years
   D. 20 years

   Answer: A

72. According to the text, adolescents raised in which of the following homes are more likely develop rigid political attitudes?
   A. authoritative
   B. authoritarian
   C. indulgent
   D. indifferent

   Answer: B

73.	Research on religious changes during adolescence indicates that _____.
	A. adolescents believe that attending church exhibits a person's religious commitment.
	B. children are more strict observers of religious customs.
	C. college students are more religiously oriented than children.
	D. religion is more important to older adolescents than to children.

	Answer: B

74.	When is an adolescent most likely to question his or her religious beliefs?
	A. during junior high
	B. during middle school
	C. during high school
	D. during college

	Answer: D

75.	During adolescence, the importance of religion _____.
	A. increases
	B. decreases
	C. decreases during early adolescence and then begins to increase
	D. remains the same

	Answer: B

Essay Questions

76. Discuss Anna Freud's view of autonomy during early adolescence. How does her perspective differ from that of contemporary writers?

Sample Answer:
Freud argued that the physical changes of puberty caused substantial disruption and conflict inside the family system, because intrapsychic conflicts that had been repressed since early childhood are reawakened at early adolescence by the resurgence of sexual impulses. The reawakened conflicts are not dealt with consciously and explicitly by the adolescent and his or her parents, but, rather, are expressed in the form of increased tension between family members. As a consequence of this tension, early adolescents are driven to separate themselves, at least emotionally, from their parents and turn their emotional energies instead to relationships with peers. Psychoanalytic theorists called this process detachment, because it appeared as if the early adolescent was attempting to sever the attachments that had been formed during infancy and strengthened throughout childhood. As an alternative to the classic psychoanalytic perspective on adolescent "detachment," some contemporary writers have suggested that we look at the development of emotional autonomy in terms of the adolescent's developing sense of individuation. The process of individuation, which begins during infancy and continues well into late adolescence, involves a gradual, progressive sharpening of one's sense of self as autonomous, as competent, and as separate from one's parents. The process does not involve breaking off relationships with parents, but rather transforming them.

Key Points
a) Physical changes of puberty cause substantial disruption and conflict inside the family system.
b) Resulting tensions lead the adolescent to peers for emotional support.
c) Other contemporary writers analyze adolescent autonomy in terms of individuation.

77. Provide three answers to the Heinz dilemma according to Kohlberg's levels of moral reasoning.

Sample Answer:
A preconventional moral reasoner would not base their answer on society's standards or rules. They would state that it is wrong to steal the drug because one could go to jail. A conventional reasoner would focus on how an individual would be judged by others for behaving in a certain way. They would state that it is wrong to steal the drug because stealing is against the law (or that one should steal the drug because that is what a good husband is expected to do). A postconventional reasoner sees society's rules as subjective. Their thinking is oriented toward the individual's personal conscience. They might state that one should steal the drug if someone's life was at stake.

Key Points
a) preconventional = not based on society's standards, rules or conventions. Should not steal drug because one could go to jail
b) conventional = focuses on how an individual will be judged by others for behaving in a certain way. One should not steal drug because stealing is against the law – or should steal drug because that is what a good husband is expected to do
c) postconventional = society's rules are seen as subjective. Should not steal drug because he violated an implicit agreement among members of society - or should steal drug because someone's life was at stake (answers are oriented toward the individual's personal conscience).

78. Define three types of autonomy and give a concrete example of each.

Sample Answer:
Three types of autonomy that develop throughout adolescence are emotional autonomy, behavioral autonomy, and value autonomy. Emotional autonomy describes the aspect of independence that is related to changes in the individual's close relationships, especially with parents. The adolescent-parent relationship changes in the expression of affection, the distribution of power, and patterns of verbal interaction. An emotionally autonomous adolescent does not generally rush to their parents whenever they have a problem. Behavioral autonomy describes the capacity to make independent decisions and follow through with them. An individual who is behaviorally autonomous is able to turn to others for advice, can weigh alternative courses of action, and can reach an independent conclusion about how to behave. Value autonomy describes having a set of principles about right and wrong. The development of value autonomy entails changes in the adolescent's conceptions of moral, political, ideological, and religious issues. Individuals with a stronger sense of value autonomy may question how just certain laws or rules are.

Key Points
a) Emotional autonomy refers to changes in the individual's close relationships.
b) Behavioral autonomy refers to the capacity to make independent decisions and follow through with them.
c) Value autonomy describes having a set of principles about right and wrong.

79. Discuss Carol Gilligan's criticisms of Kohlberg. Provide an example that displays your understanding of her criticism.

Sample Answer:
Gilligan has argued that the women and men think "in a different voice." Women, she argues, are more likely to emphasize caring when evaluating a course of action, whereas men tend to emphasize justice. From the caring perspective, the focus is on problems of abandonment and detachment, and the ideal is a morality of attention to others and responsiveness to human need. The justice orientation, in contrast, is oriented toward problems of inequality or oppression, and holds out as its ideal a morality of reciprocity and equal respect. Gilligan believes that Kohlberg places too much emphasis on justice and not enough on caring, therefore making his theory gender biased. According to Gilligan, while a man is more likely to analyze the Heinz drug story (an expensive cure was stolen for his wife) on the basis of whether or not laws were broken, a woman would be inclined to ask questions about why the druggist wouldn't lower the price. As a result, men and women would come to different conclusions (with women reaching lower levels of moral development).

Key Points
a) Woman emphasize caring when evaluating a course of action.
b) Men emphasize justice.
c) Kohlberg's theory may be gender-biased.

80. The process of individuation is integral to adolescent development. Discuss two ways in which this process is triggered, and one of the first signs that this might be taking place.

Sample Answer:
Two different models have been suggested as to the triggers of individuation, or the gradual, progressive sharpening of one's sense of self as autonomous and separate from one's parents. One model notes puberty as the main catalyst. Changes in adolescents' physical appearance provoke changes in the way that adolescents are viewed - by themselves and by their parents - which, in turn, provokes changes in parent-child interaction. A second model notes that adolescents' movement toward higher levels of individuation is stimulated by their social-cognitive development. The development of more sophisticated understandings of oneself and one's parents is one way to gain this sense of autonomy. One of the first signs that this is taking place is the de-idealization of parents, or realizing that parents sometimes make mistakes and aren't perfect.

Key Points
a) Puberty is the main catalyst.
b) There are also social-cognitive developmental changes.
c) The first sign of individuation tends to be the de-idealization of parents.

CHAPTER 10
TEST ITEMS

❖

Intimacy

Multiple Choice Items

1.   The psychosocial domain concerning the formation, maintenance, and termination of close
      relationships is called _____.
      A. attachment
      B. sexuality
      C. intimacy
      D. security

      Answer: C

2.   What statement about intimacy is _false_?
      A. Intimacy is an important concern only in adolescence.
      B. One of the central issues in the study of intimacy during adolescence is the onset of dating.
      C. Intimacy is characterized by a willingness to disclose private and occasionally sensitive topics
         and a sharing of common interests.
      D. All of the above are false.

      Answer: A

3.   Children's friendships are based on _____, while adolescents' friendships are based on _____.
      A. activities; competition
      B. activities; intimacy
      C. intimacy; competition
      D. competition; activities

      Answer: B

4.   According to Sullivan, the need for intimacy develops during _____.
      A. childhood
      B. preadolescence
      C. early adolescence
      D. late adolescence

      Answer: B

5. Which of the following children is probably experiencing for the first time the need to be intimate with a friend of the same age?
    A. Carlo, who is 7.
    B. Dierdre, who is 9.
    C. Randy, who is 11.
    D. Connie, who is 16.

Answer: C

6. Who is Julia likely to develop an intimate relationship with first?
    A. Mark; a good friend
    B. Suzanne; a good friend
    C. Steve; an acquaintance
    D. Ken; a popular boy from school

Answer: B

7. According to Sullivan, development can be best understood by examining transformations in
    _____.
    A. psychosexual needs
    B. sexual drive
    C. interpersonal needs
    D. self-conceptions

Answer: C

8. Which theorist adopted the most biological view of development?
    A. Freud
    B. Sullivan
    C. Erikson
    D. Gilligan

Answer: A

9. Sullivan emphasized the social aspects of growth, suggesting that psychological development can be best understood when looked at in _____.
    A. societal terms
    B. interpersonal terms
    C. identity terms
    D. medical terms

Answer: B

10. According to Sullivan, where does the capacity for intimacy first develop?
    A. early adolescent, same-sex relationships
    B. early adolescent, opposite-sex relationships
    C. middle adolescent, opposite-sex relationships
    D. preadolescent, same-sex relationships

Answer: D

11.   Based on Sullivan's theory of interpersonal development, intimacy is first expressed in
       _____.
       A. sexual relationships
       B. opposite-sex friendships
       C. mixed-sex relationships
       D. same-sex relationships

       Answer: D

12.   According to Erikson, what must precede the capability of real intimacy?
       A. established identity
       B. exploration
       C. powerful sex drive
       D. puberty

       Answer: A

13.   Casey and Erin are 16 years old. They have been in a romantic relationship for 5 months. They
       constantly profess their love for one another and say that they want to stay together forever, but
       when they think about post-high school plans, they have trouble making plans that include the
       other. According to Erikson, this is called _____.
       A. internal working model
       B. intimacy versus isolation
       C. psuedointimacy
       D. secure attachment

       Answer: C

14.   Sullivan believes the crisis of adolescence is _____. Erikson believes it is _____.
       A. identity; intimacy
       B. autonomy; intimacy
       C. intimacy; identity
       D. intimacy; autonomy

       Answer: C

15.   According to Erikson, the major crisis of early adulthood is _____.
       A. trust vs. mistrust
       B. identity vs. identity diffusion
       C. autonomy vs. shame and doubt
       D. intimacy vs. isolation

       Answer: D

16. According to Erikson, the major crisis of adolescence is _____ and the major crisis of young adulthood is _____.
    A. identity vs. identity diffusion; intimacy vs. isolation
    B. intimacy vs. isolation; identity vs. identity diffusion
    C. intimacy vs. isolation; autonomy vs. shame and doubt
    D. autonomy vs. shame and doubt; identity vs. identity diffusion

Answer: A

17. With which of the following statements would Erikson agree?
    A. Intimacy develops during preadolescence.
    B. An adolescent must establish a sense of identity before he or she is capable of real intimacy.
    C. Intimacy is a more fundamental concern for boys than for girls.
    D. The development of intimacy precedes the development of a coherent sense of self.

Answer: B

18. "Identity is a necessary precursor to intimacy. True engagement with others is the result and the test of firm self-delineation." Which of the following theorists is most likely to agree with this statement?
    A. Gilligan
    B. Sullivan
    C. Erikson
    D. An attachment theorist

Answer: C

19. Both Erikson and Sullivan viewed psychosocial development as _____.
    A. centered around the family
    B. biologically predetermined
    C. cumulative
    D. a function of the environment

Answer: C

20. Sullivan's theoretical view may be more applicable to _____ and Erikson's theoretical view may be more applicable to _____.
    A. early adolescence; late adolescence
    B. late adolescence; early adolescence
    C. girls; boys
    D. boys; girls

Answer: C

21. During infancy, Julia formed a secure attachment with her parents. This attachment has formed the basis for all her future approaches to interpersonal relationships. According to attachment theorists, Julia is employing _____.
   A. a Q-sort technique
   B. an intimate ideology
   C. an internal working model
   D. a social support theory

   Answer: C

22. An infant who is indifferent to his/her caregiver would have what type of attachment?
   A. secure
   B. anxious-avoidant
   C. anxious-resistant
   D. anxious-secure

   Answer: B

23. The close, significant emotional bond between parent and infant is called _____.
   A. attachment
   B. goodness-of-fit
   C. symbiosis
   D. the secure base

   Answer: A

24. A research procedure in which raters make their evaluations by determining how characteristic each of several descriptors is of the person being evaluated is _____.
   A. the Adult Attachment Interview
   B. the Q-sort
   C. the Rank Order Method
   D. an Attachment Tier Scale

   Answer: B

25. After conducting the Adult Attachment Interview, Dr. Yuen needs to interpret the answers his patient gave. A common method used to analyze the AAI is the _____.
   A. Higher Order Processing Procedure
   B. Rank Order Procedure
   C. Q-sort
   D. Bell Curve Method

   Answer: C

26. Maria is the mother of a 6-month-old baby girl, Antonia. Antonia does not seem to have a close, trusting bond with Maria. Instead, their relationship is characterized by ambivalence. What type of attachment best describes Antonia's relationship with Maria?
A. secure attachment
B. anxious-resistant attachment
C. anxious-avoidant attachment
D. indifferent attachment

Answer: B

27. Which of the following patterns of attachment is positively correlated with high sociability in childhood?
A. anxious-resistant
B. secure
C. anxious-avoidant
D. dependent

Answer: B

28. Which of the following is *not* one of Kobak's attachment classifications of adolescents?
A. secure
B. avoidant
C. dismissing
D. preoccupied

Answer: B

29. During Misha's AAI interview, he appears uninfluenced by his childhood experiences. For example, even though his mother wasn't around much during his childhood, instead of being upset, Misha replies, "No big deal, I don't need her anyway." Based on Kobak's classifications, Misha would be categorized as _____.
A. secure
B. avoidant
C. dismissing
D. preoccupied

Answer: C

30. Jennifer has been diagnosed with an eating disorder. Based on Kobak's research, Jennifer would probably fall under which of the following attachment classifications?
A. preoccupied
B. dismissing
C. avoidant
D. secure

Answer: B

31. The structured interview used to assess an individual's past attachment history and internal working model of relationships is called the _____.
   A. Adult Attachment Interview
   B. Q-sort
   C. Intimacy Measure
   D. Adolescent Security Scale

   Answer: A

32. What is the best predictor of a person's capacity for an intimate friendship?
   A. gender
   B. race
   C. socioeconomic status
   D. sex-role development

   Answer: D

33. Dr. Diamond conducts an interview with a patient in order to assess the history of the patient's attachment relationships. What method would Dr. Diamond use?
   A. the Adult Attachment Interview
   B. the Q-sort
   C. the Longitudinal Attachment Measure
   D. the Adolescent Security Scale

   Answer: A

34. Which of the following explanations of friendship would probably be associated with the oldest child?
   A. "He always wants to play with me."
   B. "He will stick up for me when a bully picks on me."
   C. "He helps me figure out how to build things."
   D. "He likes to go to the park with me."

   Answer: B

35. Allison says that Susan is her friend because she can tell Susan secrets and Susan won't tell anyone else. Allison's definition of friendship is based on _____.
   A. play
   B. prosocial behavior
   C. intimacy and trust
   D. association

   Answer: C

36. Friendships based on which of the following criteria are more likely to be found among adolescents than younger children?
   A. play
   B. association
   C. prosocial behavior
   D. loyalty

   Answer: D

37. Which of the following friendship qualities would be most important to 14-year-old Sarah?
   A. self-disclosure
   B. loyalty
   C. honesty
   D. openness

   Answer: B

38. During adolescence, intimacy with friends _____, and intimacy with parents _____.
   A. increases; decreases
   B. decreases; increases
   C. increases; remains the same
   D. remains the same; decreases

   Answer: C

39. The likelihood that an individual will turn to a peer during a time of trouble _____ in adolescence and the likelihood for turning to a parent _____.
   A. increases ; increases
   B. decreases ; decreases
   C. decreases ; remains stable
   D. increases ; remains stable

   Answer: D

40. Carol, a 14-year-old freshman in high school, is facing a big dilemma that she needs advice about. To whom is Carol likely to turn for this support?
   A. her friends
   B. her parents
   C. an adult expert outside the family
   D. depends on the specific issue at hand

   Answer: A

41. In general, which of the following relationships tends to be the closest?
   A. mother-son relationship
   B. mother-daughter relationship
   C. father-son relationship
   D. father-daughter relationship

   Answer: B

42. Which situation is more important for the psychosocial development of an adolescent?
   A. being popular
   B. having lots of acquaintances
   C. having a few acquaintances
   D. having a few close friends

   Answer: D

43. Which of the following statements about adolescents' level of interaction with parents is true?
   A. Adolescents interact more with their mother.
   B. Adolescents interact more with their father.
   C. There is no difference in adolescents' level of interaction between mothers and fathers.
   D. Sons interact more with fathers and daughters interact more with mothers.

   Answer: A

44. Ron will be going to a new school in the fall. What would be most effective in making this transition less stressful?
   A. calling the guidance counselors at the new school to alert them to Ron's arrival
   B. encouraging Ron to sever ties with his current school so that he enters his new school with no prior attachments
   C. letting Ron establish his autonomy by fending for himself
   D. providing Ron with social support and encouragement from parents and classmates

   Answer: D

45. Which of the following has a more positive impact on adolescents' psychological health?
   A. being close to one's friends
   B. being close to one's parents
   C. having social support from adults in the community
   D. having both parents present in the home

   Answer: B

46. Justin, a 16 year-old, has a substance-abuse problem. To whom is he most likely to turn for help?
   A. his teacher
   B. his friends
   C. his parents
   D. his siblings

   Answer: B

47.   Jessica's parents are verbally abusive to one another and are constantly fighting. When Jessica interacts with her boyfriend, she will probably be _____.
        A. more likely to avoid arguments
        B. less likely to talk to him
        C. more likely to talk to him
        D. more likely to fight with him

        Answer: D

48.   Zach, a college graduate, has developed a relationship with Jamie, a high school senior. They play basketball together, and Zach helps Jamie with his homework. What type of relationship is this called?
        A. guiding relationship
        B. mentor relationship
        C. attachment relationship
        D. Sullivan relationship

        Answer: B

49.   Who is Nicole more likely to have an intimate relationship with: her "favorite" sister Chrissy, or her best friend Renée?
        A. Chrissy
        B. Renée
        C. Nicole will have the same level of intimacy with Chrissy and Renée.
        D. Nicole will be closer to Chrissy during preadolescence and then become closer to Renée during late adolescence.

        Answer: C

50.   During preadolescence, _____ is the single most important determinant of friendship.
        A. gender
        B. ethnicity
        C. socioeconomic status
        D. neighborhood

        Answer: A

51.   Which of the following is the best indicator of when an adolescent will begin dating?
        A. chronological age
        B. biological development
        C. the school norm
        D. the age of his or her parents

        Answer: C

52. What period of life is considered the loneliest?
   A. late childhood
   B. early adolescence
   C. middle adolescence
   D. late adolescence

   Answer: D

53. Which of the following is the best indicator of when an adolescent will engage in sexual behavior?
   A. chronological age
   B. biological development
   C. the school norm
   D. the age of their parents

   Answer: B

54. Edna just celebrated her 80th birthday surrounded by friends and family. This birthday made her think back to the loneliest time of her life. When was this?
   A. when she was a child
   B. when she in late adolescence
   C. when her children left the home
   D. when she first retired

   Answer: B

55. Jesse is a physically immature 14- year-old who goes to school where it is expected that 14-year-olds date. Hillary is a physically mature 14-year-old who goes to school where it is expected students delay dating until age 16. Which adolescent is more likely to date?
   A. Hillary
   B. Jesse
   C. neither Hillary nor Jesse is likely to date
   D. both Hillary and Jesse are likely to date

   Answer: B

56. Who is most likely to suffer from loneliness and social isolation?
   A. Adam; a middle-aged man
   B. Lisa; a freshman in high school
   C. Hans; a freshman in college
   D. Loryn; an elderly woman

   Answer: C

57. Which college students are likely to experience loneliness?
    A. male students
    B. female students
    C. off-campus students
    D. all students are equally likely to experience loneliness

Answer: D

58. When we compare friendship patterns of high school freshmen with those of college freshmen, we find _____.
    A. the younger students have more friends
    B. friendships fluctuate more among older students
    C. friendships in the younger group do not involve intimacy
    D. the younger students experience more social isolation

Answer: A

59. Which of the following statements about loneliness is _false_?
    A. Loneliness is strongly related to students' attitudes.
    B. Although adolescents suffer from loneliness, it is more common among the elderly.
    C. Lonely individuals engage in more self-disclosure.
    D. Lonely individuals are poor judges of how intimate their relationships truly are.

Answer: B

60. What percentage of UCLA college students (1982) reported feeling lonely during their first six months of college?
    A. 10 percent
    B. 25 percent
    C. 50 percent
    D. 75 percent

Answer: C

61. Which type of development most strongly influences sexual activity?
    A. emotional development
    B. cognitive development
    C. biological development
    D. social development

Answer: C

62.   The level of intimacy Marcy expresses with her best friend will be comparable to the level of intimacy _____ shares with his best friend.
        A. Doug; a masculine boy
        B. Kent; a feminine boy
        C. Jacob; an androgynous boy
        D. none of the above; all boys generally exhibit lower levels of intimacy in their friendships than girls

        Answer: D

63.   Elise, a 13-year-old girl, has a "crush" on a boy at school. As a parent, what would be the best way to handle Elise's interest in a member of the opposite sex?
        A. Forbid Elise to engage in activities with members of the opposite sex.
        B. Encourage Elise to exclusively date this boy so that she learns the value of commitment.
        C. Allow Elise to participate in mixed-sex group activities rather than one-on-one dates.
        D. Facilitate autonomy by allowing Elise to do what she wants.

        Answer: C

64.   According to the text, young adolescent girls seem to experience _____ when they become involved in a serious dating relationship.
        A. an increase in imaginative behaviors
        B. a decline in social maturity
        C. less pressure to engage in sexual activity
        D. more interest in academic performance

        Answer: B

65.   Adolescents behave in a variety of ways within dating relationships that are shaped by _____ for how one is expected to behave.
        A. rules
        B. scripts
        C. emotional norms
        D. cultural norms

        Answer: B

66.   What represents the change in the function of dating over the past two decades?
        A. Dating has become more formal and competitive.
        B. Dating has become less frequent and important in society.
        C. Dating has become more informal and less rigidly structured by traditional sex-role stereotypes.
        D. Dating has become more centered around the family.

        Answer: C

67. Angela and Dan have been dating throughout their high school years. Angela is going away to begin college in the fall. What will most likely happen to their relationship?
A. They will break up but remain friends.
B. Angela will break up with Dan.
C. Dan will break up with Angela.
D. They will continue to date.

Answer: B

68. Charlie and Kerry have been dating throughout their high school years. What are the chances that their relationship will end within their first year of college?
A. 25 percent
B. 50 percent
C. 75 percent
D. 100 percent

Answer: B

69. Who is more likely to take breaking up the hardest?
A. men
B. women
C. Men and women react the same.
D. It depends on who initiates the break up.

Answer: D

70. The percentage of teenage marriages has _____ in recent decades.
A. increased
B. decreased
C. remained the same
D. not been documented

Answer: B

71. Statistics on the age at which young people marry indicate that _____.
A. it is approximately the same for males and females
B. girls marry younger today than their mothers' generation did
C. both males and females tend to be older at first marriage than in the 1950s
D. more males than females marry before they are 20

Answer: C

72. Who is the _least_ likely to get divorced?
A. Gideon and Cheryl; who are an older couple
B. Stuart and Lillian; who have not finished high school
C. Chuck and Sue; who had a baby at a young age
D. Pete and Darlena; who are experiencing economic problems

Answer: A

73. What is the most common reason for teenagers to get married?
   A. economic hardship
   B. pregnancy
   C. adherence to religious beliefs
   D. parental pressure

   Answer: B

74. Although the rate of early marriages has _____, the rate of divorce has _____ over the past twenty years.
   A. increased; decreased
   B. increased; stayed the same
   C. stayed the same; increased
   D. decreased; increased

   Answer: D

75. Which of the following couples has the greatest chances of marital problems and divorce?
   A. Phil and Fatima, married at age 19
   B. Carmen and Harry, married at age 23
   C. Luke and Jennifer, married at age 28
   D. Mohamed and Angie, married at 35

   Answer: A

Essay Questions

76. Betty and Barney, both 14-years-old, are "in love." How would Sullivan characterize their relationship? Erikson? Be sure to explain the development of intimacy during adolescence and any differences observed.

   Sample Answer:
   Sullivan believes that intimacy first surfaces in preadolescent, same-sex friendships and that intimacy follows a different course from sexuality. According to Sullivan, sexual desires do not emerge until early adolescence, at which point the individual must begin to learn how to integrate needs for intimacy and desires for sexuality. Thus, for Sullivan, interpersonal relations during adolescence involve integrating sexuality and opposite-sex relationships into an already established capacity for intimacy. In contrast, Erikson views intimacy as a rather late development that typically does not manifest itself until young adulthood, after the crisis of identity has been successfully resolved.

   Key Points
   a) Sullivan believes adolescent must integrate need for intimacy with desire for sexuality.
   b) Erikson believes intimacy does not emerge until after identity development.

77.   The closeness that intimacy brings to friendships also increases the likelihood of conflict in those relationships. Address the differences between close and casual friendships in the types of conflicts experienced in both forms of friendship, differences in conflict resolution, and differences between boys' and girls' conflicts with their friends.

Sample Answer:
While conflicts with close friends are less common than conflicts with casual friends, the conflicts with close friends are more emotional. Anger and hurt feelings are more common in arguments with close friends. Also, close friends are more likely to engage in efforts to restore the relationship following a conflict than are casual friends. Boys' conflicts with their friends are briefer, often focus on issues of power or control, are more likely to involve physical aggression, and are often resolved by just letting the problem pass. In comparison, girls' conflicts last longer, often focus on betrayal in the relationship, and are resolved when one friend apologizes to the other.

Key Points:
   a) Conflict is less common but more intense in close friendships than in casual friendships.
   b) More effort to resolve the conflict and restore the friendship will occur in close friendships.
   c) Boys' conflicts contrast with girls' conflicts in their duration, cause, and resolution.

78.   To what extent does intimacy with peers replace intimacy with parents over the course of adolescence?

Sample Answer:
Although intimacy with peers increases during adolescence, it appears to supplement, rather than take the place of, intimacy with parents. This can be seen in several types of studies of young people's relationships. For example, studies that question young people about the degree of closeness in their various relationships show that intimacy between adolescents and their parents remains at the same level throughout adolescence as it was during childhood, despite concomitant increases in intimacy with peers. Second, in studies asking young people to list significant others, the likelihood of naming parents does not decrease during adolescence, even though the number of peers appearing on the typical youngster's list increases. Generally speaking, research suggests an overall expansion of the individual's social world during adolescence, rather than a substitution of relations with age-mates for relations with parents.

Key Points
a) Intimacy with peers does not replace intimacy with parents.
b) Intimacy with parents remains stable throughout adolescence.
c) Intimacy with peers increases throughout adolescence.

79.   Discuss the nature and prevalence of sex differences in the development of intimacy during adolescence.

Sample Answer:
It is often noted that intimacy develops earlier in girls than in boys, that intimate relationships are more common among girls throughout adolescence, and that girls experience higher levels of intimacy in their relationships than boys do. In most respects, these observations are absolutely true. Girls list more friends than boys do, are more likely to mention intimacy as a defining aspect of close friendship, and express greater interest in their close friendships. Girls are more likely than boys to draw distinctions between intimate and non-intimate friends in the way they treat them, and girls appear to prefer having more exclusive friendships, being less willing to include other classmates in their cliques' activities. Girls also appear to develop intimate relationships with boys earlier than boys do with girls and appear to be more sensitive than boys when comforting friends who are distressed. Yet, boys and girls report similar levels of actual self-disclosure in their same-sex friendships, have equivalent degrees of intimate knowledge about their best friends, and are equally likely to help their friends. Intimacy may be a more conscious concern for adolescent girls than for boys, but the development of intimacy among males may be a quieter, more subtle phenomenon.

Key Points
a) Intimacy develops earlier in girls than in boys.
b) Girls tend to be more exclusive in their relationships than boys.
c) Both boys and girls report similar intimate behaviors with their close friends.

80.   Provide two reasons why the nature of an individual's early attachment relationships during infancy continues to have an influence on the capacity to form satisfying intimate relationships during adolescence and adulthood.

Sample Answer:
Many theorists propose that the initial attachment relationship forms the basic foundation from which all ensuing interpersonal relationships stem. This foundation is called the internal working model. An individual's internal working model determines his or her sensitivity to rejection and the ability to incorporate intimacy into relationships in adolescence and adulthood. Additionally, the initial attachment relationship is important because its effects are cumulative. Studies have found that anxiously attached infants are more likely to develop psychological and social problems during childhood, including poor peer relationships. These problems lead to problems of social competence in adolescence. Adolescence who are able to establish healthy, intimate relationships are more satisfied with their lives as middle-aged adults. This extension suggests that the initial attachment relationship continues to influence social ability throughout life.

Key Points
a) The initial attachment relationship forms the internal working model, which determines an individual's sensitivity to rejection and ability to incorporate intimacy into relationships.
b) The effects of the initial attachment relationship are cumulative, affecting the social life from infancy to childhood, adolescence, and adulthood.

CHAPTER 11
TEST ITEMS

◆

Sexuality

Multiple Choice Items

1. "Sexual socialization" refers to _____.
    A. a person's sexual orientation
    B. a person's social skills in sexual relationships
    C. the way in which an individual is educated about sexuality
    D. the degree to which an individual is comfortable with his or her sexuality

    Answer: C

2. On Steve's 13th birthday, his father wants to educate him about sex, so they sit down to have a "man to man" talk about the "birds and the bees." This process is called _____.
    A. sociosexual preparation
    B. sexual socialization
    C. permissive communication
    D. human ecology

    Answer: B

3. In the Mandingo tribe, boys and girls are separated until they have completed their religious instruction. This separation also occurs because sexual contact before marriage is strictly forbidden. According to Ford and Beach, this society would be characterized as _____.
    A. semi-restrictive
    B. permissive
    C. prohibitive
    D. restrictive

    Answer: D

4. Ford and Beach found that sexual expressions varied widely from culture to culture. Their findings suggest that _____.
    A. biology is the key to understanding adolescent sexuality
    B. adolescent sexuality may begin in biology but ends in culture
    C. sexuality cannot be fully understood cross-culturally
    D. adolescent sexuality is very uniform within cultures

    Answer: B

5.   When *Patterns of Sexual Behavior* was published in 1951, the sexual socialization of American children and adolescents was categorized as _____.
    A. prohibitive
    B. semi-restrictive
    C. permissive
    D. restrictive

Answer: D

6.   Molly and Lawrence were caught kissing in school, and were sent to the principal's office. He gave them each after-school detention (in separate rooms) and instructed them that this behavior was to cease immediately However, when the principal saw Lawrence and Molly kissing at the mall on Saturday, he ignored their behavior. This type of attitude toward sexuality is consistent with which type of society?
    A. semi-restrictive
    B. permissive
    C. prohibitive
    D. restrictive

Answer: A

7.   Having a series of relationships in which one is always faithful to one's partner is called _____.
    A. serial monogamy
    B. cohabitation
    C. semi-restrictive sexuality
    D. sexual socialization

Answer: A

8.   Marlene has had many sexual partners over the last five years, but has been monogamous within each relationship. What is this pattern called?
    A. abstinence
    B. permissiveness
    C. serial monogamy
    D. semi-restrictiveness

Answer: C

9.   Barbara's mother always felt that premarital sex was permissible for men but not for women. Today, Barbara believes that males and females should each follow the same standards for premarital sexual behavior. What is this trend called?
    A. a decline in the double standard
    B. societal permissiveness
    C. serial monogamy
    D. none of the above

Answer: A

10. Autoerotic behavior during adolescence _____.
    A. generally precedes sociosexual behavior
    B. often involves fantasies about television or movie stars
    C. appears earlier among females than males
    D. is all of the above

    Answer: D

11. When Ken is alone, he fantasizes about supermodels and masturbates. This type of behavior is called _____.
    A. nocturnal stimulation
    B. autoerotic
    C. sociosexual
    D. sensual stimulation

    Answer: B

12. Which of the following adolescents is more likely to move toward intercourse at an earlier age without as many intervening steps?
    A. Sotoko, an Asian adolescent
    B. Miranda, a Latina adolescent
    C. Carrie, an African American adolescent
    D. Torrie, a White adolescent

    Answer: C

13. While Nathan is sleeping, he ejaculates. This phenomenon is referred to as _____.
    A. autoerotic emission
    B. nocturnal orgasm
    C. twilight discharge
    D. circadian rhythm

    Answer: B

14. Which of the following illustrates the typical sequence of sexual behavior among adolescents?
    A. masturbation; necking; sexual intercourse; oral intercourse
    B. necking; masturbation; petting; sexual intercourse
    C. masturbation; necking; petting; sexual intercourse
    D. petting; necking; sexual intercourse; oral intercourse

    Answer: C

15. In males, ejaculations that occur while asleep are called _____.
    A. autoerotic
    B. nocturnal orgasms
    C. twilight discharge
    D. simultaneous climaxing

    Answer: B

16. The aspect of sexual behavior that is merged with social relationships is known as _____.
     A. sexual socialization
     B. autoerotic behavior
     C. sociosexual behavior
     D. sex-role behavior

     Answer: C

17. After the school dance, Michael kissed Becky goodnight. This type of sexual behavior can be thought of as _____.
     A. nocturnal stimulation
     B. autoerotic
     C. sociosexual
     D. sensual stimulation

     Answer: C

18. Members of which of the following racial groups are most likely to become sexually experienced at earlier ages?
     A. Anglo Americans
     B. Hispanic Americans
     C. Asian Americans
     D. African Americans

     Answer: D

19. The greatest increase in the prevalence of premarital intercourse has been among which group?
     A. males
     B. females
     C. minority males
     D. females from higher socio-economic backgrounds

     Answer: B

20. According to national surveys, sexual activity among adolescents is occurring _____ it has in past decades.
     A. later than
     B. earlier than
     C. at the same time as
     D. earlier for boys but later for girls than

     Answer: B

21.   Ann is a 17-year-old adolescent who is still a virgin. She believes sex before marriage is wrong and worries about how her parents would respond if she were to become sexually active. Ann is probably of which descent?
A. African American
B. Asian American
C. Hispanic
D. White

Answer: C

22.   Approximately what fraction of American adolescents are having intercourse for the first time before age 15?
A. one-third
B. one-half
C. two-thirds
D. three-quarters

Answer: A

23.   The major changes in sexual activity between today's adolescents and those in previous generations have not been in behaviors such as _____, but in the incidence and prevalence of _____ among teenagers.
A. necking and petting ; homosexuality
B. intercourse ; autoerotic behavior
C. sociosexuality ; necking and petting
D. necking and petting ; intercourse

Answer: D

24.   Changes in the prevalence of premarital sex among college students since the 1970s has been _____ that of high school students.
A. the same as
B. sharper than
C. less dramatic than
D. there are no differences

Answer: C

25.   Over the past 25 years, rates of premarital intercourse in different subgroups of American adolescents have _____.
A. increased
B. decreased
C. converged
D. diverged

Answer: C

26. Jeannette is a 17-year-old who has decided to engage in sexual intercourse with her boyfriend. Tammy is a 17-year-old who has decided to abstain from sex until she is older. Which adolescent is more likely to experience psychological disturbances?
A. Jeannette
B. Tammy
C. Neither Tammy nor Jeannette, because they have made mature decisions.
D. Sexual activity during late adolescence is not associated with psychological disturbance.

Answer: D

27. Tim and Carol are upset because they recently discovered that their 14-year-old daughter has already engaged in sexual intercourse. What other types of problems should they anticipate?
A. drug and alcohol problems
B. low interest in academics
C. tolerance of deviant behavior
D. all of the above

Answer: D

28. The sexual _____ of males and females may be similar, but the sexual _____ of males and females is quite different.
A. behavior; socialization
B. socialization; behavior
C. attitudes; experiences
D. experiences; attitudes

Answer: A

29. Generalizing from the text, if Nicky's parents want to slow down his sexual involvement, which of his parents should talk to him about sex?
A. his mother
B. his father
C. Both of his parents should talk to him at the same time.
D. Neither of his parents should talk to him about sex.

Answer: A

30. Fathers who talk to their sons about sex are more likely to _____ their sexual activity.
A. decrease
B. increase
C. not influence
D. postpone

Answer: B

31. What family factor appears to predict adolescent sexual involvement, especially among girls?
   A. household composition
   B. mothers employment
   C. number of siblings
   D. parenting styles

   Answer: A

32. According to the text, who is more likely to be sexually active: Ingrid who lives in a single-parent home, or Leanne who lives in a two-parent home?
   A. Ingrid
   B. Leanne
   C. Ingrid, but only immediately following her parents' divorce.
   D. Both girls are equally likely to be sexually active.

   Answer: A

33. A field of inquiry that focuses on the study of development and behavior in context is called _____.
   A. neighborhood analysis
   B. contextual tracking
   C. societal patterns
   D. human ecology

   Answer: D

34. Research on what adolescents learn about sex, and who they learn this information from, reveals that they learn _____.
   A. very little, and most is learned from peers
   B. a great deal, and most is learned from older siblings
   C. very little, and most is acquired from parents
   D. very little, and most is acquired form teachers

   Answer: A

35. Adolescents who became sexually active at an early age were found to differ from other adolescents in a number of ways. The early-active teens exhibited differences from other adolescents in all of the following areas *except* _____.
   A. personality measures
   B. perceptions of their environments
   C. physical maturity
   D. involvement in other behaviors

   Answer: C

36. Of particular importance in determining the different sexual responses of males and females are levels of _____.
   A. progesterone
   B. estrogen
   C. ACTH
   D. androgens

   Answer: D

37. For adolescent girls, which is the most important factor in determining the onset of sexual intercourse?
   A. increased levels of androgens
   B. availability of birth control
   C. the attitudes of friends toward sexual activity
   D. receiving sex education in school

   Answer: C

38. For adolescent boys, which is the most important factor in determining the onset of sexual intercourse?
   A. increased levels of androgens
   B. availability of birth control
   C. the attitudes of friends toward sexual activity
   D. receiving sex education in school

   Answer: A

39. Generalizing from the text, Zack is most likely to have his first sexual encounter with a _____.
   A. younger partner
   B. classmate
   C. casual date
   D. steady girlfriend

   Answer: C

40. Which of the following statements about boys' first sexual experience is *false*?
   A. A boy's first sexual experience is usually through masturbation.
   B. Boys typically view sex as recreation.
   C. A boy's first sexual partner is likely to be someone he's in love with.
   D. Boys are more likely than girls to keep sex and intimacy separate.

   Answer: C

41. Early sexuality for males is tinged with elements of _____, while for females it is more linked to feelings of _____.
    A. intimacy; recreation
    B. recreation; intimacy
    C. enjoyment; guilt
    D. guilt; enjoyment

    Answer: B

42. Amy, a 15-year-old, lost her virginity to her boyfriend last night. Which of the following is Amy least likely to say?
    A. "I'm in love!"
    B. "I'm so worried - what if I'm pregnant!"
    C. "I'm so glad I'm no longer a virgin!"
    D. "I'm so excited!"

    Answer: C

43. Generalizing from the text, Marge is most likely to have her first sexual encounter with a

    _____.
    A. younger partner
    B. classmate
    C. casual acquaintance
    D. steady boyfriend

    Answer: D

44. The incidence of homosexuality has, over the last twenty years _____.
    A. increased
    B. remained stable
    C. decreased
    D. increased for men but decreased for women

    Answer: B

45. Todd would rather date men than women. This is called _____.
    A. gender identity
    B. sexual preference
    C. sex-role behavior
    D. homophobia

    Answer: B

46. Michael and Kayla are concerned because they noticed their 10-year-old son, Tom, engaging in sex play with a male friend. They ask a psychologist what she thinks. What did she probably say?
   A. "Tom is probably homosexual."
   B. "Tom has been sexually abused."
   C. "Same-sex play among young adolescents is common."
   D. "Tom needs to get counseling for this unusual behavior."

   Answer: C

47. Amy is a "straight", 16-year-old adolescent. Kelly, also 16, has discovered that she has homosexual interests. Which girl is most confused about her gender identity?
   A. Amy
   B. Kelly
   C. Both Amy and Kelly will be confused because adolescence is a confusing time.
   D. Neither Amy nor Kelly has anything to be confused about.

   Answer: C

48. Pete, a 17-year-old, has just told his parents that he is gay. According to statistics, what types of problems should Pete's parents anticipate?
   A. school difficulties
   B. substance abuse
   C. running away from home
   D. all of the above

   Answer: D

49. Bill is a very feminine man. Based on this sex-role behavior, one would predict that Bill is probably _____.
   A. homosexual
   B. heterosexual
   C. bisexual
   D. There is no connection between sex-role behavior and sexual preference.

   Answer: D

50. Since Andrea is a lesbian, she is more likely to exhibit what types of behaviors?
   A. feminine behaviors
   B. masculine behaviors
   C. androgynous behaviors
   D. There is no connection between sex-role behavior and sexual preference.

   Answer: D

51. Which is *not* a risk factor for sexual abuse?
    A. living apart from one's parents
    B. living in a major city
    C. being raised in poverty
    D. having parents who abuse alcohol or other drugs

    Answer: B

52. Homosexual adolescents may be at a greater risk for all of the following outcomes *except*
    _____.
    A. suicide
    B. alcohol and drug use
    C. sexually-transmitted diseases
    D. running away from home

    Answer: C

53. Fourteen-year-old Sarah began "acting out" behaviors that her teacher had never observed in her before, such as a decline in self-esteem, sexual promiscuity, and risky behavior. Sarah's teacher suspects that Sarah is _____.
    A. pregnant
    B. fighting with her boyfriend
    C. a victim of sexual abuse
    D. questioning her sexual orientation

    Answer: C

54. Suzanne has just found out that her 13-year-old daughter had been sexually abused by her piano teacher. What type of problem is Suzanne's daughter most likely to face?
    A. drug abuse
    B. suicide
    C. academic difficulties
    D. infertility

    Answer: C

55. What is the most common method of birth control among sexually-active adolescents?
    A. condoms
    B. birth control pills
    C. withdrawal
    D. the rhythm method

    Answer: B

56. Research has indicated that many young people do not use contraception regularly because _____.
   A. their parents forbid them to use it
   B. they unconsciously desire to become pregnant
   C. contraceptives may be difficult for them to obtain
   D. they do no know how

   Answer: C

57. The best predictor of contraceptive use is _____.
   A. age
   B. IQ
   C. race
   D. socioeconomic status

   Answer: A

58. Which of the following sexually active adolescents is most likely to use contraception?
   A. Sara, a 15-year-old
   B. Leonardo, a 16-year-old
   C. Chloe, a 17-year-old
   D. Thomas, an 18-year-old

   Answer: D

59. Tyra doesn't believe that she will become pregnant because she is in love with her boyfriend, and so she doesn't bother to use contraception. Tyra is engaging in _____.
   A. rationalization behavior
   B. imaginary audience behavior
   C. a sexual script
   D. the personal fable

   Answer: D

60. Which of the following sexually transmitted diseases is caused by a virus?
   A. gonorrhea
   B. herpes
   C. chlamydia
   D. syphilis

   Answer: B

61. AIDS is transmitted through _____.
   A. casual contact
   B. bodily fluids
   C. kissing
   D. mosquito bites

   Answer: B

62. Both _____ are cause by a bacterium, while _____ are caused by a virus.
    A. chlamydia and herpes; gonorrhea and human papilloma virus
    B. gonorrhea and herpes; chlamydia and human papilloma virus
    C. human papilloma virus and gonorrhea; chlamydia and herpes
    D. gonorrhea and chlamydia; herpes and human papilloma virus

Answer: D

63. What is *not* a risk factor for contracting HIV?
    A. using drugs
    B. having unprotected sex
    C. having many sexually partners
    D. being male

Answer: D

64. Sexual activity in the United States is _____ in other industrialized countries, and the rate of pregnancy is _____.
    A. higher than; higher
    B. lower than; the same
    C. comparable; the same
    D. comparable; higher

Answer: D

65. Which country has the highest rate of teen pregnancy?
    A. Sweden
    B. United States
    C. England
    D. France

Answer: B

66. Although the rate of sexual activity among adolescents in the U.S. does not differ much from that reported by other industrialized countries, the rate of teenage pregnancy in the U.S. is _____.
    A. in the top third of all industrialized countries
    B. in the bottom third of all industrialized countries
    C. the highest in the world among industrialized countries
    D. average as compared to other industrialized countries

Answer: C

67. What percentage of adolescents who become pregnant get an abortion?
    A. less than 2 percent
    B. 10 percent
    C. 40 percent
    D. 70 percent

Answer: C

68. The birth rate among adolescent women today is _____ than in previous eras, and the proportion of teenage childbearing that occurs out of wedlock is _____.
   A. higher; higher
   B. lower; lower
   C. higher; lower
   D. lower; higher

   Answer: D

69. Alice, a 16-year-old, gave birth to a baby boy last year. How will this affect the likelihood that her 13-year-old sister, Marie, will have a baby?
   A. It will increase.
   B. It will increase only if Marie is already sexually active.
   C. It will be unaffected.
   D. It will decrease.

   Answer: A

70. Who is the least likely adolescent to bear her first child while married?
   A. Maria; a Mexican-American
   B. Alisha; an African-American
   C. Francine; an Asian-American
   D. Sylvia; a Caucasian American

   Answer: B

71. Who is more likely to exhibit negative psychological effects two years later: Beth who aborted her pregnancy, or Jenny who gave her child up for formal adoption?
   A. Beth
   B. Jenny
   C. Neither Beth nor Jenny will show negative psychological effects.
   D. Beth will suffer short-term problems whereas Jenny will exhibit long-term problems.

   Answer: C

72. Nancy, a 13-year-old, has recently become pregnant. Statistically, who is most likely the father of her child?
   A. Anthony; a 10-year-old
   B. Zack; a 13-year-old
   C. Daryl; a 17-year-old
   D. Clarence; a 20-year-old

   Answer: D

73. Who is the most likely, after becoming pregnant, to have an abortion?
   A. Jamie; a White female living in the suburbs
   B. Kimberly; a White female who dropped out of high school
   C. Dotty; a Black female who dropped out of high school
   D. Tara; a Black female living in poverty

   Answer: A

74. Research on teenage mothers indicates that _____.
   A. their infants are at heightened risk for school problems and other behavior problems in childhood
   B. most of them unconsciously "wanted" to have a baby
   C. within two to three years, their lives are similar to those of their peers who did not bear a child
   D. they are better off psychologically than teenagers who had aborted their pregnancy

   Answer: A

75. According to research cited in the text, what is the main reason sex education programs fail?
   A. They are taught before children are sexually mature.
   B. Teachers are uncomfortable talking about the subject with students.
   C. Talking about sex increases promiscuity among adolescents.
   D. They emphasize biological over emotional aspects of sex.

   Answer: D

Essay Questions

76. Adolescents' stance on premarital intercourse has changed over the past three decades. Discuss three specific trends that define attitudes toward intercourse.

   Sample Answer:
   Adolescents have more readily engaged in premarital intercourse over the past several decades than ever before. Three trends have notably contributed to this rise in acceptance of premarital intercourse. First, the overall percentage of American adolescents who have engaged in the premarital sex accelerated markedly during the early 70s, stabilized during the early 80s, and then increased again during the late 80s. Second, the median age at which adolescents first engage in intercourse has declined since the early 70s. Third, the greatest increase in the prevalence of premarital intercourse has been among females. Not only are more adolescents from all groups engaging in premarital sex more, but they start younger, and more young females are engaging in sex than ever before.

   Key Points
   a) First trend: The overall percentage of American adolescents who have engaged in premarital sex accelerated markedly during the early 70s, stabilized during the early 80s and then increased again during the late 80s.
   b) Second trend: The median age at which adolescents first engage in intercourse has declined.
   c) Third trend: The greatest increase in the prevalence of premarital intercourse has been among females.

77.   Michelle, a 16year-old adolescent, is the only one in her circle of friends who has not yet had sex. She is beginning to feel pressured to have sex. Discuss two ways that her friends are influencing her attitude toward sex.

Sample Answer:
Adolescents often influence each other's sexual attitudes just as they influence each others tastes and behaviors. Michelle is probably feeling pressured to become sexually experienced like her friends because of two reasons. First, because all of her close friends have experienced intercourse, they have established a normative standard that having sex is acceptable. Therefore, if and when Michelle does decide to have sex, she knows that she will have a group of friends who will support and condone her decision. Second, Michelle's friends are probably directly influencing her sexual attitudes through direct communication. Peers often engage in lengthy conversations about sexual experiences and Michelle might feel like she stands out, or her friends might directly point out that she is at a different place than the others.

Key Points
a) When an adolescent's peers are sexually active, they establish a normative standard that having sex is acceptable.
b) Peers influence each other's sexual behavior directly through communication.

78.   Why have many sex education programs failed? Discuss the major features of a good sex education program.

Sample Answer:
Until very recently, most evaluations of formal sex education programs were quite negative. Many experts believe that early sex education programs failed because they emphasized the biological aspects of sex over the emotional aspects of sexual activity. Newly designed sex education programs have received more positive evaluations, however. These programs attempt to increase adolescents' knowledge about sex as well as teach them decision-making and interpersonal assertiveness skills. It also has been suggested that contraceptive services for teenagers be expanded. In particular, school-based clinics in combination with sex education programs provide a more effective means of deterring adolescent pregnancy than does sex education by itself.

Key Points
a) Emphasized the biological rather than the emotional aspects of sexual activity.
b) New programs are trying to increase both knowledge and teach interpersonal skills.
c) School based clinics may be an effect means of providing education.

79.   Provide three reasons why growing up in a single-parent home affects girls' sexual behavior more than boys.

Sample Answer:
Social influences on girls' sexual behavior are in general stronger and more varied than are the influences on boys' behavior. Boys' parents may not attempt to exert great control over their sexual activity, regardless of whether the household has one parent or two. A second reason is that single-parent mothers are more likely to be dating than married mothers, and may inadvertently be role models of sexual activity to their adolescents. To the extent that this modeling effect is stronger between parents and children of the same sex, we would expect to find a more powerful effect of growing up in a single-parent home on the sexual behavior of daughters than sons. A third reason is that girls are more likely than boys to respond to problems at home by turning outside the family for alternative sources of warmth and support.

Key Points
a) The social influences on girls' sexual behavior are stronger and more varied than boys.
b) Single-parent mothers are more likely to be dating than married mothers, and therefore may inadvertently be role models of sexual activity.
c) Girls are more likely than boys to respond to problems at home by turning outside the family for support.

80.   It is well known that adolescent contraceptive use tends to be infrequent and irregular. Why is this the case?

Sample Answer:
Social scientists point to several important factors. First, for many adolescents, contraceptives are not readily available, or if they are, young people may not know where to go to obtain them. This is likely to be an especially important barrier among younger adolescents, who may feel uncomfortable discussing their sexual activity with parents or other adults whose help or consent may be necessary in order to obtain birth control. Second, many young people do not fully understand that the likelihood of pregnancy varies over the course of a woman's menstrual cycle. Third, although it is certainly a misconception that many young women unconsciously "want" to become pregnant, many young people nevertheless do not recognize the seriousness of pregnancy and take the possibility lightly. Fourth, the limited ability of young adolescents to engage in long-term hypothetical thinking and their occasionally egocentric tendency to believe that they are immune from the forces that affect others may impede their consideration of pregnancy as a likely outcome of sexual activity. Finally, many adolescents fail to use birth control because doing so would be tantamount to admitting that they are planfully and willingly sexually active. For many young people, this is an extremely difficult realization to face.

Key Points
a) Contraceptives are not readily available.
b) Many youth are insufficiently educated about reproduction.
c) Adolescents take the possibility of pregnancy lightly.
d) Engage in personal fable behavior.
e) Having birth control would suggest that the adolescent was "planning"" to have sex.

CHAPTER 12
TEST ITEMS

◆

Achievement

Multiple Choice Items

1. Achievement concerns the development of motives, capabilities, interests, and behavior that relate to _____ in evaluative situations.
    A. performance
    B. outcomes
    C. scores
    D. none of the above

    Answer: A

2. Alice has worked all evening on a psychology assignment that is not being graded. She has a very strong _____.
    A. need for approval
    B. need for achievement
    C. need for fulfillment
    D. need for success

    Answer: B

3. Amy gets extremely nervous during exams and never does as well as she should because of these anxious feelings. She has a very strong _____.
    A. fear of rejection
    B. fear of testing
    C. fear of failure
    D. fear of evaluation

    Answer: C

4. Al's parents expect him to receive all A's on his report card, play quarterback for the football team, and win the election for senior class president. When Al came home with a B+ on his report card, his parents grounded him for a month. Al probably will develop _____.
    A. a high need for achievement
    B. a fear of failure
    C. an intrinsic type of motivation
    D. learned helplessness

    Answer: B

5. Adolescents who come from family environments in which parents have set unrealistically high standards for their children's achievement and react very negatively to failure are most likely to develop _____.
   A. intrinsic motivation
   B. a fear of failure
   C. Type-A personality characteristics
   D. a high need for achievement

   Answer: B

6. Which statement is true about achievement in adolescence?
   A. Achievement only occurs through external forces.
   B. Achievement takes place most often in the classroom.
   C. "The rich get richer and the poor get poorer."
   D. Each person has a maximum level of achievement that they can attain.

   Answer: C

7. The extent to which an individual strives for success is referred to as _____.
   A. mood composition
   B. need for achievement
   C. personality structure
   D. self-orientation

   Answer: B

8. The intrinsic desire to perform well is called _____.
   A. achievement motivation
   B. mastery motivation
   C. evaluation anxiety
   D. desensitization

   Answer: A

9. Whitney's present goal is to get good enough at spelling to earn the school's spelling trophy. Whitney's ambition is an example of _____.
   A. intrinsic motivation
   B. ego motivation
   C. self-regulation
   D. extrinsic motivation

   Answer: D

10. Alicia has trouble persisting at tasks and fears failure. Her grades are far lower than one would expect based on her intellectual ability. She is a(n)_____.
    A. failure
    B. underachiever
    C. delinquent
    D. normal adolescent

    Answer: B

11.	Leroy plays video games not because he will win anything by doing well, or because anyone approves of his increasing skill, but because he enjoys getting better at the games. His behavior is an example of _____.
A. intrinsic motivation
B. temperament
C. learned helplessness
D. extrinsic motivation

Answer: A

12.	Motivation based on the pleasure one will experience from mastering a task is called _____.
A. extrinsic motivation
B. intrinsic motivation
C. intuitive motivation
D. instinctive motivation

Answer: B

13.	Motivation based on the rewards one will receive for successful performance is called _____.
A. extrinsic motivation
B. reward-punishment theory
C. extraneous achievement
D. intrinsic motivation

Answer: A

14.	Sonya has scored in the top one percentile on an IQ test. Yet, she gets below average grades in school. What is true about Sonya?
A. she has a learning disorder
B. she has low self-esteem
C. she is a delinquent
D. she is an underachiever

Answer: D

15.	Jacob and Stephen just got a project back from their teacher that they had worked on together. They received a "D" on the project. Jacob said that it was because of the project was too hard. Stephen said it was because they hadn't worked hard enough on the project. Which adolescent is most likely to try harder on future projects?
A. Stephen
B. Jacob
C. Both boys will try harder next time.
D. Neither boy will try hard next time because they failed this time.

Answer: B

16. Lorraine believes that she can succeed at most things if she tries hard enough. Mandy doubts her abilities, and feels that trying harder will not make her more likely to succeed. Lorraine is more likely to be _____ and Mandy is more likely to be _____.
    A. extrinsically motivated; intrinsically motivated
    B. extrinsically motivated; anxious and hesitant
    C. intrinsically motivated; extrinsically motivated
    D. intrinsically motivated; unmotivated

    Answer: C

17. Bill approaches new tasks with the attitude that he can master them, and he tries to do so because he wants to gain new skills. Bill is motivated by _____.
    A. intrinsic forces
    B. extrinsic forces
    C. fear of failure
    D. learned helplessness

    Answer: A

18. Every time Frank receives an A on his report card, his grandmother gives him $50. However, if Frank receives a C, he is grounded for two weeks. Frank will probably develop _____.
    A. a high need for achievement
    B. intrinsic motivation
    C. extrinsic motivation
    D. Type-A Behavior

    Answer: C

19. Tory is extrinsically motivated and believes that intelligence is fixed trait. Based on this combination, Tory probably focuses on _____.
    A. performance goals
    B. learning goals
    C. self-regulatory goals
    D. mastery goals

    Answer: A

20. Ivan, who believes that intelligence is a malleable trait, is enrolled in several advanced placement classes. Mastering the subject material is more important to him than getting good grades. Ivan probably emphasizes _____.
    A. performance goals
    B. learning goals
    C. self-regulatory goals
    D. evaluation goals

    Answer: B

21. Marty's main concern in playing soccer is whether his performance will be good enough to win his father's attention and approval. Marty's behavior is being motivated by _____.
   A. intrinsic forces
   B. extrinsic forces
   C. temperament
   D. crystallization

   Answer: B

22. Fear of success is most prevalent among _____.
   A. males
   B. females
   C. blacks
   D. whites

   Answer: B

23. Antonio is very confident about his abilities; he has a strong sense of _____.
   A. academic success
   B. self-efficacy
   C. self-awareness
   D. social desirability

   Answer: B

24. Students' motivation and school performance _____ when they enter into secondary school.
   A. remains the same
   B. increases
   C. decreases
   D. increases sharply and then plateaus

   Answer: C

25. Which of the following is *not* likely to predict students' achievement-related behavior?
   A. whether the student has experienced a failure
   B. whether the student believes intelligence is fixed or malleable
   C. whether the student is intrinsically or extrinsically motivated
   D. whether the student is confident in his/her abilities

   Answer: A

26. Shawn is told by his teacher that the task he is working on is too difficult for him. Therefore, Shawn believes that failure is inevitable. He is likely to develop _____.
   A. learned helplessness
   B. attribution biases
   C. achievement attributions
   D. none of the above

   Answer: A

27. Generally speaking, when a boy fails at a task, he tends to look for a(n) _____ cause; when a girl fails, she tends to seek a(n) _____ cause.
A. temporary; permanent
B. external; internal
C. internal; external
D. gender-related; gender-independent

Answer: B

28. Boys seem less prone to learned helplessness than girls because they attribute failure to _____ causes and attribute success to _____.
A. external; ability
B. internal; luck
C. stable; intelligence
D. internal; external causes

Answer: A

29. The belief or expectation that one cannot control the forces in one's environment is called
_____.
A. underachievement
B. fear of failure
C. learned helplessness
D. temperament

Answer: C

30. Paul won't even try to learn how to swim because when he has tried before, he has not done very well and he is now convinced that no matter what he does, he will never learn to swim. Paul's situation is an example of _____.
A. ego deflation
B. Type-A Behavior
C. learned helplessness
D. temperament

Answer: C

31. Which of the following parenting styles is associated with adolescents' development of strong needs for achievement?
A. permissive
B. authoritative
C. authoritarian
D. demonstrative

Answer: B

32.   Which type of parenting is linked to school success during adolescence?
       A. authoritarian
       B. authoritative
       C. indulgent
       D. neglectful

       Answer: B

33.   Who is most likely to suffer from parental gender stereotyping?
       A. Lionel, whose parents are divorced.
       B. Kevin, whose parents are married.
       C. Rebecca, whose parents are divorced.
       D. Rhonda, whose parents are married.

       Answer: C

34.   Who will probably have the poorest school performance?
       A. Luanne, whose parents are consistently authoritative.
       B. Dierdre, whose parents are consistently authoritarian.
       C. Bobby Jo, whose parents are consistently indulgent.
       D. Sally, whose parents are sometimes authoritarian and sometimes indulgent.

       Answer: D

35.   Which of the following parenting styles is most often associated with adolescents' dropping out of high school?
       A. authoritative
       B. authoritarian
       C. permissive
       D. autocratic

       Answer: C

36.   Lydia's family is always going to art shows, concerts and poetry readings. They have a large amount of _____.
       A. societal influence
       B. social capital
       C. cultural capital
       D. monetary success

       Answer: C

37.   Jane's community does a lot to support and encourage adolescent's success in school. This community has a large amount of _____.
       A. societal influence
       B. social capital
       C. cultural capital
       D. monetary success

       Answer: B

38.   The impact of friends on adolescents' school performance depends on what factor(s)?
      A. the academic orientation of the peer group
      B. the number of extracurricular activities in which they participate
      C. the size of the peer group
      D. All of the above.

      Answer: A

39.   The resources provided within a family allowing the exposure of the adolescent to art, music, and literature are called _____.
      A. special education
      B. social cultivation
      C. artistic refinement
      D. cultural capital

      Answer: D

40.   During the school year, Titus' parents took him to the theater and the opera. In addition, they bought him an encyclopedia for his birthday. The treatment Titus is receiving is an example of
      _____.
      A. special education
      B. social cultivation
      C. artistic refinement
      D. cultural capital

      Answer: D

41.   Which of the following is the best example of cultural capital?
      A. Art's father takes him to museums during the summer.
      B. Chip's parents bought him a computer.
      C. Henry's mother has a masters degree in Shakespearean drama.
      D. Crystal's parents buy her expensive earrings.

      Answer: A

42.   Which of the following is an example of school performance?
      A. Kelly received a C on her report card.
      B. Naomi received a 1200 on the SAT.
      C. Mel has been in school for 7 years.
      D. Vinny has an IQ of 105.

      Answer: A

43.   Which type of educational achievement has important implications for subsequent earnings?
      A. school performance
      B. academic achievement
      C. educational attainment
      D. all of the above

      Answer: C

44. Which of the following is an example of academic achievement?
   A. Kelly received a C on her report card.
   B. Naomi received a 1200 on the SAT.
   C. Mel has been in school for 7 years.
   D. Vinny has 3.7 GPA.

   Answer: B

45. Recent studies have shown that there has been a decline in minority student college enrollment. What factor probably contributed to this decline?
   A. a lost connection between educational attainment and future success
   B. decline in cultural capital in the African-American community
   C. cutbacks in financial aid
   D. decline in minority work ethic

   Answer: C

46. In a study on the effect of early intensive education on later school performance among children in poverty, which intervention had the greatest impact on performance in high school?
   A. the preschool intervention
   B. the elementary school intervention
   C. each intervention was equally effective
   D. neither intervention affected high school performance

   Answer: A

47. Studies show that disadvantaged youth perform more poorly in school than their advantaged counterparts. Which of the following reasons best accounts for this disparity?
   A. Poor adolescents begin school at a distinct academic disadvantage.
   B. Poor adolescents have more stress.
   C. Parents from higher social classes are more involved in the school.
   D. All of the above.

   Answer: D

48. Socio-economic status is to educational achievement as family background is to _____.
   A. educational achievement
   B. academic achievement
   C. occupational achievement
   D. school performance

   Answer: A

49. A factor presumed to form an intervening link between two variables that are causally-connected is called a _____.
   A. mediating variable
   B. moderating variable
   C. correlational variable
   D. a regression variable

   Answer: A

50. According to research conducted by Felner, what variable mediates the relationship between social class and math grades?
    A. drug and alcohol use
    B. stress
    C. pregnancy
    D. gender

Answer: B

51. Cole has a high need for achievement. What is probably _not_ true about his family?
    A. His parent have high performance standards.
    B. Cole feels enormous pressure from his parents to excel.
    C. He has been rewarded for achievement success during childhood.
    D. His parents have encouraged autonomy and independence.

Answer: B

52. Mary comes from an economically disadvantaged household. Her mother went to the school counselor to find out what could be done to help Mary overcome her disadvantage. What did the counselor suggest would help?
    A. positive relations at home
    B. extra tutoring
    C. an after school job
    D. special education classes

Answer: A

53. According to the text, Asian children tend to attribute success to _____.
    A. external causes
    B. hard work
    C. inherited intelligence
    D. luck

Answer: B

54. Across all ethnic groups, studies indicate that which of the following measures helps students to achieve?
    A. a sense of belonging to the school
    B. a perceived connection between academic accomplishment and future success
    C. parental monitoring of behavior and schooling
    D. all of the above

Answer: D

55. Kim, an African American adolescent, believes that she is the victim of discrimination. How will this probably affect her school performance?
    A. Her level of effort will increase in order to overcome discriminatory barriers.
    B. Her grades will decline because she does not believe that educational success will pay off.
    C. Her grades will not be affected.
    D. Her grades will improve, but her self-esteem will suffer.

Answer: B

56. Levels of educational attainment in America have _____ over the past six decades.
    A. risen substantially
    B. remained stable
    C. declined dramatically
    D. declined slightly

Answer: A

57. Compared with their counterparts twenty years ago, today's adolescents have _____ levels of educational attainment and _____ levels of academic achievement.
    A. lower; lower
    B. lower; higher
    C. higher; higher
    D. higher; lower

Answer: D

58. The modest gains in achievement that have occurred during the past decade or so have been in the area of _____.
    A. higher order thinking
    B. relatively simple skills
    C. computer training
    D. specialized science fields

Answer: B

59. All of the following have been cited as possible explanations for low achievement scores among American students *except* _____.
    A. teachers do not spend enough time on basic instruction
    B. students do not take advanced courses when they are offered
    C. parents do not encourage academic pursuits at home
    D. students spend too much time involved in extracurricular activities

Answer: D

60. Raul, a Latino youth, has decided to drop out of high school. According to the studies, what is likely to be the reason for his desire to drop out?
A. He is not proficient in English.
B. He has a low IQ.
C. He has social problems at school.
D. He needs to earn money for his family.

Answer: A

61. In recent years, among black youth, high school graduation rates have _____ and college enrollments have _____.
A. increased; increased
B. decreased; remained stable
C. increased; decreased
D. remained stable; decreased

Answer: C

62. What percentage of students who complete high school go on to college?
A. 10 percent
B. 25 percent
C. 50 percent
D. 75 percent

Answer: C

63. High school dropout rates are highest among _____ adolescents.
A. Black
B. Hispanic
C. White
D. Asian

Answer: B

64. What percentage of students drop out of high school?
A. less than 5 percent
B. 10 percent
C. 25 percent
D. 45 percent

Answer: C

65. Which of the following is the best predictor of occupational success?
A. school performance
B. educational attainment
C. academic achievement
D. motivation

Answer: B

66.   Who is most likely to attain occupational success?
        A. Francesca, who earned good grades in college
        B. Luke, who received a high score on the SAT
        C. Karen, who has a master's degree
        D. Ruben, who has a high IQ

        Answer: C

67.   Which of the following has _not_ been identified as a factor in determining the likelihood of dropping out of high school?
        A. socioeconomic status
        B. repeating a grade
        C. achievement test scores
        D. gender

        Answer: D

68.   According to Super, the stage during which individuals first begin to formulate their ideas about appropriate occupations (typically between the ages of 14 and 18) is called _____.
        A. crystallization
        B. specialization
        C. orientation
        D. specification

        Answer: A

69.   According to Super, the stage during which individuals first begin to consider narrowly defined occupational pursuits (typically between the ages of 18 and 21) is called _____.
        A. crystallization
        B. specialization
        C. orientation
        D. specification

        Answer: D

70.   Harry has decided he wants to go into the field of medicine but has not decided what he will specialize in. Based on Super's stages of occupational development, Harry is in the _____.
        A. composition stage
        B. specification stage
        C. self-directed search stage
        D. crystallization stage

        Answer: D

71. Akira wants to be an occupational therapist specializing in the rehabilitation of the hand. Based on Super's stages of occupational development, Akira has reached the _____.
   A. composition stage
   B. specification stage
   C. self-directed search stage
   D. crystallization stage

Answer: B

72. Who espoused the idea that individuals should select careers that match their personalities?
   A. Super
   B. Holland
   C. Felner
   D. Dweck

Answer: B

73. Which of the following is most likely to influence a teenager's occupational choice?
   A. parents
   B. part-time work
   C. courses in school
   D. peers

Answer: A

74. Margaret, age 17, wants to be a physician. If she is a typical adolescent, she is most likely to have _____.
   A. thoroughly researched the occupational requirements of a physician
   B. determined exactly what schooling is required
   C. selected this profession because it is the opposite of what her parents do
   D. underestimated the amount of education necessary

Answer: D

75. Which statement represents an important goal of career educators helping adolescents with their future plans?
   A. Help adolescent find a job right after high school.
   B. Help adolescents achieve the highest score possible on the SAT's.
   C. Help adolescents make informed choices about their career and free them from stereotypes that constrain their choices.
   D. Help adolescents form lasting relationships with teachers and administrators.

Answer: C

Essay Questions

76.   Discuss some of the reasons that boys and girls show different patterns of math and science achievement during high school.

> *Sample Answer:*
> *Despite an absence of sex differences in ability, girls in general are less likely than boys to pursue advanced courses in math and science, and are more likely to drop out of such courses. This may be partially explained by sex differences in social consequences of succeeding in such classes. Sometime in adolescence, girls may receive a message that competition in such courses is aggressive and unfeminine, and that it may threaten their heterosexual relationships. A second explanation for these differences may be that girls are less likely to believe that taking math classes will be useful in their future careers. As a result, they may be more likely to drop such classes. Both boys and girls probably pick up these messages from parents, teachers, and counselors, who attribute success in boys to ability, but success in girls to hard work, and who support math achievement among boys but discourage it among girls.*

> Key Points
> a) Girls are less likely than boys to pursue math and science courses.
> b) Girls are less likely than boys to believe math will help them in their future careers.

77.   As a guidance counselor at a large public high school, you notice that achievement test scores are very low. From your knowledge of the recent research, suggest four reasons for this disturbing fact.

> *Sample Answer:*
> *Recent research suggests several reasons why achievement test scores are so low. First, teachers are not spending enough time on basic instruction. Second, there has been a pervasive decline in the difficulty of textbooks. Third, parents are not encouraging academic pursuits at home. Finally, students know that, thanks to "grade inflation," they can earn good grades without working very hard.*

> Key Points
> a) Teachers are not spending enough time on basic instruction.
> b) The decline in difficulty of textbooks
> c) Parents are not encouraging academic pursuits at home.
> d) Students are not spending enough time on studies outside of the classroom.
> e) Grade inflation

78. Michael and Selma are the parents of 13-year-old Luisa. They understand that the home environment they create can affect their daughter's achievement. What three steps can they take to positively influence Luisa's achievement?

> *Sample Answer:*
> *Researchers have found that important aspects of the home environment are good predictors of adolescents' academic achievement. Michael and Selma can help improve Luisa's chances of achieving by doing three things. First, they should encourage school success by setting high standards for Luisa's school performance and homework completion as well as have high aspirations for her. Second, they should support values that are consistent with doing well in school. For example, they should structure their home environment so that the messages Luisa hears at school are echoed at home. Third, they should become involved in Luisa's education. Parents who encourage success are more likely to attend school programs, help in course selection and main interest in school activities and assignments.*

> Key Points
> a) They can encourage achievement by setting high standards and aspirations for performance at school.
> b) They can support values expressed at the school by echoing school messages at home.
> c) They should become involved in the school and their daughter's education.

79. Discuss the development of occupational plans during the adolescent years according to the theory of Super.

> *Sample Answer:*
> *According to Super, occupational plans develop in stages, and two such stages occur during adolescence. Between ages 14 and 18, individuals first begin to crystallize a vocational preference. During this period of "crystallization," individuals begin to formulate ideas about appropriate work and begin to develop occupational self-conceptions that will guide subsequent educational decisions. Although adolescents may not settle on a particular career at this point, they do begin to narrow their choices according to their interests, values, and abilities. Following the period of crystallization is a period of "specification," occurring roughly between the ages of 18 and 21. During this period, the young person recognizes the need to specify his or her vocational interests and begins to seek out appropriate information to accomplish this.*

> Key Points
> a) The adolescent first crystallizes a vocational preference.
> b) After crystallization, the adolescent specifies his or her vocational interests.

80.   Ricky is 16 years old, yet he is just a freshman in high school because he was held back a grade in elementary school. Recently, Ricky has decided to drop out of school. Discuss the likely origins of his decision and the general factors that lead students to drop out.

Sample Answer:
When considering the origin of Ricky's decision to drop out, it is important to remember that his decision is not so much made during adolescence as it is the culmination of a long process that begins early on. Ricky's decision probably has a lot to do with the fact that he was held back a grade in elementary school. Having been held back is one of the strongest predictors of dropping out among adolescents. There are, however, many other reasons that may lead to dropping out. Dropping out is a process characterized by a history of repeated academic failure and increasing alienation from school. Adolescents who leave high school before graduating are more likely to come from lower socioeconomic levels, poor communities, large, single-parent, or non-demanding families, and households where little reading material is available.

Key Points
a) Dropping out is not so much a decision made during adolescence as it is the culmination of a long process that begins early on.
b) Having been held back is one of the strongest predictors of dropping out among adolescents.
c) Adolescents who drop out are likely to come from households with limited social and cultural capital.

CHAPTER 13
TEST ITEMS

◈

Psychosocial Problems in Adolescence

Multiple Choice Items

1. Which scenario best represents adolescent alcohol use in today's society?
    A. Dahlia started using alcohol at age 17 and usually drinks it a few times each year.
    B. Brian first tried alcohol as an early adolescent and now, at age 17, uses it only occasionally.
    C. Julia, a high school senior, has never tried alcohol
    D. Michael, a 13 year old, drinks alcohol almost every day with his friends.

    Answer: B

2. Which of the following adolescent problems is likely to be resolved by adulthood?
    A. substance abuse
    B. delinquency
    C. unemployment
    D. all of the above

    Answer: D

3. Denise has just been caught vandalizing for the fourth time this year. What is probably true of her early home and school life?
    A. Her problems have emerged only during adolescence.
    B. Her early home and school life were average.
    C. She probably had problems at home and school at an early age.
    D. Home and school life have not been shown to be connected to delinquency.

    Answer: C

4. Peter's parents are worried that their son is drinking too much. They think his alcohol use might turn into a long-term problem. Which theory best illustrates the nature of adolescent drug use?
    A. Many problems experienced by adolescents are relatively transitory in nature.
    B. Adolescent alcohol use is the first sign of long-term problems with drugs.
    C. Adolescent alcohol use is a clear indication of permissive parenting techniques.
    D. None of the above are true.

    Answer: A

5.   Carol has just learned that her son, Mike, has been caught shoplifting for the fifth time. Carol told the police that Mike's just reacting to the stress of going through puberty. How accurate is Carol's idea?
A. Carol is probably correct, adolescence is a very confusing time
B. Adolescent stress can only be part of the problem. There must be some problems at home as well.
C. Carol is incorrect. Problem behavior is virtually never a direct consequence of going through the normative adolescent changes.
D. Mike's problem behavior is difficult to trace to just one cause.

Answer: C

6.   Christi suffers from depression. She also gets in fights at school to express her anger and sadness. Christi's problems fall into which category?
A. internalizing disorder
B. externalizing disorder
C. comorbidity
D. substance abuse

Answer: C

7.   Greg suffers from depression. His friend Matthew also suffers from depression as well as conduct disorder. Which boy probably had worse family experiences?
A. Chris
B. Matthew
C. both Chris and Matthew
D. neither boy, these problems cannot be attributed to the family

Answer: B

8.   Alice has a substance abuse problem. Which of the following problems is she also likely to have?
A. internalizing disorder
B. externalizing disorder
C. Both of the above.
D. None of the above.

Answer: C

9.   _____ is an example of an internalizing disorder; _____ is an example of an externalizing disorder.
A. Depression; psychosomatic disturbance
B. Anxiety; drug and alcohol abuse
C. Drug and alcohol abuse; delinquency
D. Truancy; psychosomatic disturbance

Answer: B

10. Dara suffers from depression. What type of disorder does she probably have?
    A. an externalizing disorder
    B. a psychosomatic disorder
    C. an internalizing disorder
    D. a personality disorder

Answer: C

11. Theodore has been referred to as an "acting out" adolescent. He engages in delinquent behavior. Theodore is exhibiting _____.
    A. an externalizing disorder
    B. a psychosomatic disorder
    C. an internalizing disorder
    D. a personality disorder

Answer: A

12. The theory that suggests that the covariation among various types of externalizing disorders results from an underlying trait of unconventionality is called _____.
    A. problem behavior theory
    B. biological risk theory
    C. social control theory
    D. gateway theory

Answer: A

13. Which of the following individuals is most likely to engage in risk-taking behaviors?
    A. Marco, who is tolerant of deviance
    B. Karen, who is not highly connected to school or to a religious institution
    C. Patrick, who is very liberal in his social views
    D. All of the above.

Answer: D

14. According to social control theory, delinquency is caused by_____.
    A. unconventionality in the adolescent's personality
    B. an inherited predisposition toward deviance
    C. biologically based differences in arousal and sensation-seeking
    D. a lack of bonds to the family, the school, or the workplace

Answer: D

15. What would a social control theorist say about an adolescent who engages in risk-taking behavior?
    A. They have a biological predisposition toward risky behavior.
    B. They are inherently unconventional.
    C. They have a weak attachment to society.
    D. They have authoritarian parents.

Answer: C

16. Externalizing problems is to antisocial syndromes as internalizing problems is to _____.
   A. negative affectivity
   B. social control
   C. risk-taking behaviors
   D. comorbidity

   Answer: A

17. Characterized by high levels of subjective distress, _____ is considered one of the underlying causes of internalizing disorders.
   A. the hostile attributional bias
   B. negative affectivity
   C. temperament
   D. fatalistic disposition

   Answer: B

18. Which of the following is considered an "internalizing disorder"?
   A. drug abuse
   B. anxiety
   C. truancy
   D. delinquency

   Answer: B

19. Which drugs are the most commonly used and abused among adolescents?
   A. alcohol and nicotine
   B. marijuana and alcohol
   C. nicotine and marijuana
   D. alcohol and cocaine

   Answer: A

20. Alcohol and nicotine are the most common drugs used by adolescents in which category?
   A. prevalence
   B. recency of use
   C. both a and b
   D. neither category

   Answer: C

21. Jim and his mom are in an argument because his mom found out that Jim has smoked marijuana. Jim's defense is, "Half the senior class is doing it!" How accurate is Jim's statement?
   A. It is very inaccurate; only 10 percent of high school seniors have tried marijuana.
   B. It is inaccurate because half of all Americans have tried marijuana, not half of high school seniors.
   C. It is accurate, about half of all high school seniors have tried marijuana.
   D. Statistics about marijuana use are too inconsistent to know.

   Answer: C

22. Which of the following sets of drugs is correctly ranked from most to least popular among adolescents?
    A. alcohol, cigarettes, marijuana, inhalants
    B. cigarettes, alcohol, cocaine, marijuana
    C. alcohol, marijuana, cigarettes, cocaine
    D. cigarettes, alcohol, marijuana, inhalants

    Answer: A

23. Which of the following statements about adolescent cigarette use is true?
    A. Cigarette tax increases has led to a sharp decrease in the percentage of smoking adolescents.
    B. Anti-smoking campaigns have contributed to the steady decline of cigarette use among adolescents.
    C. Despite massive anti-smoking efforts, cigarette use among teenagers has continued to increase since early 1993.
    D. Despite changes in tobacco industry policies, the percentage of smoking adolescents has remained stable over two decades.

    Answer: C

24. According to recent surveys, which drug is used most on a daily basis by high school students?
    A. marijuana
    B. alcohol
    C. tobacco
    D. cocaine

    Answer: C

25. What drug has been used by the largest percentage of American adolescents?
    A. cocaine
    B. marijuana
    C. alcohol
    D. LSD

    Answer: C

26. Which of the following drugs has increased in use over the past decade?
    A. alcohol
    B. LSD
    C. cocaine
    D. All of the above

    Answer: B

27. Which statement is most likely true about American adolescents today?
    A. Adolescents are experimenting with drugs at later ages.
    B. Marijuana is the only substance used by a substantial number of high school seniors daily.
    C. Adolescents are experimenting with drugs at earlier ages.
    D. A large proportion of adolescents use hard drugs.

    Answer: C

28.   Corrina is concerned because she learned that her 15 year-old son Henry has started smoking and her 14-year-old son Hector has started drinking. Which boy is most likely to continue his habit into adulthood?
      A. Hector
      B. Henry
      C. Both boys will be addicted and continue drug use into adulthood.
      D. Neither boy, these are both cases of adolescent experimentation.

      Answer: B

29.   Alejandra, a Hispanic adolescent, is best friends with Mina, a foreign-born adolescent. Which statement is most likely true about their drug use?
      A. Alejandra will use less drugs than Mina.
      B. Alejandra and Mina will use the same amount of drugs.
      C. Alejandra and Mina will use more drugs than their friend Susan, a White adolescent.
      D. Mina will use less drugs than Alejandra.

      Answer: D

30.   Which of the following adolescents is _least_ likely to use drugs?
      A. Mike, a White adolescent
      B. Li, an exchange student from China
      C. Emily, an Asian American adolescent
      D. Hector, an African American adolescent

      Answer: B

31.   Who is the most likely to abuse alcohol?
      A. Caroline; a Hispanic adolescent
      B. Lynne; a White adolescent
      C. Betty; an African American adolescent
      D. Isabelle; a Native American adolescent

      Answer: D

32.   Which minority ethnic group has the highest proportion of drug users?
      A. African Americans
      B. Asians
      C. Hispanics
      D. American Indians

      Answer: D

33.   Most adolescents who abuse hard drugs often began their drug use with alcohol and marijuana which is why they are considered _____.
      A. gateway drugs
      B. highly addictive
      C. illegal
      D. status offenses

      Answer: A

34. Mark and Kathleen have discovered that their son Dylan has been abusing alcohol and marijuana. They went to a doctor to find out what types of problems this may cause for Dylan. What did he probably say they should expect?
A. Dylan will have problems at school.
B. Dylan will experience depression.
C. Dylan is at risk to engage in sexual activity.
D. All of the above.

Answer: D

35. Ben was a maladjusted child and scored low on measures of psychological adjustment. Which statement is most likely true about his drug use as an adolescent?
A. No relationship can be determined.
B. Ben is a frequent user of drugs.
C. Ben does not use drugs.
D. Ben uses drugs only occasionally.

Answer: B

36. The early initiation of drug use among young teenagers and preadolescents is especially disturbing for all of the following reasons *except* _____.
A. Heavy drug use may interfere with the adolescent growth spurt.
B. Younger adolescents may lack the psychological maturity of judgment necessary to use drugs in moderation.
C. Younger adolescents may face unique developmental challenges with which drug use interferes.
D. Heavy drug use may hurry adolescents through the psychosocial tasks of adolescence at too fast a pace.

Answer: A

37. Of the following adolescents, who will be the most well-adjusted?
A. Mavis, who is a frequent drug user
B. Jennifer, who abstains from drugs due to an irrational fear
C. Vicki, who uses drugs occasionally
D. None of the above.

Answer: C

38. Which of the following is *not* a risk factor for developing substance abuse problems?
A. having excessively permissive parents
B. having easy access to drugs
C. working more than twenty hours per week
D. being involved in a sexual relationship

Answer: D

39. Which is _not_ considered a risk factor for substance abuse in adolescence?
     A. psychological factors
     B. interpersonal factors
     C. contextual factors
     D. environmental factors

     Answer: D

40. What is one of the most important risk factors for adolescent substance abuse?
     A. having a peer who abuses drugs or alcohol
     B. having a sibling who abuses drugs or alcohol
     C. having a parent who abuses drugs of alcohol
     D. having protective factors

     Answer: C

41. Which of the following are psychological risk factors for substance abuse?
     A. anger
     B. impulsivity
     C. academic difficulties
     D. All of the above.

     Answer: D

42. Glen and Laura ask a counselor what they can do to help protect their teenage son, Jason, from abusing drugs. What might the counselor have suggested?
     A. Enroll Jason in a private school.
     B. Get Jason involved at the church.
     C. Punish any deviance very heavily.
     D. Make sure Jason gets an after-school job.

     Answer: B

43. Which of the following is a likely reason that African American youngsters have a lower rate of drinking than their White counterparts?
     A. They don't have money to purchase alcohol.
     B. They are biological unable to process alcohol.
     C. Their parents are less likely to drink and tolerate drinking.
     D. Their celebrity role models do not drink.

     Answer: C

44. Which of the following methods has been found effective in reducing adolescent drug and alcohol use?
     A. drug and alcohol education
     B. raising the price of alcohol and cigarettes
     C. scare tactics
     D. increasing adolescents' self-esteem

     Answer: B

45. Which factor is _not_ focused on in the prevention of substance use and abuse among teenagers?
A. the supply of drugs
B. the environment in which teenagers may be exposed to drugs
C. characteristics of the potential drug user
D. family characteristics

Answer: D

46. Which prevention program is most likely to be successful?
A. One that focuses on community-wide intervention aimed at adolescents.
B. One that focuses on social competence training.
C. One that focuses on community-wide intervention aimed at parents and teachers.
D. All of the above.

Answer: D

47. Individuals under the age of 24 account for what percentage of all violent crimes in the United States?
A. 10 percent
B. 25 percent
C. 50 percent
D. 75 percent

Answer: C

48. Kristin has just been the victim of a mugging. Her parents are concerned about how she will react to the crime. What is a likely response?
A. She will develop post-traumatic stress disorder.
B. She will be depressed.
C. She will have academic problems.
D. All of the above.

Answer: D

49. Cliff is 16 years old, is truant from school, drinks alcohol regularly, and has run away from home. Legally speaking, Cliff is a(n) _____.
A. ADHD child
B. habitual criminal
C. sociopath
D. status offender

Answer: D

50. Which of the following would be considered a status offense?
A. using cocaine
B. truancy
C. vandalizing property
D. All of the above.

Answer: B

51. Who is the most likely to be a victim of a violent crime?
    A. Jeffrey; an African American adolescent living in the suburbs
    B. Rose; an elderly Caucasian woman living in the city
    C. Elaine; a Caucasian adolescent living in the country
    D. Mitch; a Hispanic adolescent living in the city

    Answer: D

52. Charlie is a violent and aggressive adolescent. Which of the following is also most likely true about him?
    A. He lives in an impoverished neighborhood.
    B. He lives with only one parent.
    C. He has many siblings.
    D. He is a heavy drug user.

    Answer: A

53. Jeremy, a 15-year-old African American, and Craig, a 15-year-old European American, were both caught shoplifting. Who is more likely to be arrested?
    A. Jeremy
    B. Craig
    C. Both are equally likely to be arrested.
    D. Unable to determine.

    Answer: A

54. In general, the earlier an adolescent's criminal career begins _____.
    A. the easier it is for that person to be treated
    B. the more likely the adolescent is to stop the criminal behavior on his or her own
    C. the less likely he or she is to be arrested
    D. the more likely he or she is to become chronically delinquent

    Answer: D

55. The main antecedents of chronic delinquency appear to be rooted in _____.
    A. relations with peers during childhood
    B. relations with parents during childhood
    C. academic failure in junior high school
    D. pessimistic attitudes about employment prospects

    Answer: B

56. The biologically-based psychological disorder characterized by impulsiveness, inattentiveness, and restlessness is called _____.
    A. schizophrenia
    B. nervosa
    C. attention deficit/hyperactivity disorder
    D. oppositional defiant disorder

    Answer: C

57. As a child, Carlos had a hard time sitting still and was highly aggressive. As an adolescent, he is extremely impulsive and is more likely to engage in delinquent behavior. Carlos probably suffers from _____.
   A. antisocial nervosa
   B. obsessive/compulsive disorder
   C. attention deficit/hyperactivity disorder
   D. oppositional defiant disorder

   Answer: C

58. The tendency to interpret ambiguous interactions with others as deliberately antagonistic is called _____.
   A. attention deficit disorder
   B. negative affectivity
   C. hostile attributional bias
   D. oppositional defiant disorder

   Answer: C

59. While Alan is waiting in line for tickets to the show, the man behind him bumps into him. Even though the man apologizes, Alan becomes extremely upset and pushes him back. Alan is probably suffering from _____.
   A. attention deficit disorder
   B. negative affectivity disorder
   C. hostile attributional bias
   D. status offense syndrome

   Answer: C

60. Vince engaged in delinquency as an adolescent and has continued to be in trouble with the law ever since. What type of behavior is this?
   A. life-course persistent antisocial behavior
   B. comorbidity
   C. externalizing disorder
   D. adolescent limited antisocial behavior

   Answer: A

61. Some people who are delinquent as adolescents grow up to be law-abiding adults. What type of pattern is this?
   A. transitory delinquency
   B. negative affectivity
   C. diathesis-stress model
   D. adolescent limited antisocial behavior

   Answer: D

62. According to recent research, what percent of adolescents have attempted suicide?
    A. between 1 and 5 percent
    B. between 5 and 10 percent
    C. between 10 and 15 percent
    D. between 15 and 20 percent

Answer: B

63. Which would *not* be considered a vegetative symptom of depression?
    A. insomnia
    B. loss of appetite
    C. pessimism
    D. fatigue

Answer: C

64. Boys are more likely to suffer from _____ disorders, and girls are more likely to suffer from _____ disorders.
    A. externalizing; internalizing
    B. internalizing; externalizing
    C. internalizing; internalizing
    D. externalizing; externalizing

Answer: A

65. Many experts endorse a model of depression that suggests individuals who are predisposed toward internalizing problems will develop depression when they are exposed to chronic or acute stressors. This is called _____.
    A. emotion-focused coping
    B. diathesis-stress model
    C. epidemiology
    D. problem behavior theory

Answer: B

66. Which of the following statements about suicide is *false*?
    A. Adults complete suicide more often than adolescents.
    B. Females attempt suicide more often than males.
    C. Suicide rates have increased among adolescents .
    D. Adults attempt suicide more often than adolescents.

Answer: D

67. Who is the most likely to succeed in his or her suicide attempt?
    A. Joseph; an adolescent
    B. Heather; an adolescent
    C. Drew; an adult
    D. Laurie; an adult

Answer: C

68. Dr. Herman is a psychologist who treats depression among adults. He notices that many of his patients suffered from depression as children. As a result, Dr. Herman decides to create a program aimed at adolescents who are at risk for developing depression. This type of approach is called _____.
   A. primary prevention
   B. secondary prevention
   C. emotion-focused coping
   D. problem-focused coping

   Answer: B

69. During the school year, a counselor for the health clinic gives a presentation to the student body about depression. This type of approach is called _____.
   A. primary prevention
   B. secondary prevention
   C. emotion-focused coping
   D. problem-focused coping

   Answer: A

70. Dr. Brussel is studying the clustering of adolescent suicide in a small Midwestern community. By studying the spread of this problem, we can conclude that Dr. Brussel studies _____.
   A. entomology
   B. epidemiology
   C. sociology
   D. ecology

   Answer: B

71. Felicia is worried she may be pregnant. She decides to go to the store and purchase a pregnancy test. This type of coping is called _____.
   A. protective focused
   B. event oriented
   C. problem-focused
   D. emotion-focused

   Answer: C

72. Xavier is receiving chemotherapy treatments for cancer. He decides to listen to soft music during the session. This type of coping is called _____.
   A. protective focused
   B. affection oriented
   C. problem-focused
   D. emotion-focused

   Answer: D

73. Both Yvette and Becky have parents who are currently getting divorced. Yvette also has to move into a different house. Which adolescent is at higher risk for developing psychological problems?
    A. Becky
    B. Yvette
    C. Both girls have high risk.
    D. This cannot be predicted.

Answer: B

74. Which of the following methods is the best for dealing with controllable stress?
    A. problem-focused
    B. emotion-focused
    C. protective focused
    D. affection oriented

Answer: A

75. When stress is uncontrollable, the best method of coping is _____.
    A. problem-focused
    B. emotion-focused
    C. protective focused
    D. affection oriented

Answer: B

Essay Questions

76. Discuss several points of confusion that often surface in discussions of adolescent problem behavior and that lead to exaggerations of its prevalence and seriousness.

Sample Answer:
Four points in particular are important. First, one needs to distinguish between occasional experimentation and enduring patterns of dangerous or troublesome behavior. Research shows that rates of occasional, and usually harmless, experimentation far exceed rates of enduring problem behavior. Second, one needs to distinguish between problems that have their origins and onset in adolescence and those that have their roots in earlier periods of development. The fact that a problem may be displayed during adolescence does not mean that it is a problem of adolescence. Third, it is important to remember that some, though not all, of the problems experienced by adolescents are relatively transitory in nature and are resolved by the beginning of adulthood with few long-term repercussions in the majority of cases. Finally, problem behavior during adolescence is virtually never a direct consequence of the normative changes of adolescence itself.

Key Points
a) Distinguish between occasional experimentation and enduring delinquent behavior.
b) Some problems begin before adolescence and other emerge at the onset of adolescence.
c) Most problems are transitory in nature.
d) Problem behavior is not associated with the normative changes of adolescence.

77. Bryce, a 13-year-old, has been experimenting with drugs for a few years, but is not a heavy user. Connor, his older brother tried smoking marijuana for the first time as a senior in high school. Which brother is at a greater risk for drug abuse and why?

Sample Answer:
Recent research suggests that early experimentation with drugs is more harmful than experimentation at a later age. Therefore, Bryce is at greater risk because he is younger. Younger adolescents may lack the psychological maturity of judgment necessary to use drugs in moderation or under safe circumstances. Additionally, younger adolescents may face unique developmental challenges that drug use interferes with. Finally, there is some evidence that heavy drug use may "hurry" adolescents through the psychosocial tasks of adolescence at too fast a pace, thereby interfering with the normal developmental timetable.

Key Points
a) Bryce, because he is younger
b) Younger adolescents lack the psychological maturity of judgment.
c) Younger adolescents face unique developmental challenges.
d) Heavy drug use may rush adolescents through the psychosocial tasks of adolescence.

78.   You are a school counselor. One day, a set of parents bring their young child into your office because he has been acting up. They want to know if this problem behavior will progress into delinquency. Discuss four sets of characteristics that help you determine an individual's potential for delinquent activity.

Sample Answer:
Aside from family factors, there are four sets of individual characteristics that distinguish potential delinquent youngsters from their peers, at a relatively early age. First, children who become delinquent have histories of aggressive and violent behavior that are identifiable as early as age 8. Second, delinquent teens were more impulsive as children and more likely than their peers to suffer from hyperactivity, or ADHD. Third, children who become delinquent are more likely than their peers to score low on standardized tests of intelligence and to perform poorly at school. Finally, aggressive adolescents often have a prior history of poor relations with peers.

Key Points
a) Delinquent teens often have histories of aggressive and violent behavior as children.
b) Delinquent teens were more impulsive as children.
c) Child who become delinquent perform poorly on intelligence tests and in school.
d) Aggressive adolescents often have prior history of poor relations with peers.

79.   Why might there be an increase in the prevalence of depression at adolescence?

Sample Answer:
A variety of theoretical arguments have been made to explain the increase in depression at adolescence, or, more specifically, around the time of puberty. Biological theorists point to the hormonal changes of puberty, which are likely to have implications for neuroendocrine activity. Cognitive theorists point to the onset of hypothetical thinking at adolescence, which may result in new (and perhaps potentially more depressing) ways of viewing the world. Theorists who emphasize environmental factors draw attention to the new environmental demands of adolescence, such as changing schools or beginning to date, all of which may lead to feelings of loss, heightened stress, or diminished reinforcement. Thus there are many good reasons to expect that the prevalence of depression would increase as individuals pass from childhood into adolescence.

Key Points
a) Hormonal changes associated with puberty
b) Cognitive changes that allow the adolescent to think differently about the world
c) Societal demands and pressure on adolescents

80. Based on what you know about adolescent drug use, design an effective drug prevention program. Describe the components that make it effective.

Sample Answer:
The most encouraging results regarding drug prevention programs have been found in programs that combine some sort of social-competence training with a community-wide intervention aimed not only at adolescents, but also at their peers, parents, and teachers. In order to have an effective program, it must have two components. First, the program would include workshops that address social-competence skills like how to handle social situations where drugs and alcohol are involved. It would also distinguish the difference between drug use and drug abuse. The second component that would make the program effective is a training session for parents and teachers that empower them to change the community environment at the school and home so that adolescents can successfully avoid drug abuse.

Key Points
a) The program must combine social competence training with a community wide intervention aimed at adolescents and their peers, as well as teachers and parents.
b) The program must distinguish between drug use and drug abuse.
c) The community environment must be changed in order to support adolescents in their effort to avoid drug abuse.